Interior finishes & fittings for historic building conservation

This book is part of a series on historic building conservation:

Understanding Historic Building Conservation
Edited by Michael Forsyth
9781405111720

Structures & Construction in Historic Building Conservation
Edited by Michael Forsyth
9781405111713

Materials & Skills for Historic Building Conservation
Edited by Michael Forsyth
9781405111706

Other books of interest:

Managing Built Heritage: the role of cultural significance
Derek Worthing & Stephen Bond
9781405119788

Conservation and Sustainability in Historic Cities
Dennis Rodwell
9781405126564

Building Pathology
Second Edition
David Watt
9781405161039

Architectural Conservation
Aylin Orbaşli
9780632040254

Urban Heritage Management: best practice from UNESCO sites worldwide
Francesco Bandarin & Ron van Oers
9780470655740

Interior finishes & fittings for historic building conservation

Edited by

Michael Forsyth
**Department of Architecture and Civil Engineering
University of Bath**

&

Lisa White
Furniture and Interiors Historian

WILEY-BLACKWELL

A John Wiley & Sons, Ltd., Publication

This edition first published 2012 © 2012 Blackwell Publishing Ltd

Blackwell Publishing was acquired by John Wiley & Sons in February 2007. Blackwell's publishing program has been merged with Wiley's global Scientific, Technical and Medical business to form Wiley-Blackwell.

Registered office:
John Wiley & Sons, Ltd, The Atrium, Southern Gate, Chichester, West Sussex, PO19 8SQ, UK

Editorial offices:
9600 Garsington Road, Oxford, OX4 2DQ, UK
The Atrium, Southern Gate, Chichester, West Sussex, PO19 8SQ, UK
2121 State Avenue, Ames, Iowa 50014-8300, USA

For details of our global editorial offices, for customer services and for information about how to apply for permission to reuse the copyright material in this book please see our website at www.wiley.com/wiley-blackwell.

The right of the author to be identified as the author of this work has been asserted in accordance with the UK Copyright, Designs and Patents Act 1988.

Library of Congress Cataloging-in-Publication Data

Interior finishes & fittings for historic building conservation / edited by Michael Forsyth and Lisa White.
    p. cm.
Includes bibliographical references and index.
ISBN 978-1-4051-9022-0 (hardback)
1. Building fittings. 2. Finishes and finishing. 3. Interior decoration. 4. Historic buildings–Conservation and restoration. I. Forsyth, Michael, 1951- II. White, Lisa, 1950- III. Title: Interior finishes and fittings for historic building conservation.
    TH6010.I54 2011
    747–dc22
    2011010022

A catalogue record for this book is available from the British Library.

This book is published in the following electronic formats: ePDF 9781119979333; Wiley Online Library 9781119979364; ePub 9781119979340; Mobi 9781119979357

Set in 10 on 12.5 pt Avenir by Toppan Best-set Premedia Ltd.
Printed and bound in Singapore by Markono Print Media Pte Ltd.

1   2012

Contents

Preface

This volume on the historic interior is the fourth of a series on Historic Building Conservation that combine conservation philosophy in the built environment with knowledge of traditional materials and structural and constructional conservation techniques and technology. The chapters are written by leading conservators, historians, architects and related professionals, who together reflect the interdisciplinary nature of conservation work.

While substantial publications exist on each of the subject areas – some by the authors of the Historic Building Conservation series – few individuals and practices have ready access to all of these or the time to read them in detail. The aim of the series is to introduce each aspect of conservation and to provide concise, basic and up-to-date knowledge within four volumes, sufficient for the professional to appreciate the subject better and to know where to seek further help.

This interiors volume is of course mindful of the National Trust's magisterial *Manual of Housekeeping* (Elsevier Butterworth-Heinemann, Oxford, 2006) and the aim throughout has been to complement, rather than overlap with, the information and advice the *Manual* offers on housekeeping and maintenance, largely by augmenting the understanding of the history and character of interior elements through previously unpublished material and offering current building conservation principles and techniques.

Of direct practical application in the field, the books are structured to take the reader through the process of historic building conservation, presenting a total sequence of the integrative teamwork involved. Of the other complementary volumes, *Understanding historic building conservation* provides understanding of the planning, legislative and philosophical background, followed by the process of researching the history of a building and the formulation of a conservation policy and plan. *Structures & construction in historic building conservation* traces the history of structures in various materials and contains much guidance on the survey, assessment and diagnosis of structures, the integration of building code requirements within the historic fabric and much else besides. *Materials & skills for historic building conservation* provides, within a single volume, essential information on the properties of traditional external building materials, including their availability and sourcing, the causes of erosion and decay, the skills required for their application on conservation projects and the impact the materials have on the environment. The present volume, *Interior finishes & fittings for historic building conservation*, complements *Materials & skills for historic building conservation*, combining the history and application of each material with current knowledge of maintenance and conservation techniques.

The series is particularly aimed at construction professionals – architects, decorative arts historians and specifiers, surveyors, engineers – as well as postgraduate building conservation students and undergraduate architects and surveyors as specialist or optional course reading. The series is also of value to other professional groups such as commissioning client bodies, managers and advisers, and interested individuals involved in house refurbishment or setting up a building preservation trust. While there is a focus on UK practice, most of the content is of relevance overseas (just as UK conservation courses attract many overseas students, for example from India, China, Australia and the USA).

Michael Forsyth

Contributors

Patrick Baty

Joined family business, Papers and Paints, after leaving the army. For many years has run a consultancy that advises on the use of paint and colour in historic buildings. Projects have ranged from private houses to palaces, museums to London housing estates. Recent restoration projects include Kew Palace and the Royal Festival Hall. Lectures widely and has published numerous articles. Trustee of the Georgian Group. In 2007 the firm was granted a Royal Warrant of Appointment to Her Majesty the Queen.

David Bostwick

Formerly Keeper of Social History at Sheffield Museums, and now a free-lance lecturer and consultant in the Cultural History of the Medieval, Tudor and Stuart periods. His particular interest is in how buildings and objects were used, and he is currently researching the meanings of 'vulgar' carvings in churches.

David Drewe

Head of Building Services Engineering & Safety Team, English Heritage. He joined English Heritage in 1998 as a Senior Mechanical & Electrical Engineer and in 2005 was appointed Head of Team. In addition to the general management of building services engineers, fire and health & safety advisers, most of his work involves providing advice on the application of building services in historic interiors and structures, and developing standards and guidance to further the understanding of the relationship of services and historic buildings and the impacts that their provision can have. He is much involved with energy, environmental and sustainability issues as they relate to the management of historic buildings.

James Finlay

Adviser to the National Trust on Interior Decoration since 1998. James Finlay set up his own business in 1983 soon after graduating from Manchester University with a degree in History of Art. He offers specialist, practical and design advice to owners and guardians of historic buildings based on detailed research, and manages projects from concept to completion. There has been a broad spectrum of commissions involving churches, museums, colleges, country houses, and industrial and vernacular buildings at places such as Wrotham Park, Clifton Hampden Church, Chillington Hall, the Beatles' houses in Liverpool, Kedleston Hall, Sidney Sussex College, Penrhyn Castle, the Archbishop's House in Westminster, Quarry Bank Mill and Belton House.

Michael Forsyth

Architect and director of the postgraduate degree course in the Conservation of Historic Buildings, University of Bath. Studied at Liverpool University, held the Rome Scholarship in Architecture and, after residence in Italy, moved to Canada, working on the design of the new concert hall for the Toronto Symphony Orchestra with the architect Arthur Erickson. Lectured at University of Bristol, 1979–89 and has lived and practised in Bath since 1987. Books include *Pevsner Architectural Guides: Bath* (Yale University Press, 2003) and *Buildings for Music: The architect, the musician, and the listener from the seventeenth century to the present day* (MIT Press and Cambridge University Press, 1985), which won the 19th Annual ASCAP-Deems Taylor Award; translations in French, German, Italian and Japanese. Edited the three other volumes in the Historic Building Conservation series (Blackwell Publishing, 2007–2008).

Ian Hume

Structural conservation engineer. Worked for English Heritage for twenty-two years, ten as Chief Engineer, and was project engineer for work at Ironbridge, Castle Howard Mausoleum, the National Gallery, the British Museum and the Palace of Westminster. Advised on projects ranging from prehistoric to the 1960s, including earth, stone, brickwork, timber, iron and modern materials. Took early retirement in 1997 and is now in private practice. Lectures to postgraduate students and organises courses on Conservation Engineering. Chairs the Conservation Accreditation Register for Engineers (CARE).

Peter Norris

Chartered surveyor and an Approved Inspector and fire safety adviser. Started career in building control in 1975 working in West Dorset with its abundance of vernacular buildings, then moved to Bath City Council in 1986 specialising in major projects and historic buildings. Co-founded Rexon Day Building Control in 1997. Lectures on the Building Regulations and Fire Safety at the University of Bath for the postgraduate degree course in the Conservation of Historic Buildings and to the RIBA Part 3 students. Also an art historian; holds a degree in art history and is the biographer of the artist Arthur Henry Knighton-Hammond.

Treve Rosoman

Curator of English Heritage's Architectural Study Collection since 1986. The Architectural Study Collection, of which the wallpapers are part, is a collection of architectural fragments reflecting London's building history consisting of some 4000 objects. It is due to go online in early 2012 as part of English Heritage's project to make their collections more accessible. An antique dealer for ten years before joining the Historic Buildings Division of the Greater London Council. As part of the English Heritage's curatorial team responsible for the London houses, Chiswick, Marble Hill, Kenwood, and Ranger's House, he was in charge of refurnishing the Art Deco Eltham Palace. In 1992 he put on an exhibition of historic wallpapers in the Heinz Gallery of the RIBA and the accompanying catalogue, *London Wallpapers: Their manufacture and use, 1690-1840*, has just gone into a second edition. He has written widely on furniture history and interiors.

Annabel Westman

Independent textile historian and consultant on the restoration of historic interiors. Since 1980, has worked on a large number of historic furnishing projects for heritage bodies including the National Trust, English Heritage and Historic Royal Palaces, historic house trusts, and major museums in the UK and USA. Lectures regularly on university-accredited and museum decorative art and interior courses and has contributed numerous articles to art history publications including the *Burlington* and *Apollo* magazines. Director of Studies for the Attingham Trust for the Study of Historic Houses and Collections since 2005, and former Director of the Attingham Summer School 1992–2005.

Lisa White

Furniture and interiors historian, Director of the Attingham Summer School for the Study of Historic Houses and Collections 2004–10. Studied at Oxford University, trained as a curator at the Victoria and Albert Museum and subsequently taught at Bristol University (History of Art Department), University of Buckingham (MA in Decorative Art and Interiors) and University of Bath (MSc in Conservation of Historic Buildings, MSc in Conservation of Historic Gardens and Landscape); Curator of Decorative Art, The Holburne Museum, Bath, 2000–06; Chairman of the National Trust Arts Advisory Panel. Published *The Pictorial Dictionary of Eighteenth Century Furniture Design* (Antique Collectors' Club, 1990) and numerous articles on furniture history.

1 Conservation of the historic interior

Michael Forsyth

Introduction

The House Improved, published in 1931 by *Country Life* and written by Randall Phillips, Hon. ARIBA, the editor of *Homes and Gardens*, explains for owners of an old building how to make an 'ordinary' panelled door flush by nailing plywood over the top and how to box in the turned balusters up the staircase. It also gives several designs for encasing marble chimney-pieces in wood and fitting a gas fire insert. It illustrates how to improve a Georgian townhouse by demolishing part of the front façade and adding a bay window on the ground floor – and how to convert a Victorian Italianate villa into a bungalow with a mansard roof.

Just two year previously – in 1929 – A.R. Powys published his seminal book, *Repair of Ancient Buildings*. This was the first text, in the wake of William Morris, to lay out the principles of conservation that we still use today. So building conservation as we know it has a very short history, and the sort of vandalism advocated in *The House Improved* was still current in the 1970s, though boxing in architectural features is at least for the most part reversible – many of us have taken a claw hammer to sheets of plywood as the first step after moving in to an unrenovated house – whereas the wholesale demolition of historic buildings that continued into the 1970s was anything but reversible.

The presentation of historic interiors

The first volume in this series, *Understanding historic building conservation* (Chapter 1, 'The past in the future'), briefly reviews the growth of the heritage society in the 1970s including the adoption of the country house style

Interior finishes & fittings for historic building conservation, First Edition. Edited by Michael Forsyth & Lisa White. © 2012 Blackwell Publishing Ltd. Published 2012 by Blackwell Publishing Ltd.

for interiors, with scrubbed pine and flowered wallpaper, the rise in popularity of visiting National Trust properties and the success of upstairs-downstairs films. When the National Trust acquired Erddig at Wrexham, North Wales, in 1973, the new interest in upstairs-downstairs was reflected in the presentation of the house, with the servants' quarters and kitchens being emphasised. At Dyrham Park, near Bath, Gloucestershire, another of the Trust's flagship properties, in the early twenty-first century the visitor route underwent substantial revision to display restored Victorian domestic rooms, including the kitchen, bells passage, bakehouse, larders, tenants' hall and Delft-tiled dairy, while the kitchens, nurseries and servants' quarters at Lanhydrock, Bodmin, Cornwall, rebuilt after a devastating fire in 1881, have for many years been a major visitor attraction.

The presentation of National Trust country houses open to the public is a good reflection of the changing approaches to heritage and conservation. Interiors in houses belonging to the Trust formerly received a ruthless and rather standardised redecoration, but later on things changed. Kingston Lacy, where the Victorian character of the saloon was restored in 1982, was the first National Trust property to retain a sense of the history of the house.

The conserve-as-found approach was then taken much further at several properties: for example, by English Heritage in the 1980s at Brodsworth Hall, in South Yorkshire, where every stained patch of wallpaper and rusty picture hook was carefully removed while the building was renovated then reinserted back into place exactly as found. A similar approach was taken at Calke Abbey, Derbyshire, donated to the National Trust in 1985 by the Harpur-Crewe family (the house is situated on the site of an Augustinian priory, but was never actually an abbey). The eccentric Harpur-Crewe family had lived there for 360 years and had acquired an immense assortment of artefacts as they never threw anything away, and no redecoration had been carried out at least since 1924. When the Trust opened the house to the public in 1989, having stabilised the building but without carrying out any restoration, it was said to be 'a time capsule' and 'the house where time stood still'.

Chastleton, a splendid Jacobean house near Moreton-in-Marsh, Oxfordshire, built between 1607 and 1612 for Walter Jones, a wealthy wool merchant, came to the National Trust in 1991 after 400 years of continuous ownership by an increasingly impoverished family who could do no more than 'make do and mend'. The Trust carefully avoided restoration, retaining everything as found, from the kitchen's soot-blackened ceiling, to the peeling 1960s wallpaper in the library and abandoned slipper bath under the rafters; the house feels lived in, with fires in the hearths and no ropes or barriers.

When the National Trust for Scotland acquired Newhailes House, near Edinburgh, in 1997, the Trust did much to stabilise the house and prevent deterioration, while doing as little as possible to alter or restore the property and its contents. The last owner's electric fire and television were all kept in place; the railings up to the entrance were stabilised but kept rusty; and after the building was renovated the library furniture, instead of being arranged in the room, was carefully piled up in a dusty heap in a corner, just as it was when the Trust took over.

The National Trust (of England) also implemented a conserve-as-found renovation at the very grand Victorian country house, Tyntesfield, at Wraxhall, North Somerset, acquired in 2002. However, as James Finlay asserts in Chapter 13, the conserve-as-found approach records only the decline of a once-great house, and its chief merit is in preserving evidence of an interior for future generations. But the great presentational innovation at Tyntesfield was to keep the house open during the conservation work, making the repair work visible to the public as part of the Trust's educational remit. Visitors can climb a viewing tower to see the roof repairs and meet specialist conservators carrying out work ranging from re-roofing to rolling carpets.

Croome Court, Croome d'Abitot, near High Green, Worcester, Worcestershire, was purchased in 2007 by the Croome Heritage Trust, working in partnership with the National Trust. The house with its surrounding estate was 'Capability' Brown's first major commission in 1751 and helped establish his reputation together with that of Robert Adam, who designed part of the Court's interiors. The debate at the time of writing is how to present the interiors when eventually restored. Should the interiors be furnished in an appropriate if conjectural manner, or presented as a sequence of sparse architectural spaces? In recent years the house was a centre for the Hare Krishna movement, and one room was bizarrely but finely decorated by the Hare Krishna. Should the existing interior decorative scheme revert to an original style, but a conjectural one, or remain as part of the history of the building?

A very different approach to conserve-as-found had to be taken by necessity at Uppark, West Sussex, after a major fire caused by a workman's blowtorch completely destroyed the interior on 30 August 1989. Most of the pictures and furniture in the house were saved and the house was rebuilt in replica, re-opening its doors in 1995.

Managing change

In the field of repair and presentation of historic interiors – indeed, in the conservation world as a whole – the ground is always shifting as conservation philosophy evolves, and as knowledge and understanding improves and better repair techniques are developed. The only certainty is that in twenty or fifty years' time whatever we did today will be dateable to our own era.

The classic interiors of the decorator John Fowler (1906–77), in the third quarter of the twentieth century, transformed dreary pre-wartime interiors with vivid colours, informality, rich twentieth-century textiles and deeply upholstered soft furnishings, all projecting a sense of ease and comfort and historic association for his clients, many of whom had downsized with the disappearance of servants and country house life. Fowler, working with society decorator Lady Sibyl Colefax and later with his business partner,

Nancy Lancaster, lent freshness and liveliness to historic interiors, though the freedom of treatment and the use of subtly varying multiple tones and stippled paint effects may seem today to lack an academic approach, and in some of his private commissions to be over elaborate. However, Fowler's work itself evolved and his later, extensive work for the National Trust became more serious and historical, though without becoming lifeless.

Most historic interiors themselves have evolved over time. In the present day, decorative schemes are changed particularly frequently as property changes hands – it is very rare today for a family to occupy the same house even for one whole generation. It is vital that buildings are allowed to continue to adapt to changing needs and circumstances and to remain alive. After all, the interiors of Bath's Georgian houses were frequently modified and refurnished from Georgian through to Victorian times to remain up to date for rental by the upmarket London grandees coming to the city to socialise and take the waters. It is a common misconception among householders that if their home is listed they will not be allowed to make any changes whatsoever: the reality is that the legislation protecting historic buildings is not about *preventing* change but about the *management* of change, as buildings must accommodate owners' changing needs and lifestyles – and sometimes complete changes of use (though it is important for the householder to understand that the listing applies to the entire building and everything within its curtilage, not just to items that are described in the listing schedule).

One of the chief reasons for more major rebuilding work to historic interiors was to repair fire damage. It is remarkable that, along with smaller historic properties, nearly every country house has suffered fire damage – and not just in the era of lighting by open flames, with in the past two or three decades major fires at Hampton Court (1986), Uppark, West Sussex (1989), Prior Park, Bath (1991), Windsor Castle (1992) and Moreton Hall, Warwickshire (2008), one of the country's best Edwardian houses. On 30 June 2011 fire destroyed much of the 16th-century manor house former home of Augustus John, one of Britain's leading portrait painters, at Fordingbridge, Hampshire.

Building history and understanding significance

With old buildings care has to be taken over the question of authenticity because, especially in the case of buildings that have suffered fire damage, what you see can be misleading: sometimes the rebuilding was in the original style and sometimes in a contemporary style. Before applying for listed building consent to carry out alteration work to a historic interior, it is essential to understand the significance of the building through a combination of observation on the ground and a desktop study to reveal the building's history and to understand what in the interior is authentic. This, together with the formulation of a policy towards the proposed works – the conservation philosophy to be adopted in terms of approach, techniques and technology, and proposed structural interventions such as floor strengthening – will result in a justification statement in the case of small buildings and a conservation plan, sometimes preceded by a synopsis of the plan in a conservation statement, in the case of major buildings, together with a Conservation Management Plan for large sites that will map how the heritage asset will be cared for in the future.

The desktop study will often involve a combination of primary sources, such as documents and drawings, and secondary sources, for example history books, listed building descriptions, Pevsner's The Buildings of England series, dictionaries of architects including Howard Colvin's A Biographical Dictionary of British Architects 1600–1840, 4th edition (2008), and websites such as www.imagesofengland.org.uk. The archives that may be valuable include local record offices and libraries and national resources including the National Register of Archives; the National Monuments Record; the public archive of English Heritage, in Swindon; the British Library and the Public Record Office, Kew; Lambeth Palace Library; and the Church of England Record Centre. Private sources for major houses may include family archives with deeds, letters, building accounts, estate maps and photographs. The history of lesser houses may be investigated through deeds held by the owners or local record offices (though many deeds have been destroyed since the Land Registration Act 1925, as property is transferred), street directories, electoral registers, census returns (from 1841), rate books, estate maps, tithe maps (by parish, c.1840), early large-scale early Ordnance Survey maps (which are highly accurate), land tax assessment and building control records (kept, for example, in Bath from 1865, usually with drawings of proposed changes or additions to buildings), while record offices and libraries often have useful published prints, engravings, newspapers and sales particulars, sometimes illustrated with plans. Different building types, such as commercial and industrial buildings, public buildings and churches, have further sources of information that can be investigated and on which archives can advise.

The study may require some complex detective work to unravel the history of the building – investigative work that occasionally involves more than one building. Following an earlier devastating fire at Prior Park, Bath, in 1836, much rebuilding was carried out using components – decorative features, windows and other elements – sold to the then owner, Bishop Baines, that had been salvaged from the late eighteenth-century Huntstrete House, near Marksbury, Somerset. As with churches, early country houses sometimes underwent major programmes of restoration work in the nineteenth century. Frederick Leyland, a nineteenth-century lessee of the outstanding Tudor timber-framed Speke Hall, Liverpool, and a shipping magnate and patron of the arts, carried out major restoration work on the ground-floor rooms in 1867–78 that now forms a significant part of the history of this National Trust house. At another National Trust property, Great Chalfield Manor near Bradford-on-Avon, Wiltshire, Sir Harold William Brakspear carried out sympathetic restoration work in 1905–11 that is architecturally interesting in itself, with careful Arts and Crafts detailing and reconstructing demolished parts of the building, working from drawings made by Pugin's pupil, Thomas Larken Walker, in 1836 when the building was still in its original state.

'Reading' the classical interior

When 'reading' a classical interior, another aspect of the investigation – especially important in reconstructing a decorative scheme – is to establish the original use of rooms. Frequently in classical Georgian interiors the iconography of decorative elements may give the vital clue, such as gesso work on chimneypieces and details of decorative plasterwork. Rooms in a house were given a particular character relating to their function in accordance with the fundamental, but now deeply unfashionable, eighteenth-century concept of propriety, the notion of what is appropriate to a room, to a person's status or to social behaviour. Interiors were broadly masculine or feminine in character, and decorated accordingly, though the entrance and stairway to a Georgian townhouse was perceived as an 'outdoor' or public space, especially in the case of rooming houses that were let as multiple occupancy. These areas would be sparsely furnished with a stone floor and the walls painted a stone colour, sometimes blocked to resemble ashlar, or the walls might actually be clad in ashlar. Libraries and dining rooms – where the chimneypiece might have bacchanalian suggestions or sheaves of wheat or garlands of fruit – were perceived as masculine, and were decorated in sober tones, the dining room especially avoiding fabrics that were thought to harbour cooking smells. In Victorian country houses, the billiard room and smoking room were of course most strictly male domains. Drawing rooms, on the other hand, were feminine places and were decorated and furnished accordingly, while a music room might have a pine and gesso chimneypiece with depictions of lyres or clusters of musical instruments, and bedrooms might have iconic clues in the decorative scheme such as images of Venus.

One difficulty with determining the original use of rooms and thus decorating them appropriately is that architectural features are often peripatetic, as Georgian chimneypieces and the like have frequently been removed illegally, or, until recent years, imported from Ireland and sold through architectural salvage yards – a ruthless and regrettable trade – then installed elsewhere, often inappropriately. Many of the finest architectural elements were removed from the 750 major country houses prior to their demolition in the years between 1945 and 1973, a sad period that was graphically depicted in Marcus Binney's tide-changing exhibition of 1974 at the Victoria and Albert Museum, 'The Destruction of the Country House', with grim pictures of decaying and crumbling houses. Cities fared no better, with great swathes of Georgian Liverpool, Bath and elsewhere being cleared.

The fall and rise of craftsmanship

Traditionally, craft skills and the use of traditional tools were passed from one generation to the next. Boys of fourteen might be apprenticed to men in their eighties – still working in pre-pension days – and the boys themselves might work to a similarly venerable age, so that over two generations alone there could be the best part of 130 years of unbroken skills and knowledge. This perception of craftsmanship as a continuum is very different from the 'filing cabinet' approach to architectural history – the largely Victorian conception still in use today – of compartmentalising architectural styles into periods of fixed dates when change supposedly took place. Indeed, in the case of minor rural dwellings that have no documentation and where deeds are not available, dating on stylistic grounds may be deceptive as building traditions often had continuity to the extent that a provincial house built around 1900 might be mistakenly dated as c. 1780.

Despite this, however, craftsmanship did begin a terminal decline during the Industrial Revolution. The Regency saw a growth in mass production and the consequent availability of artefacts, from architectural fittings to fabrics and household goods (as well as the rapid dissemination of the latest styles and fashions in architecture and furnishing through publications such as Rudolph Ackerman's influential British periodical *Repository of Arts*, published from 1809 to 1829, which could reach America or Hong Kong within weeks of publication). With decorative plasterwork, for example, the exquisiteness of Georgian freehand in situ modelling with heavy undercutting became replaced by moulded plasterwork, where a little undercutting was possible using several piece moulds, but without the three-dimensionality of the earlier work – typical, for instance, of Jeffrey Wyatville's work at Windsor Castle. Victorian plasterwork is perfect and hard, but lacks even further the liveliness of earlier craftsmanship.

Rebuilding works after the fires at Uppark and elsewhere were largely responsible for the revival of traditional craftsmanship in the United Kingdom; of skills that had been all but lost in the twentieth century with the use of Portland cement instead of lime products, and mass production of components and new methods of construction including reinforced concrete and steel framing.

In present-day conservation and restoration work, however, modern methods are often used to achieve a visual result similar to that of original work at a much lower cost; in the rebuilding of Windsor Castle after the fire, the term 'equivalent restoration' was coined. Instead of traditional methods of plastering, for instance, where gypsum or lime plaster with hair reinforcement is applied onto riven oak or chestnut laths, fibrous plaster with hessian reinforcing may be used, with one mould able to be reused many times. Such work may shrink and crack over time and tends to be visually dull compared with traditional work, albeit redeemed at Windsor by copious gilding.

Joinery detailing: a case study

Whatever the repair method used, it is essential that the detailing is correct. One of the key elements of the historic interior is joinery. When refurbishing an interior the decision must be made whether to reinstate original detailing, or to retain later alterations where – with decorative plasterwork and other elements – these are so extensive and complete that it would be nonsense to reinstate original joinery details. With Georgian houses, broadly speaking, it is desirable to do the latter, and essential for instance in the case of a Georgian house where rooms may have been subdivided and original joinery altered piecemeal. The Victorians frequently removed dado rails (which went out of fashion in the Regency period) and installed picture rails. With the latter removed, the dado rail should be reinstated to the correct height and profile. Too often dado rails have been replaced too high, while the exact correct position can often be determined as the original fixing battens are usually to be found behind Victorian plaster skim; as a general guide, the dado rail aligns with the windowsill and the profile is usually an inversion of the skirting. The exception is the staircase, where the skirting is normally bull-nosed and the dado rail is positioned at balustrade height and is profiled as a half balustrade. The Victorians frequently replaced glazing bars with plate glass after the mid-1840s, when the tax on glass by weight was removed. When reinstating glazing bars it is vital that the thickness and profile is correct for the period of the building (the profile does of course face the room interior, except for shop fronts, where the joinery profile faces the street). Early eighteenth-century glazing bars in Bath were 1½ inches (38 mm) thick, of ovolo profile, set within small 'nine-over-nine' sashes, and they became increasingly thin and elegant as the century progressed. The post-1755 houses of Bath's Gay Street have 1⅛ inch (29 mm) bars, and by the 1760s and 1770s (e.g. Brock Street, Royal Crescent and Rivers Street) these are ¾ inch (19 mm). The most elegant bars, with their reflection of light off curved surfaces, are astragal and hollow, used in the 1790s and early 1800s and just ⅝ inch (16 mm) thick, with meeting rails of ¾ inch (19 mm). The entire sashes were often replaced by the Victorians with a heavier profile and with 'horns', the extension of the styles beyond the mortice and tenon of the meeting rail to strengthen the frame to take heavy sheets of plate glass.

Finding 'forgotten spaces'

We emphasised earlier the need to keep buildings alive through a process of carefully managed change. With important, usually large-scale, public buildings another way of breathing new life into historic interiors is by finding 'forgotten' exterior spaces and enclosing them with a contemporary intervention, which may not only extend the accommodation to provide much-needed public facilities and substantially improve internal circulation; this concept also allows the experience of the historic interior to remain undisturbed. There are several significant examples in London, principally the Queen Elizabeth II Great Court at Sir Robert Smirke's British Museum, designed by Foster and Partners in the late 1990s based on a 1970s proposal by Colin St John Wilson. In the vast central quadrangle, commonly known as 'the Great Court', an accretion of additions were demolished to reveal the drum-like Reading Room and the space enclosed by a fully tessellated glazed roof designed by Buro Happold. Besides providing retail, catering and other facilities, the vast enclosure 'resolves' the circulation whereby the visitor can enter any part of the existing building without relying on the entirely linear circulation as before. At the Wallace Collection, Marylebone, Rick Mather Architects enclosed the dank and disused court-yard (1993–2000) with a glass roof to form a badly needed restaurant with educational and exhibition spaces below.

The architects Dixon Jones have completed several conceptually similar projects. Their work at the Royal Opera House (1983–99; in collaboration with Building Design Partnership, as Dixon Jones BDP) adapted and extended the historic interiors, which included linking the building with the adjacent Floral Hall – another 'forgotten' space – to form a spectacular atrium, while the building was democratised by forming a single main entrance for all ticket prices. The main auditorium was enhanced, mean-while, by decorative scheme by David Mlinaric, without any alteration to its character. At the National Portrait Gallery in St Martin's Lane, a once-dingy service yard that separated the Gallery from the National Gallery next door was enclosed to form the Ondaatje Wing (1994–2000), a triple-height hall that improved the circulation system without altering the essen-tial experience of the three main levels of picture galleries. At the National Gallery, in the newly pedestrianised Trafalgar Square (built in 1832–8), Dixon Jones created (2003–2005) a new entrance, alternative to the main entrance at the central portico, through an access passage and opening up the ground floor for public facilities including a refurbished café, a shop and a double-height top-lit atrium, originally an external courtyard. This was achieved while maintaining the integrity of the richly ornate interiors of the existing galleries, which were refurbished to their original decorative appearance in the 1990s by the conservation architects Purcell Miller Tritton, using rich figured silks and restoring many of the ceilings' original decorative schemes.

Conclusion

In conclusion, it is essential in any interior conservation scheme first of all to understand the process. This involves recognising the importance of the initial investigation into the history and fabric of the building and the estab-lishment of a philosophical approach and a policy towards the work. It is necessary to make a diagnosis of problems that may exist and an assess-ment of what work is required. Finally, it is essential to recognise the divi-sion of responsibility, when the work is carried out, between management, professional consultants, specialist conservators, contractors and others who may be involved.

Further reading

Specialist books are noted by chapter, but among general books, James Ayres, *Building the Georgian City* (Yale University Press, 1998), provides a systematic explanation of eighteenth-century building trades and methods and an understanding of traditional tools and craftsmanship. Geoffrey

Beard, *Craftsmen and Interior Decoration in England, 1660–1820* (Holmes & Meier Publishers Inc., 1981), is a rich source of information on the very finest work. Of the many books on the history of interior design, the first to draw widespread attention was Mario Praz, *An Illustrated History of Interior Decoration* (Thames & Hudson, 1964), and Peter Thornton, *Authentic Décor: The Domestic Interior 1620–1920* (Weidenfeld & Nicolson, 1984) and John Fowler and John Cornforth, *English Decoration in the Eighteenth Century* (Barrie & Jenkins, 1974) remain among the best. John Cornforth, *The Inspiration of the Past: Country House Taste in the Twentieth Century* (Viking in Association with Country Life, 1985) gives much information on the influential decorator, John Fowler. Dan Cruickshank and Neil Burton, *Life in the Georgian City* (Viking, 1990) explains how Georgian houses functioned domestically. There are few books on the humble interior, and James Ayres, *Domestic Interiors: The British Tradition 1500–1850* (Yale University Press, 2003) fills this gap.

2 Stone floors

Lisa White

Introduction

Stone has long been used as an interior finish for walls, especially where environmental conditions limit the use of additional surfaces such as plaster or paint, for instance in basement service areas. It has also been used aesthetically, to link the exterior finish of a building with the immediate rooms of an interior, and particularly in entrance halls and passages.[1] It is an ideal, hard-wearing surface for floors in areas where exposure to moisture may be considerable although its weight means that it is usually confined to use on ground floor and basement levels.

Materials

In general before 1660, stone for the interior was sourced locally: Isaac Ware pointed out in his *A Complete Body of Architecture* (1756) 'that all stones stand better, and serve for purposes of strength and beauty both, much more successfully upon or near where their quarries are, than elsewhere'.[2] But stone was carried or shipped from other parts of Britain if local materials were unavailable, or where a client required a particular finish. Historic shipping routes across the River Severn from the Forest of Dean to Bristol, and from Yorkshire and the Portland peninsula in Dorset to London, provided important cities with essential supplies for street paving and durable floors for public and domestic building.[3] Slate from Cornwall, Wales and Cumbria was used extensively, either on its own or interspersed with lighter-coloured stone. English coloured marbles also provided builders with decorative stone for interior finishes. The best of these fine-grained limestones that contain a high level of calcium carbonate were found in Kent, Derbyshire, Sussex, Surrey and Dorset (Purbeck). Not only could these marbles take a high polish, but they were also beautifully patterned, often with swirling patterns of fossilised crustaceans. Many fine examples can still be seen in the columns of medieval cathedrals and grander parish churches.

Interior finishes & fittings for historic building conservation, First Edition. Edited by Michael Forsyth & Lisa White. © 2012 Blackwell Publishing Ltd. Published 2012 by Blackwell Publishing Ltd.

After c. 1660, coloured stones and marbles from other parts of Europe were imported in increasing quantities for the finishing of historic interiors in Britain, in response to prevailing fashions for classical decoration. These were used domestically for patterned floors (discussed below), for chimneypieces (see Chapter 7 of this volume), for interior architectural elements such as columns, and even on occasion as a veneer for walls. By the nineteenth century not only were Italian marbles imported in vast quantities, but skilled Italian craftsmen came too. In 1841 the Roman craftsman Leonardi laid the brightly coloured pavement of the newly enclosed colonnade of the courtyard at Chatsworth, Derbyshire.

British patterned stones, alabasters and marbles continued to be used for decorative finishes throughout the eighteenth and nineteenth centuries, and particularly when foreign supplies were difficult to obtain during wartime naval blockades. Magnificent use was made of Derbyshire alabaster for door-cases for the State Apartment at Chatsworth, c. 1694, and Nottinghamshire alabaster was used for the twenty columns of Kedleston's immense hall in 1763, quarried from another family property. Understanding the sources of decorative stones used in historic buildings is a vital part of research for any conservation plan: colour schemes and patterns used in such permanent decoration may provide essential clues about other lost or obscured elements in an interior.

Floors

Traditional stone floors in Britain were created by using large 'flags' or panels of stone, finished on the upper side only, and bedded into a lime-and-sand mortar (Figure 2.1). The stone surface would be left in its natural state and cleaned with fresh water, brushes or sand, giving lighter-coloured natural stone floors a bright appearance.

Over a long period of time, however, dirt can penetrate deep into stone flags, especially those made of more porous materials such as Cotswold and Bath stone, so that surfaces gradually become permanently darkened. More invasive proprietary nineteenth- and twentieth-century cleaning agents have also damaged the surfaces of older stone floors, and hard wear over centuries has worn down the stones of passages, stairs and doorways. More damaging have been attempts to 'seal' stone floors with modern resins, which result in moisture being trapped within the stone itself, causing deterioration. Careful investigation of the age, material and condition of historic natural stone floors is vital in any conservation scheme. Retaining and conserving old stone can preserve the character of a building, especially when replacement stone can no longer be sourced from the original quarry.

From 1500 onwards, fashionable European interiors were increasingly fitted with patterned stone floors for principal ground-floor rooms, particularly entrance halls. In Britain after 1600, patterns were taken from Continental, mainly Italian, published sources dating from the mid-sixteenth century onwards: for example, Book IV of Sebastiano Serlio's *Architettura*

Figure 2.1 Natural stone floor, 1765, Countess of Huntingdon's Chapel, Bath, showing signs of heavy wear and recent repair. The Building of Bath Collection (Bath Preservation Trust).

(1559–62) and Andrea Palladio's famous *Quattro Libri*, first published in 1570 and published in English translations from the 1660s onwards.[4] Godfrey Richards's translation (1663) included additional designs for floor patterns.[5] Inigo Jones's design for the marble floor of the Queen's House, Greenwich, laid by the mason Nicholas Stone in 1636–7, is an early example of the sophisticated use of Italianate design in England. The Little Castle at Bolsover, Derbyshire (1612–14), retains a chequered black-and-white marble floor in the Marble Closet on the first floor, and a stone floor arranged in geometric patterns in the Pillar Parlour, originally the 'lower dining room' (Figure 2.2).

Charles-Augustine Daviler's *Cours Complet d'Architecture* (1691) provided clients and craftsmen with up-to-date, fashionable patterns for marble and stone floors, for example at Petworth House, Sussex, laid by James Sayers in 1692 (Figure 2.3). These patterns remained in use throughout the eighteenth century. Large square or lozenge shapes were considered suitable for churches and large public spaces, while more complex and intricate patterns using circles, hexagons, octagons, triangles and rectangles, with interlace borders, were available for domestic halls, passages and terraces, faithfully evoking Roman mosaics.

The use of marble patterned floors became far more widespread in England after 1660, and they were highly admired. The floor of the Sheldonian Theatre, Oxford, designed by Christopher Wren and built in

Figure 2.2 Stone floor in geometric patterns, 1612–14, in the Pillar Parlour, Bolsover Castle, Derbyshire. Courtesy of English Heritage.

Figure 2.3 Marble Hall, Petworth House, Sussex; the floor laid by James Sayers, 1692. Courtesy of the National Trust.

1663–8, was paved with black and white marble, and Celia Fiennes commented that the floor of the chapel at Chatsworth (1690–91) 'is black and white marble vein'd lay'd longwayes in large stones all of the same'.[6] Throughout the eighteenth century patterned stone and marble floors were regarded as essential for fashionable houses built in the classical style in all parts of the country. Many beautiful examples survive in country house halls and garden buildings. Great attention was paid to the cutting, laying and bordering of such floors, as in the black-and-white marble floor of the Octagon at Orleans House, Twickenham, designed by James Gibbs in 1720, or the multicoloured marble floor of Vanbrugh's Temple of the Four Winds at Castle Howard, Yorkshire, finished in 1736. Both native and imported marbles were used for these major commissions: Italian marbles were regarded as the finest by house-owners who had seen them during the Grand Tour. In 1732 the 4th Duke of Beaufort ordered to be sent back to England sufficient Italian marble to line the floor and walls of an entire Cabinet Room at Badminton House. Much of the marble is now

Figure 2.4 Batty Langley, decorations for 'Cabinet-Works, Floors, Ciellings &c', Plate XCVI of *The Builder's and Workman's Treasury of Designs* (1739).

Figure 2.5 Stone and slate floor designed by Robert Adam for the hall, Osterley Park House, Middlesex, 1763. Courtesy of the National Trust.

fitted into Badminton Church. Many English designers plagiarised or adapted Italian and French designs for their own publications during the middle years of the century. Most memorable among these are John Carwitham's *Various Kinds of Floor decorations . . . whether in Pavements of Stone, Marble or with Painted Floor Cloths* (1739) and Batty Langley's *City and Country Builder's and Workman's Treasury of Designs* (1740) (Figure 2.4).

Robert and James Adam perfected the use of marble and stone floors in their numerous commissions between 1760 and 1780, carefully balancing the patterns of both floor and ceiling, as at Osterley Park (1767). Adam's designs for the floors at Osterley Park House in 1763 demonstrate the minute consideration he gave to the floor surfaces in such grand schemes (Figure 2.5). The hall floor at Syon was cut and laid in bold black-and-white marble, while that in the anteroom next door was executed in *scagliola*, a composition material of pulverised selenite (gypsum) which can be coloured, fired and polished to resemble inlaid marble. By the late eighteenth century the use of decorative marble floors for grand houses, both public and private, was thoroughly established and continued through the nineteenth century.

Marble floors respond rapidly to changes in temperature and humidity, allowing condensation to form on them and become slippery. Over the years many have suffered from abrasion, breakage of the surface when heavy objects have been dragged across or dropped on them, or incursion of dirt into the mortar between the different stones. When stone and marble floors ceased to be so fashionable in the later Victorian period and the twentieth century, they were covered with carpet or matting, often adding to the problems of condensation. Perhaps worst of all has been careless damage caused by the installation of central heating systems, when floors have been wantonly chopped through to allow the laying of pipework beneath them. The conservation and restoration of such floors can be expensive, but the results are always rewarding.

Endnotes

1. See *Materials and skills for historic building conservation*, Chapter 2, pp. 5–46, for full discussion of stone types and use for buildings.
2. Isaac Ware, *A Complete Body of Architecture* (1756), Book I, Chapters III, IV, V, pp. 41–46.
3. James Ayres, *Building the Georgian City* (Yale University Press, 1998), Chapter 4, pp. 66–72.
4. Andrea Palladio, *I Quattro Libri dell'Architettura* (Venice, 1570).
5. *The First Book of Architecture, By Andrea Palladio, Translated out of Italian . . . to which are added Designes of Floors lately made at Somerset-House . . . London, printed by J.M and sold by G. Richards* (1663).
6. Christopher Morris, *The Illustrated Journeys of Celia Fiennes, c. 1682–c. 1712* (Macdonald & Co., 1982), p. 106.

3 Cantilever or hanging stone stairs

Ian Hume

Cantilever (or hanging) stone stairs are fascinating (Figure 3.1). They are so very slender and graceful by comparison with modern reinforced concrete staircases. These stairs have a long and distinguished history, being illustrated in Palladio's book *I Quattro Libri dell'Architettura*, published in 1570. The first example built in this country was, seemingly, the Tulip Staircase in the Queen's House, Greenwich, by Inigo Jones in 1629–35 (see Figure 6.2). It is also understood that an example was reported in a fourth-century BC watchtower at Naxos.

There are straight flights, curved flights, flights with winders and even 'flying' flights that sail across window openings with only a minimal stone or cast iron beam for support. There are flights on the grandest scale in palaces, and workaday servants' back stairs in Georgian terraced houses. All are intriguing, many exciting to see.

How do they work?

Stairs of this type neither cantilever nor do they hang; neither do they gain any real support from the handrail, but each tread bears on the tread below and relies on torsion at the point where it is built into the wall (Figure 3.2).

Stepping on one tread passes load to the next, and that passes on to the next, and so on. The load must be carried back to the wall within a few treads; if it were not, the load at the bottom of a very long spiral flight would clearly be unsustainable. The act of one tread applying load to the back of the tread below tends to rotate the lower tread, but as this is, or should be, solidly built into the wall, it cannot turn. Torsion plays a major role in the action of this type of construction.

Some of the more elaborate stairs (also known in Scotland as 'Pencheck stairs') have an element of interlock between adjacent treads, but as many

Interior finishes & fittings for historic building conservation, First Edition. Edited by Michael Forsyth & Lisa White. © 2012 Blackwell Publishing Ltd. Published 2012 by Blackwell Publishing Ltd.

Figure 3.1 A splendid example of a cantilever or hanging staircase.

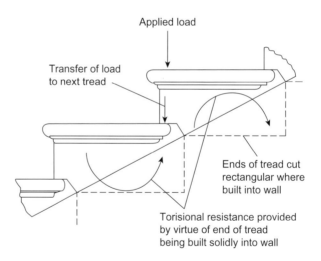

Figure 3.2 How cantilever stairs work.

of the simpler types do not have this, the existence of such an interlock cannot be critical.

The fact that the treads are buried only perhaps 120 mm into the supporting wall while they may be well over 1 m long indicates that they cannot possibly cantilever. Without the mutual support of each other, they would simply tear from the wall under their own weight.

Landings

Landings are also a source of wonder. They are often no more than 130 mm thick, sometimes less. Half landings also rely on interlock between the stairs and the various slabs from which they are constructed. Long landings must cantilever from the wall and are, as a consequence, usually much thicker than half landings.

Sources of problems

The main problem with this type of staircase is wear to the nosing of the treads, and where this has already been repaired by the insertion of a replacement nosing, the staircase is very much at risk (Figure 3.3). This was the root cause of the collapse of an office building staircase some time ago. The staircase had fractured along a line close to the supporting wall and coincident with the end of the nosing replacement. Cutting out the worn nosing dramatically reduces the strength of the stair and should never be done under any circumstances.

Cutting holes for the insertion of services is very likely to threaten the stability of the staircase. While the requirement to put holes through stairs must be resisted, it is equally undesirable to put holes through landing slabs, which will themselves be of minimal thickness (100 mm is perhaps the norm) and an integral part of the stability of the staircase.

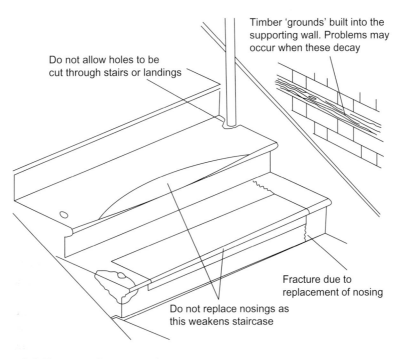

Timber 'grounds' built into the supporting wall. Problems may occur when these decay

Do not allow holes to be cut through stairs or landings

Fracture due to replacement of nosing

Do not replace nosings as this weakens staircase

Figure 3.3 Danger points to watch.

Failure of supporting walls due to decay of any timber embedded in the wall or due to foundation movement that thus allows the wall to settle a little will disturb the stairs, seriously weakening them. Sudden impact, such as might be caused by bumping a safe or heavy furniture down the stairs, can easily cause fracturing. Scaffolding should never be erected on this type of staircase even if it is supported from below as this puts a high and localised load on the staircase that it may be unable to resist.

Investigation

As with all problems in buildings, unless there is a proper and careful investigation there is unlikely to be a correct diagnosis, and without the correct diagnosis the correct solution is unlikely to be found.

The investigation should begin with a thorough and close look for cracking, paying particular attention to the stair/wall junction, the tread-to-tread junctions and the stair-to-landing junction. Excessive movement between treads should be looked for; some movement is quite common but an excessive gap allows the tread above to become a pure cantilever. If replacement nosings are discovered then a very careful search for cracking must be made. Such cracking will be found through the original tread at the end of the replacement nosing close to the supporting wall. Carpets must always be lifted and a good torch used for proper inspection of the underside and dark corners. Landings should likewise be carefully inspected.

A staircase that has no signs of cracking, movement or replacement nosings is likely to be satisfactory.

Repairs

The introduction of a carpet is a good basic step to prevent further wear to the nosings of the treads. If treads are worn badly and to a point where they are dangerous to use, it is quite feasible to rebuild the worn surface using a resin-based mortar. If the result of this is unsightly (although it should be possible to achieve a reasonably satisfactory appearance) then the stair could be carpeted. As discussed above, on no account should the nosing be cut back to allow a replacement stone nosing to be inserted.

Cracks in treads can be repaired by resin injection with the addition of thin stainless steel dowels drilled in, but this not be attempted when the crack is close to the wall. When a tread has cracked part way along its length, it is possible – although difficult owing to tight tolerances – to slide out the broken length and to refix it to its stub by resin-fixed dowels. This is not recommended when the fracture is within one-third of the tread length of the wall. Treads with fractures close to the wall should be replaced in their entirety. The replacement step must be tightly embedded into the wall and be a good fit to its neighbours.

If the step-to-step rebate is excessively wide, injection of resin into the cleaned-out gap can serve to restore the integrity of this joint, and it may sometimes be necessary to tighten the bedding of the treads into the wall in order to restrain torsion forces.

Putting stringers under a flight of stairs is very much a last resort as the result can rarely be anything but most unsightly. It may, however, be the only alternative to putting in a new staircase.

Cracks in landing slabs should also be of concern, and joints between landing slabs should be as near to their original condition as possible.

The whole structure must remain rigid. Stone cantilever staircases are one of the few parts of traditional buildings that do not benefit from being flexible; they must be rigid, tight to their neighbours and firmly embedded into the supporting wall.

Load testing

Load testing can be a means of justifying the unjustifiable. It must be done with great care and under proper supervision. English Heritage has carried out a number of load tests on cantilever staircases, usually on staircases that because of a change in visitor circulation were to be put into public use for the first time in a long life. A scaffold shoring system was erected beneath the staircase not quite touching the stairs to act as a 'safety net' in case of disaster and the stairs loaded to well beyond the British Standard required loading. The movement, measured on highly accurate dial gauges, was, in each case, almost imperceptible.

A further test carried out by the English Heritage Conservation Engineering Team involved a staircase that was to be demolished. It was decided to load this staircase to destruction to determine the failure mode. If a staircase is crowded it might carry as much as $3.0\,kN/m^2$. This staircase was loaded to $10\,kN/m^2$, but very little happened. Slight downward movements at the edges of the treads were noted, but the attempt to determine the failure mode was a complete washout. However, a very important lesson was learnt – these sometimes delicate-looking stairs are, when in good order, immensely strong.

Timber cantilever stairs

Also in existence are a much smaller number of 'cantilever' staircases constructed from timber. In some examples each tread is made from timber planks formed into a rectangular box that is then built into the wall, and the whole assembly acts exactly as described above. However, as the construction is of timber held together with glue and nails it is doubtful whether the carrying capacity of such staircases is anything like as high as that of their much more robust stone cousins. This type of wooden staircase seems to be found in grand houses. In more simple situations treads are constructed as triangular boxes, but instead of being built into the wall they are supported by a timber stringer, perhaps only 25 to 30 mm thick, fixed to the wall. This latter type of staircase is likely to be quite frail as it relies on a stringer, which will be susceptible to decay and shrinkage.

Conclusion

As with conservation in general, these staircases are best left well alone if at all possible. Inspect them carefully; ensure that they are rigid and that they will serve well. Do not worry unduly, but just admire their beauty and the daring of those who built the early ones.

4 Decorative plasterwork: materials and methods

David Bostwick

Introduction

Decorative plasterwork has been used as an interior finish since the mid-sixteenth century. It is well known that Henry VIII's Nonsuch Palace, Surrey, built in the 1540s, employed Italian plasterers who were skilled in creating figurative panels of plasterwork for the exterior of the building. Not so well known is the fact that the interior walls of the palace were also treated with elaborate schemes of plaster decoration. Henry VIII had further exterior plasterwork at Whitehall, shown in a painting of 1545, and Cardinal Wolsey's closet at Hampton Court still survives with its interior plasterwork ceiling. So, the fashion was set for others to copy, and native plasterers soon began creating elaborate interior effects for wealthy clients, such as Sir Thomas Eames's pendant plasterwork ceiling at Heslington Hall, York, in 1568 (Figure 4.1).

Exterior plasterwork is nowadays known as 'pargetting', and is found chiefly in the East Anglia region. However, panels of plasterwork with dates can be found in the Lake District at Troutbeck, and Henry Cave's etchings of 1810 show several houses in York smothered in exterior decorative plasterwork. The term 'pargetting' comes from the practice of parging chimneys – that is, plastering the interior of canopied and inglenook fireplaces to prevent sparks setting fire to wooden elements. In the wet plaster it was natural to inscribe a pattern to decorate the hearth or, perhaps, employ a butter print or gingerbread mould to create an embossed design. This practice extended to exterior decoration and the term 'pargetting' became the name for this work too. At Belton House, Lincolnshire, the chequer-pattern wattle-weave pargetting of Anthony Salvin's boathouse has recently been expertly repaired.

Interior finishes & fittings for historic building conservation, First Edition. Edited by Michael Forsyth & Lisa White. © 2012 Blackwell Publishing Ltd. Published 2012 by Blackwell Publishing Ltd.

Figure 4.1 Pendant plasterwork ceiling, Heslington Hall, York, 1568. Photo: David Bostwick.

Materials

In both exterior and interior work, the plaster used was created by burning limestone – or more rarely seashells – in a kiln fired with wood.[1] High temperatures convert the limestone into lump lime or quicklime, which is highly caustic. Great heaps of such quicklime used commonly to be seen in farmers' fields, slaking in the rain before being used to enrich the soil. Builders and plasterers, however, dug pits in which the quicklime was tipped and then slaked with the addition of water. The chemical reaction turns the quicklime into a lime putty, which has the consistency of a good Greek yoghurt. This lime putty, after being sieved to remove any unslaked lumps, could be mixed with sands, gravels and other aggregates to make building mortar, or combined with chopped cow hair and fine sands to make a plaster known as 'coarse stuff', or used on its own as 'fine stuff' (Figure 4.2).

Lime plaster sets slowly and shrinks slightly as it dries, so the addition of cow hair renders the mixture more flexible and less inclined to crack. The microscopic barbs on the hairs hook on to the plaster particles and thus prevent large cracks opening as the fibres form a matrix with the plaster. Over time, by re-absorbing carbon dioxide from the air, lime plaster turns back into limestone – a very hard material capable of withstanding exposure to harsh weather over many years, as can be seen in the late sixteenth-century work at Hardwick Old Hall, and the early eighteenth-century work at Sutton Scarsdale Hall, both in Derbyshire (Figure 4.3).

Figure 4.2 Fragment of seventeenth-century plaster cornice from a house in Somerset, showing the imprint of laths, 'coarse stuff' with chopped cow hair and 'fine stuff'. Private collection.

Figure 4.3 Plasterwork overmantel by Abraham Smith in the Hill Great Chamber, Hardwick Old Hall, Derbyshire, 1587–96. Courtesy of English Heritage.

By adding quick-setting gypsum plaster, made by burning gypsum or alabaster, to the basic lime plaster, it is possible to speed up the setting process. These quick-setting plasters, such as plaster of Paris, expand slightly as they set and are used extensively today by commercial fibrous plasterers in the workshop to create lengths of ceiling cornice and elaborate ceiling roses strengthened with hessian scrim and sawn lath. Skilled traditional plasterers could mix lime plaster with a small amount of gypsum plaster in order to finely balance the shrinkage of the one against the expansion of the other to prevent cracking. Equally, plasterers who through long experience came to know the 'feel' of the plaster mix might add 'glovers' spetches' (rabbit-skin glue) to retard the set, especially if modelling the plaster in situ. Another widely used retardant was wine. Among the plaster-working tools preserved in Exeter Museum that belonged to the seventeenth-century Devon plasterer John Abbott is his wine bottle with his initials upon it. Perhaps the phrase 'getting plastered' has something to do with all this.

Methods

Decorative plasterwork can be hand-modelled, using little modelling spatulas, plasterers' leaves or trowels, knives and stilettos, or can be cast from moulds, or run as cornice and ceiling ribs using profile moulds (Figure 4.4).

Profile moulds are made from wood with a metal profile cut to the precise outline required, and in sixteenth- and seventeenth-century ceilings

Figure 4.4 Running a cornice using a profile mould. The Building of Bath Collection (Bath Preservation Trust).

Figure 4.5 Boxwood moulds for plaster enrichments. The Building of Bath Collection (Bath Preservation Trust).

the round-bottom ribs and flat-bottom ribs set with ornament in the soffit could either be run directly on the ceiling or formed on the bench as a precast rib and then cut to size and stuck on. Since at least the late seventeenth century the cornice profile mould, known as a 'horse', was moved along guide rails temporarily fixed to wall and ceiling. Plaster was added as the 'horse' was moved along, leaving the resultant cornice behind. For deep cornices with considerable profiles it was necessary, from the sixteenth century, to create a wooden superstructure on which the moulding could be built. Normally, struts of wood were nailed at intervals across the right angle from ceiling joist to wall and then riven oak laths were nailed to these, forming the inclined plane on which the cornice would be run.

Moulds for making plasterwork ornament such as flowers, leaves and fruit could be created by cutting a design into a block of fine-grained wood, such as boxwood or limewood, and then filling the recess with plaster (Figure 4.5). Once set, the plaster 'enrichment' could be removed from the mould. Great care had to be taken not to undercut the timber, or else it would be impossible to remove the ornament.

An alternative process was described as early as 1594 when Hugh Platt recommended carving the desired ornament in wood and then forming a mould over this made from a mixture of glue and beeswax. Having removed the carved original, the resulting mould could then be filled with gypsum plaster to produce dozens of the same ornament time after time. The moulds were flexible and could be bowed backwards or slit, 'therby the esilyer to get out the patterns without danger of breaking it, and yet the mold wil returne to his first shape'.[2] When the flexible mould began to break down, it could be melted and a new mould created around the original carving. The wooden carvings were kept for many years while the particular ornament was still considered fashionable, and could be utilised for new commissions long after the original creation. Consequently, in the absence of inscribed dates, one has to be very careful in attributing decorative plasterwork of a particular style to a certain period. It may well be the case that out-of-fashion ornaments were deliberately chosen by a client for good reason. In old age, Archbishop Accepted Frewen had the hall at Bishopthorpe Palace, York, encrusted with a decorative plaster ceiling and frieze in the 1660s using patterns that had been fashionable thirty years before – that is, before the bishops were ousted by the Parliamentary regime, and their re-instatement at the Restoration in 1660. Perhaps it was his way of rewriting history.

On a related point, it is worth noting that in the early seventeenth century the widespread use of moulds for plaster ornament meant that coats of arms and heraldic badges could be turned out readily for use in gentlemen's houses. However, these heraldic ornaments can also be found in houses not owned by the bearer of the arms displayed, so a degree of caution is called for in attributing house ownership on the basis of plasterwork heraldry. As an example, in the 1580s Sir John Savile of Methley, Yorkshire, and his wife Jane Garth of Morden, Surrey, had their arms cast from a mould at Methley Hall. A distant cousin, George Savile of Wakefield, a wealthy wool merchant, had the same coat of arms cast from the same mould and installed in an elaborate plaster ceiling in his house, Haselden Hall, Wakefield, in 1584. Some years later, in 1618, his daughter Dorothy's son, John Rodes, evidently proud of his maternal family lineage, had the same coat of arms cast from the same mould and installed in his new house, Barlborough Old Hall, Derbyshire, within the Great Chamber overmantel (Figure 4.6). Historians have assumed that Barlborough Old Hall was built for Sir John Savile and Jane Garth, just because their arms are displayed there in plaster, when this was clearly not the case.

Large decorative plasterwork contracts in the eighteenth century, such as that for Nostell Priory, Yorkshire, meant that repetitive bands of egg-and-dart and guilloche and individual paterae could be cast from moulds on site. Elsewhere, and on smaller commissions, mould-cast ornaments made from quick-setting plaster were easily transported from workshop to site and were readily set into a freshly screeded backing layer of lime plaster. The reverse of the ornaments was often scored while setting in the mould to ensure a good bond. Some particularly bulbous and heavy enrichments have protrusions created on the reverse to bed them deeply in the backing plaster (Figure 4.7).

The ornaments, being dry, would suck moisture from the backing plaster and thus achieve good adhesion. Sometimes a sticky, glue-rich layer of plaster was applied over the backing layer to ensure that precast sections of ribwork and large precast ornaments would adhere the better. Occasionally, the backing layer of the plaster would be brushed all over with glue-size to ensure that the surface layer of the plaster formed a good

Figure 4.6 Mould-cast fleur-de-lis from Clarke Hall, Wakefield, showing protrusions on the reverse to better support the bulbous ornament. Photo: David Bostwick.

Figure 4.7 Arms of Savile on the Great Chamber overmantel, Barlborough Old Hall, Derbyshire, 1618. The mould for this coat of arms was carved before 1584. Photo: David Bostwick.

bond. In the same way, builders today will brush a wall or ceiling with a thin solution of PVA adhesive before applying the finish coat.

Ceiling construction

Early wooden ceilings, such as that from Bridgwater, Somerset, but now in the Burrell Collection, Glasgow, show how a framework of floor joists covered with wooden floorboards above could be made attractive from below by nailing wooden ribs onto the undersides of the floorboards and fixing wooden carved enrichments at the junctions of the ribs. Dust would sift through the floorboards from above, so the next development was to lath the underside of the floorboards and plaster over them, or to lath the underside of the floor joists and plaster over them but still retain the pattern of wooden ribs on the surface. Ceilings such as this can still be seen at Pottergate, Norwich, and Sizergh Castle, Cumbria. As such ceilings were invariably whitewashed – wooden ribs and all – the next stage of development involved dispensing with the wooden ribs and planting plaster ones in their place, as is commonly found.

In creating these plaster ceilings, the plasterer would first lath the underside of the ceiling joists with riven oak laths, closely spaced, fixed by iron nails (Figure 4.8). A backing layer of plaster – often a mix of clay, lime, sand and cow hair – was then spread over the ceiling and squeezed through the gaps between the laths, thus forming plaster 'keys' on the reverse.

Figure 4.8 Section through plasterwork ceiling in Exeter Museum, showing the method of construction. Photo: David Bostwick.

The surface was then heavily scored to create a rough finish to receive the next layer of plaster. At this stage, strings would be run from diagonal corners to identify the perfect centre of the ceiling. Then a design could be carefully marked out. In early ceilings a pattern of ribwork would form the design and enrichments would be placed within the compartments and at junctions of the ribs. Having set the ribs and enrichments in place, a surface layer of pure lime plaster could be applied to disguise all the mitring of the ribs and any sharp edges around the enrichment. The ceiling then needed to dry before a cosmetic coat of whitewash was applied.

Design

An influential source for plasterwork ceiling designs, published in 1615, was Walter Geddes's *A Book of Sundry Draughts principally serving for glaziers and not impertinent for plasterers and gardeners*. Although by 1615 decorative plasterers are here described simply as plasterers, the ceiling ribs that they created were known as 'frets' and the plasterer creating this 'fretwork' was known as a fretter. They were specialised joiners, and their ability to carve wooden moulds, mitre ribwork and so on proves this. John Rose, owner of an extensive plasterwork business, was called a 'joiner' when he died in 1615. In 1672, when his grandson Thomas died, he was referred to as a plasterer. Both joinery and plasterwork were being produced by the same workshop, in much the same way that Thomas Gunby, joiner, and his brother Francis Gunby, plasterer, worked together at Gawthorpe Hall, Lancashire, in 1604, producing plastered and panelled rooms. This close association between the two crafts can be witnessed in the sixteenth and seventeenth centuries from the evidence of carved patterns on oak panelling and oak furniture and cast and moulded ornament in plaster employing the same designs in the different regions of the country. This local vocabulary of ornament – with, in addition, ornament found carved on gravestones – is highly important in enabling moveable items of carved oak furniture to be attributed to their place of manufacture. Sixteenth- and seventeenth-century Mannerist plasterwork still in situ, together with its recreations from the nineteenth and twentieth centuries, remains a significant resource for vernacular furniture studies.

Chamberlayne, writing in 1687, remarked how 'the rooms within are ceiled with plaister, excellent against the rage of fire, against the cold, and to hinder passage of all dust and noise'.[3] He also should have mentioned that plasterwork was appreciated for its ability to reflect light. Gloomy sixteenth-century hammer-beam roofs in halls, such as at Burghley House, Lincolnshire, could be underdrawn with light-reflecting plasterwork ceilings, as at Knole House, Kent (1604). Dingy parlours with painted ceilings as at Haddon Hall, Derbyshire, could be transformed with white plasterwork into bright sunny rooms as at Benthall Hall, Shropshire. Not just ceilings, but also plasterwork friezes and overmantels all reflected light. In the sixteenth and seventeenth centuries paint colour was rarely applied to decorative plasterwork, except on coats of arms, where the correct heraldic tincture to distinguish one family's achievements from those of another were essential. At Canons Ashby House, Northamptonshire, the fireplace overmantel in the Great Chamber has marbled plasterwork columns (1590s), and the Star Chamber ceiling in Bolsover Castle, Derbyshire (1621), is painted blue with gilded stars. These are significant exceptions, although there were probably many other examples that have been lost. Certainly the sketchbooks of John Abbott, the seventeenth-century Devon plasterer, contain recipes for making colours.

Finishes

A whitewash finish was usual in early work. Writing to George Villiers, Duke of Buckingham, in 1625, his agent Balthasar Gerbier remarked, 'I am very desirous of your presence, but I should be glad not to see you for three weeks, for we are whiting the ceilings, which had not been whitewashed before so we have got scaffolding everywhere.'[4] However, coloured plasterwork was enjoyed by the 1760s in the ceilings designed by Robert Adam, whose drawings reveal the colours that the plasterwork was to be painted (Figure 4.9). This taste for colour continued through into the nineteenth century, with rich colours and gilding, as at Alnwick Castle, Northumberland.

Figure 4.9 Design for the ceiling of the Dining Room, Kedleston Hall, Derbyshire, 1762, by Robert Adam. Pen, ink and watercolour. The yellow may represent gilding. Courtesy of the National Trust.

In the second half of the twentieth century many country house interiors with seventeenth- and eighteenth-century plasterwork, such as the stunning ceiling by Edward Goudge's follower, David Lance, in the chapel at Grimsthorpe Castle, Lincolnshire, had their white ceilings cleverly and subtly altered by the decorator John Fowler. He employed a palette of different shades of white and cream to emphasise the sculptural quality of the plasterwork and to enhance the delicacy of its detail.

Perhaps the most striking example of contemporary colour applied to historic decorative plasterwork is to be seen in the frieze of trees, animals and huntsmen in the High Great Chamber at Hardwick Hall, Derbyshire (Figure 4.10). Dating from the 1590s, this remarkable piece of work possibly served as the model for simpler woodland friezes in the Arts and Crafts style in the libraries at Welbeck Abbey, Nottinghamshire, and Tissington Hall, Derbyshire. In both these cases, however, the shallow-relief friezes are pure white, relying entirely on their sculptural quality for their effect.

By 1620, most of the techniques employed in creating decorative plasterwork for ceilings, friezes and fireplace overmantels were known. While mould-cast enrichments were a relatively quick and easy way of creating a highly decorative effect, hand-modelling was invariably used in conjunction with this for the creation of more sculptural forms, such as the mermaids for the frieze at Gawthorpe Hall, Lancashire (1604), or the Nine Worthies

Figure 4.10 The coloured plaster frieze depicting Diana the Huntress, High Great Chamber, Hardwick Hall, Derbyshire, c. 1590, by Abraham Smith and assistants. Courtesy of the National Trust.

in the great chamber frieze at Aston Hall, Birmingham (1620). In both cases, armatures made from wire or wood form cores upon and around which the figures are sculpted. Armatures of a different magnitude were needed at Hardwick Old Hall, Derbyshire, where in the 1580s Abraham Smith and his team created the frieze in the Forest Great Chamber: here, plasterwork trees are modelled around real tree trunks which serve as supports.

Plasterwork pendants, such as those in the ceiling at Gilling Castle, Yorkshire (1585), or Canons Ashby, Northamptonshire (1632), were modelled on wooden armatures fixed to the ceiling joists above. Vaulted ceilings, as at Belton House, Lincolnshire (1770s), also required skilful carpentry, with wooden joists following the curve of the vault, as also did the fantastic fan-vaulting worked in plaster at Arbury hall, Warwickshire (1773). As early as 1555 Sir William Cavendish, in a letter to Sir John Thynne at Longleat House, details the importance of the carpentry and highlights the commissioning exercise:

> Sir I understand you have a connyng plasiterer at Longlete which haith in your hall and in other places of your house made diverse pendaunts and other prettye thynges; I woold pray you that I might have hym into Darbyshere for my hall is yet onmade. And therefore nowe might he devyse with my own carpenter howe he should frame the same that it myght serve for his worke . . . [5]

By 1665 at Astley Hall, Lancashire, the exuberant plasterwork with life-size putti in the hall and drawing room is supported on wire and wooden armatures fixed by lead rivets to the ceiling (Figure 4.11). Much use is made here of leather for creating scrolls, which could then be brushed with

Figure 4.11 Plasterwork ceiling in the hall, Astley Hall, Lancashire, 1665. Photo: David Bostwick.

plaster and whitewashed. Similar effects were created at Great Castle House, Monmouth in the 1670s, where plasterwork garlands of fruit and flowers dangle from the ceiling with seemingly little support.

The same techniques were employed at Sudbury Hall, Derbyshire in 1672 by the plasterers Bradbury and Pettifer. The delicacy of their work owes much to their ability to wrap wires with hessian scrim, which could then be bent to shape and dipped in plaster to form stems and tendrils. Flowers, with petals hand-modelled in plaster, hair and glue-size, were built upon wooden pegs with sharp points for sticking into the ceiling wreaths of the Long Gallery and Saloon ceilings. By the eighteenth century, trophies of arms or musical instruments on ceilings could readily utilise real items dipped in plaster.

Significance

Decorative plasterwork has always been an indication of the polite function of the room in which it is found, be it an Elizabethan great chamber, a Georgian drawing room or a Victorian front parlour. In real terms, decorative plasterwork acts as a barometer of quality, reflecting the relative status of the rooms concerned. Starting at the bottom of the scale, ceilings in cellars and pantries are found with the floorboards of the room above visible at the ceiling joists. In those houses with plaster floors laid on riven laths, the laths are visible from below. Slightly higher-status rooms, such as kitchens and attic rooms, are found with the joists still visible but the underside of the laths plastered over. The next stage is marked by rooms such as bedrooms, where the ceiling joists are lathed on the underside to take a flat plastered ceiling. Better rooms are further enhanced by the addition of moulded plaster cornices and, finally, the very best rooms are given decorative work on the ceiling itself.

Just as the relative importance of rooms can be gauged by the presence of decorative plasterwork, so, too, its appearance in the historic interior is a sign of the status of the people who commissioned it. Every room in the state apartment at Kedleston Hall in Derbyshire is graced with the finest-quality neoclassical plasterwork to designs by Robert Adam. His client, Sir Nathaniel Curzon, later 1st Lord Scarsdale, was arguably building the finest Palladian mansion in England in the 1760s to house his collection of pictures and sculpture and to entertain important guests. By way of contrast, less than a hundred years earlier and at a considerably lower social level, Elizabeth Rhodes, a widow at Washford Bridge, Sheffield, had a new house built on her retirement from managing the family knife-grinding works. In the parlour she had a fireplace overmantel in decorative plasterwork with her initials and the date 1676. The plaster ornaments she chose had in her youth been the height of fashion in the homes of the local gentry, whom she now aimed to emulate. Alas, sixty years later, the work was decidedly old-fashioned – so much so that the frieze, cast from the same mould that had first been used at Haddon Hall, Derbyshire, in 1600, was unfamiliar to the plasterers and they fitted it upside down.

Decorative plasterwork, along with other historic finishes, is subject to changes in fashion. The early seventeenth-century plasterwork at Temple Newsam House, Yorkshire, was largely destroyed or concealed behind fashionable improvements in the eighteenth century. Then the pendulum of fashion swung back in the nineteenth century and entire rooms were re-plastered with Jacobean Revival ceilings and friezes, mostly imitating original plasterwork surviving behind Georgian ceilings or concealed in closets. Window tax rather than fashion was responsible for the concealment of plasterwork at Carbrook Hall, Sheffield, where blocked windows were later turned into fitted cupboards, one of whose soffits sports a plasterwork oak tree dropping acorns. Such plasterwork fragments may appear unimportant, but in fact they can provide vital clues not only to a pre-existing scheme but to the significance of the ceiling design itself. Here, the oak tree dropping acorns is copied from a seventeenth-century emblem, and one that featured in Francis Bacon's house at Gorhambury: 'on the wall over the chimney is painted an oak with acorns falling from it; the words Nisi quod potius (Failing better things)'. This design clearly had considerable meaning for the owner at Carbrook Hall, Sir Stephen Bright, a noted Parliamentarian and Puritan.

It is particularly during the sixteenth, seventeenth and eighteenth centuries that decorative plasterwork was used as a vehicle to express ideas and attitudes through the subject matter represented. At Wentworth Castle, Yorkshire, the early eighteenth-century state dining room ceiling is appropriately decorated with a plasterwork representation of Ceres, her cornucopia overflowing with the fruits and produce of the earth. Haddon Hall, Derbyshire, has a plasterwork overmantel of Orpheus playing his lyre and charming the beasts in what was the Elizabethan Great Chamber, a room where music and dancing were enjoyed.

Among the exuberant Restoration period plasterwork at Sudbury Hall, Derbyshire, are hints of the religious leanings of the client, George Vernon. In the 1670s he employed the London team of Bradbury and Pettifer to create stunning floral and foliate plasterwork. On the drawing room ceiling, winged cherubim consort with the pelican, emblems of Christ's sacrifice on the cross; in the saloon can be seen personifications of the Theological Virtues; in the staircase hall, on the ceiling that forms the soffit of the first-floor landing, are tiny dragons among the foliage. Standing on this landing George Vernon was, literally as well as metaphorically, trampling the dragon underfoot in line with the injunction in Psalm 91, verse 13: '..and the dragon shalt thou trample under feet'.

One room in an English country house in which decorative plasterwork could have fun playing on the 'inside-outside' theme was the long gallery. At Knole House, Kent, the Cartoon Gallery ceiling of 1608 features compartments with sprigs of flowers reflecting the real flowers seen in the garden from the gallery windows. At Haddon Hall, Derbyshire, the window bay in the long gallery has a ribwork ceiling of c. 1582, whose pattern may have matched that of the knot garden laid out below. Blickling Hall, Norfolk, has plasterwork fish caught on lines depicted in the soffit of the long gallery window of 1620, from which ladies could angle for fish in the moat. Similarly

Sudbury Hall, Derbyshire, has grasshoppers modelled in plaster on the ceiling centrepiece of the bay window in the Long Gallery (1672), from which real grasshoppers could be heard chirruping in the garden below.

Endnotes

1. *Materials and skills for historic building conservation*, Chapter 4, pp. 56–91.
2. Hugh Platt, *The Jewel House of Art and Nature*, 1594; The Fourth Book, Facsimile reprint (Theatris Orbis Terrarum, Amsterdam, 1979), p. 57.
3. J. Chamberlayne, *Anglia Notitia or, The Present State of England*, quoted in M. Harrison and M. Royston, *How They Lived: An anthology of original accounts written between 1485 and 1700*, Vol. 3 (Blackwell, Oxford, 1965), p. 40.
4. Quoted in Bernard Denvir, *From the Middle Ages to the Stuarts: Art, design and society before 1689* (Longman, London, 1988), p. 175.
5. Quoted in Geoffrey Beard, *Decorative Plasterwork in Great Britain* (Phaidon, London, 1975), p. 26.

5 Woodwork

Lisa White

Introduction: timber

Oak and pine were the timbers most commonly used for interior finishes before the eighteenth century in Britain: the first for its strength, figure, colour and versatility, the latter for its availability and relative cheapness. English oak was available in great quantities, especially in the west and south-west of England and in Wales, but Norwegian and Spanish oak was imported, as well as Danish oak, which was known to be reliable and resistant to warping. By far the largest amount of deal and pine came through Britain's extensive trade with the Baltic States from the Middle Ages onwards, imported in planks or boards of standard lengths and thickness. Norway deals were usually shipped in lengths of 10 or 12 feet (3 or 3.6 m), while deals from the Baltic coast and the White Sea measured from 14 to 20 feet (4.3–6 m) in length. Sawn boards were generally between 7 and 11 inches (18 or 28 cm) wide, while those over 11 inches (28 cm), listed as 'plank', attracted a higher import duty charge.

Home-grown and imported walnut was used during the sixteenth and seventeenth centuries, but supplies of European walnut were relatively limited and always expensive, and the timber was reserved for the showiest interiors. John Evelyn described it as 'of singular account with the joyner, for the best grain'd and colour'd wainscot'.[1] By 1700 supplies of American walnut and cedar were shipped from the British colonies, especially Virginia and Maryland, and were used for fine interior woodwork in London and in some country houses. After 1730 West Indian mahogany became increasingly available for both furniture and interior joinery and within twenty years was regarded as the most fashionable timber for doors and staircases (Figure 5.1).

Other timbers may also be found in the historic interior, including elm, sycamore, chestnut, lime and beech, but usually for more specific purposes than oak and pine. Isaac Ware stated in 1756 that '[t]here are old houses in the country floored with sycamore, and wainscoted with poplar; the wainscot has never been painted, but retains a good colour, and floors

Interior finishes & fittings for historic building conservation, First Edition. Edited by Michael Forsyth & Lisa White. © 2012 Blackwell Publishing Ltd. Published 2012 by Blackwell Publishing Ltd.

Figure 5.1 Baulks of mahogany in the West Indies. The rich, red colour prized for interior woodwork in the eighteenth century is obscured by the rough grey bark.

stand excellently and are very pretty', and English lime may 'be serviceable for many kinds of inside work, and particularly is excellent for carving; much superior to deal and to most other woods'. Chestnut 'is very sound, strong and durable . . . in old houses it is often mistaken for oak, even by good workmen, it so greatly resembles it in colour, in substance and in its qualities'. Maple 'would answer excellently for the finest of the inside work in buildings', and even English yew 'would be worthy to be introduced into the finest ornamental parts of the most elegant building, where it would be as lasting as beautiful'.[2] After many decades or centuries of wear, polishing or discoloration, it is not always easy to identify some timbers. But it is important to do so in order to establish their original colour and finish in any conservation scheme.

Floors

From the early medieval period onwards, boarded floors were usually made of oak or elm and were intended to be left exposed. For smaller rooms of less than 15 feet (4.6 m) in span, full-length boards could be laid over joists from one wall plate to another. For rooms wider than 15 feet (4.6 m), joists would be supported on summer beams and boards laid over them with ends butted against each other. Oak boards were often quarter-cut to give greater resistance to abrasion and to show a better figure than straight-cut timber. Iron nails were driven through the boards into the joists to secure them, and their heads left exposed in the surface. For finer floors, oak dowels might be used to join boards together and to secure them to the joists.

In the eighteenth century joiners mastered the art of cutting oak boards to follow the curves of quadrant passages between different parts of a great house, as can be seen at Kedleston Hall, Derbyshire.[3] According to William Salmon, such work would double the price of straight work.[4] Oak boards were usually left in a 'dry' finish and could be cleaned by sweeping, or by rubbing over with abrasive rushes or sand. As a result, most oak boards had a fairly pale colour and silvery finish. Elm boards would resist more regular washing or mopping with water or a diluted lime and water mixture. By the nineteenth century many older oak floors had darkened with age and dirt impregnation. By that date they were also more regularly finished with highly polished beeswax, hard varnishes or shellac coatings, and new oak floors for Victorian houses in historic styles were waxed and polished, which gave them a yellow, glossy finish, very different from their original appearance.

Deal boards were less expensive than oak or elm, and were used for all wooden floors of lesser-quality houses or for the lesser rooms (on bedroom and service floors) of grander houses (Figure 5.2). At Temple Newsam House, Yorkshire, in the 1740s oak boards were used in the best rooms, where they were occasionally covered with loose carpets; the lesser rooms were boarded with deal and covered with fitted carpets or floor cloths.[5]

Figure 5.2 Traditional pine floorboards and nails. The Building of Bath Collection (Bath Preservation Trust).

Deal boards wear more rapidly, are prone to splintering or 'tearing', are easily stained or damaged by water, and were not intended to be seen or admired before the mid-twentieth-century fashion for 'stripped pine'. In 1803 Thomas Sheraton observed that 'since the introduction of carpets, fitted all over the floor of a room, the nicety of flooring anciently practised in the best houses, is now laid aside'.[6] However, pine boards were occasionally displayed when painted in oil paints, and in the nineteenth and early twentieth centuries were stained with 'Darklene' to a dark brown colour, to resemble oak, around the borders of rooms where loose carpets were used.

In the first decades of its general use in England, mahogany was used for flooring a few expensive houses, as for instance in the Great Room or Saloon at Marble Hill, Surrey (begun in 1724), and at Claydon House, Buckinghamshire, where in the 1760s the main rooms were laid with mahogany boards up to 9 inches (23 cm) in width. More mahogany floors may have been laid in the middle of the eighteenth century but their survival is rare.

During the last quarter of the seventeenth century, some luxurious English interiors were fitted with very expensive parquetry floors. This followed fashions that had developed in Italy and France in the previous century and were thought to have been introduced into England by Henrietta Maria, Queen Consort of Charles I. A rare survival is the dais of the Queen's bedchamber at Ham House, Surrey, made in the 1670s by Henry Harlow at a cost of 35 shillings per square yard.[7] It is created from walnut and cedar, incorporates the cipher and ducal coronet of the Earl of Lauderdale, and was originally equipped with leather covers for protection from light, dust and wear, in the same manner as expensive pieces of furniture. The small closet beyond this room has a similarly inlaid floor. Both were carefully preserved during later alterations to the house. Exceptionally fine inlaid floors dating from the late 1720s and early 1730s survive in rooms at Davenport House and Mawley Hall, Shropshire, both in the Continental fashion, and in another room at Ham House, Surrey (Figure 5.3). A simulated parquetry floor, executed in paint, exists at Belton House, Lincolnshire.[8]

A number of houses still contain inlaid floors on the landings of their main staircases, as at Beninborough Hall, Yorkshire, dated 1716, and at Dyrham House, Gloucestershire, and the one at Broadlands, Hampshire was noticed by Celia Fiennes during her travels, but these elegant floors are unusual.[9] One of the finest eighteenth-century inlaid staircases can still be seen at Claydon House, Buckinghamshire. The common practice in English country houses of the eighteenth century was to keep floors plain and undecorated, in contrast with much European fashion. Some early nineteenth-century parquetry borders for important rooms, such as Nash's great Picture Gallery at Attingham Park, Shropshire (1806), the Waterloo Gallery at Apsley House, London (the Duke of Wellington's town house) and Kingston Lacy, Dorset, are significant as all three owners had experience of, and a predilection for, European fashions.

From the mid-nineteenth to mid-twentieth centuries, parquetry floors of all types were popular, from the specially commissioned borders

Figure 5.3 Section of parquetry floor in the Dining Room, Ham House, Surrey, 1756. Courtesy of the National Trust.

incorporating rare and expensive timbers in the main rooms at Tyntesfield, Somerset, created in the 1860s for Henry and Blanche Gibbs, to 'off the peg' parquet floors for middle-class homes marketed by such firms as Bennet's 'Tungit' Flooring Company of Stratford, East London.

Staircases

Decorative timber staircases became an important feature in the domestic interior from the late sixteenth and early seventeenth century, with the development of rooms of entertainment and show on upper floors of the house. Before that date steps were generally of stone or solid oak set into the walls of dedicated staircase 'wells', with no space for decorative balusters or rails. A fine set of solid oak and elm steps survive at Broughton Castle, Oxfordshire. By 1600 the fashion for highly decorative carving and painting in Renaissance and Mannerist styles encouraged the development of elaborate staircases with ornate balusters and balustrades, newel posts, heraldic beasts and armorial emblems. Staircases became more than functional and were now used to display the wealth and status of their owners. Subsidiary and much plainer staircases were used for access to lesser apartments and service areas of the house. Magnificent examples of great staircases survive at Knole, Kent (1605–1608) (Figure 5.4), Hatfield House,

Figure 5.4 The Staircase, Knole House, Kent, 1605–08. Courtesy of the National Trust.

Hertfordshire (c. 1611), Blickling Hall, Norfolk (1620s; reconstructed in 1767) and Castle Ashby, Northamptonshire (c. 1635).

Most timber staircases were built in oak in joiners' workshops where they were assembled 'dry' before being dismantled, transported to the site, reassembled and fixed permanently in situ, and given their final finish of decorative carved panels and paint. In the 1630s new classical styles appeared, for instance in the use of carved and pierced panels of trophies of arms on the great staircase at Ham House, constructed in 1638–9 by Thomas Carter for William Murray, and finished with graining to resemble walnut. Carved panels of swirling foliate ornament and armorial and hunting trophies decorated some of the most fashionable staircases of the later seventeenth century (Sudbury Hall, Derbyshire, c. 1676, and Dunster Castle, 1683–4) and form part of the *oeuvre* of the great Baroque master carvers of the generation of Grinling Gibbons (Figure 5.5).

During the eighteenth century most standard British timber staircases were constructed to fill specific staircase halls, usually side-lit by windows on each landing, with flights of steps supported on joists at half landings, with regular turned wooden balusters and handrails. Oak was used for the most solid and durable construction of flights of steps and for balusters

Figure 5.5 Carved panel of the Great Staircase, Ham House, Surrey, 1638–9. Courtesy of the National Trust.

and rails from 1700–c. 1750. Other fashionable timbers were also used on occasions. At Dyrham Park, Gloucestershire, William Blathwayt commissioned two fine staircases for the two stages of building that took place in the 1680s and after 1700: one is made of Virginian Walnut, the other of American cedar. Both are now extremely fragile and their conservation is problematical. Thereafter mahogany was used for elegant turned and carved balusters and handrails, and turned painted pine or beech for simpler versions, before cast iron became a fashionable alternative from the 1770s (Figure 5.6). Numerous instruction and pattern books gave directions for planning and building staircases in a variety of shapes from square to circular and oval. Early staircases tended to have balusters jointed to continuous timber base boards, but from the 1720s balusters were fitted directly to the ends of steps and neat carved scrolls applied to the ends of risers.

The varied styles of balusters became the main indication of changing fashion during the period. In general, larger, heavier balusters were abandoned by 1760–70 for lighter, thinner versions. They were grouped in sets of two or three per tread, depending on the scale and grandeur of the staircase as a whole. Particular attention was paid to the finish of the scroll-ended handrail at the foot of a staircase: some were fitted with small pieces of brass, ivory or mother-of-pearl, which would be a reflective guide for the night-time user. By 1800 wooden staircases for modest town houses might be very simple, with plain square-section balusters and no carved ornament. However, the introduction of steam-powered lathes and moulding planes in the early nineteenth century allowed the development of

Figure 5.6 Wooden balusters from a staircase in Bath, c. 1770. The Building of Bath Collection (Bath Preservation Trust).

cheap ornamental staircase balusters and polished hardwood handrails, illustrated in the many builders' manuals and catalogues published throughout the period. Where balusters have been removed and replaced, such catalogues can provide nearly all the necessary information for replacing original materials correctly.

Pine staircase treads and risers were usually covered in narrow carpet strips, fixed in place by brass stair rods secured into eyes which were fixed to the timber treads. Service stairs were covered in heavier duty druggets, oil cloth or linoleum, sometimes with extra brass or rubber nosings fixed to the fronts of treads to protect them from very heavy wear. Exposed areas of treads and risers were stained, grained or painted to imitate a dark oak. When full-width carpeting became available after c. 1950, carpet gripper-rods were usually used to hold carpet in place; the fixing nails for these rods have often caused considerable damage to old steps and risers and will need careful remedial treatment if woodwork is to be re-exposed.

Panelling

Since medieval times wooden panelling has been used as a warmth-retaining and decorative treatment for interior walls. The term 'wainscot' (for oak panelling) is found as early as 1352,[10] and has generally been the province of joiners – that is, craftsmen able to 'join' together pieces of timber using mortice-and-tenon techniques. Basic construction is relatively simple. Stone or brick walls or studwork (a framework of wooden posts and rails) all formed a suitable backing to which panelling could be fixed. To create the panelling, a joiner would cut the relevant timber into stiles (uprights) and rails (horizontals) and groove the edges to receive thin boards, usually of oak (Figure 5.7). The stiles and rails were joined by mortice-and-tenon joints and fixed with wooden dowels. Iron nails or screws were avoided, allowing the timber to expand and contract naturally according to the seasons, temperature and humidity.

Oak boards were often quarter-sawn to expose fine patterns in the timber and to reduce the warping that often affected straight-grain timber, and planed down at the edges to fit snugly into the framework. When first cut oak is of a pale golden colour, so rooms panelled in that timber would have been lighter in colour than they are now, and there is plenty

Figure 5.7 Oak panelling, early seventeenth century. Barrington Court, Somerset. Courtesy of the National Trust.

of evidence to show that panelling was painted and even gilded with heraldic devices, religious mottoes and symbols, and other devices.

Oak panels were also carved: in the early sixteenth century a favourite pattern was 'linenfold' or 'drapery fold' (the original term), where the carver imitated the folds of linen fabric. When fresh and light in colour, linenfold panelling must have looked very similar indeed to the material it imitated. Some fine examples even imitate 'stitching' around the edges of the folds.[11] By the 1530s 'Romayne work', with classical Roman heads carved in profile, reflected the growing taste for Renaissance decoration in the interior, in both ecclesiastical and secular houses. During the Elizabethan and Jacobean periods (1558 – 1627), carved panelling developed into a major decorative element in the interior, with massive hall screens, chimneypieces and long galleries carved with heraldic, classical, naturalistic and fanciful figures and features surrounded by highly worked borders of interlace, guilloche or strapwork ornament. The regular panels of oak were divided by decorative pilasters and surmounted by elaborate friezes below plaster ceilings with similar patterns: the sense of ceaseless surface ornament was dominant. Carvers absorbed and adapted designs for such work from the many sheets and books of ornament available for all forms of decorative art from the 1560s, printed in Germany, France and the Low Countries (now Holland and Belgium).[12] Local styles of carving developed, especially in the south-west and north-west of England and in East Anglia. Some of these carving traditions travelled with emigrant craftsmen to New England after 1630 and continued to be used by subsequent generations well into the eighteenth century.

After 1660 the general style of panelling changed to a scheme of larger 'fielded' panels set into bolder frames, well illustrated in Joseph Moxon's *Mechanick Exercises* of 1694 (Figure 5.8).

Panels were not always rebated into rails and stiles in the old manner, but might be simply butted against the frame or each other, and the joints covered with bolection mouldings. Cedar and walnut were used for the finest work, for instance in the halls and great rooms of London livery companies and in great houses. Celia Fiennes commented on the walnut and mulberry panelling she saw at Chippenham Park, Suffolk, in the 1690s.[13] Oak remained a standard material for good panelling. These fine timbers were left in their natural colour and finished with a light waxing for protection and reflection. In addition, carved ornaments were applied to the most decorative panels for grand rooms. The work of Grinling Gibbons in a highly naturalistic Anglo-Dutch style of carving is the best known, for instance at Petworth House, Sussex, in the 1690s. Other teams of carvers worked in the same manner – for example, Samuel Watson, Lobb and Davis for the Duke of Devonshire at Chatsworth from 1692–4. Gibbons carved his enrichments in English lime wood which when first cut is very pale, and when finished with an abrasive Dutch rush (the forerunner of sandpaper) had a silvery look.[14] Pinned against the pale oak of the main panelling of a room, the original colour combination must have been one of natural silver and gold, very different from the discoloured details now seen against darkened oak. Recent conservation of such panelling at Petworth and Lyme

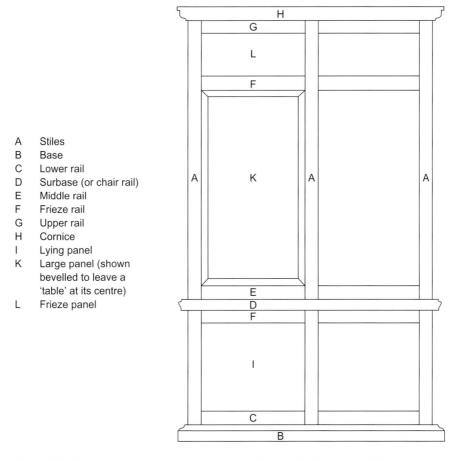

A   Stiles
B   Base
C   Lower rail
D   Surbase (or chair rail)
E   Middle rail
F   Frieze rail
G   Upper rail
H   Cornice
I   Lying panel
K   Large panel (shown
     bevelled to leave a
     'table' at its centre)
L   Frieze panel

Figure 5.8 Wainscotting, after Joseph Moxon's *Mechanick Exercises*, 1694.

Park, Cheshire, has succeeded in reviving some colour and richness in the timber[15] (Figure 5.9).

From the 1680s an increasing amount of pine was used for less expensive work. When cut and fitted to a room, the pine panelling would be 'stopped' and any holes or blemishes filled before it was painted with lead-based oil paints, which gave a slight sheen and reflective finish that enhanced the shape of the large bolection mouldings. Earth colours, stone colours, greens, blues and dark reds were all 'common' colours used on such panelling. Finer examples were grained to imitate more expensive woods – as, for example, at Ham House, Surrey, in the 1670s. Doors, shutters and cupboards would all be treated alike, giving such interiors a fully integrated appearance – a tradition that lasted through the eighteenth century in the American colonies. Many early eighteenth-century panelled eating or dining parlours were fitted with wooden 'buffet niches' with enclosing doors and candle slides for the storage and display of family silver and porcelain, often placed on either side of a projecting chimney breast. Successive layers of overpainting have often obscured the clean lines and

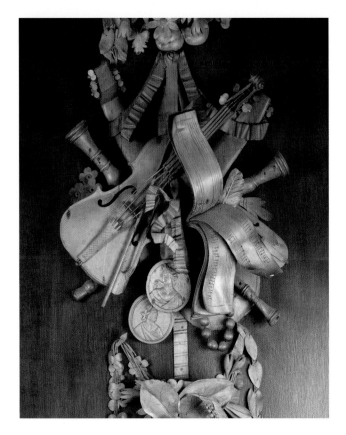

Figure 5.9 Limewood carving in the Music Room, Lyme Park, Cheshire, attributed to Grinling Gibbons. Courtesy of the National Trust.

architectural quality of such panelling. Careful thought needs to be given to the question of removing early toxic layers of paint in any conservation scheme.

During the eighteenth century a gradual change in fashion took place, away from fully panelled rooms – with the exception of dining rooms, where panelling was often retained for warmth and decoration in a space where textiles were considered unsuitable as they might retain food smells. A beautiful example of a mid-eighteenth-century panelled dining room, carved with elaborate trophies of game in a delightfully expressive Rococo manner, survives in Royal Fort House, Bristol. The Chinoiserie tea room at Claydon House, Buckinghamshire, is one of the most extraordinary creations of the mid-eighteenth century: here, as elsewhere in the house, the carver Luke Lightfoot gave free range to his imagination in an elaborately carved and painted pine alcove for a sofa and tea tables, surmounted by Chinese canopies, bells and lattice work. Other exceptions were music rooms, where timber panelling was thought to have a beneficial acoustic effect. A notable survivor is the Music Room from Norfolk House, St James's Square, London, now in the Victoria and Albert Museum. For this room the French-trained Jean Cuenot carved all the elaborate musical trophies, classical heads, raffle leaves and so on between 1753 and 1756.

The musical trophies alone cost £60.15s to carve, and £20.15s to gild.[16] A similar room, also intended for music, survives at Petworth House, Sussex, carved by Thomas Watts between 1757 and 1758. It is significant that both these rooms were further embellished with additional carving when 'Rococo Revival' styles became immensely fashionable in the early nineteenth century.

For most mid- and late eighteenth-century rooms, however, wooden panelling was reduced to become a more functional feature below the dado rail, usually made of pine and finished with regular decorative mouldings. Painted plasterwork, textiles and, most significantly, paper became the favoured wall coverings of the period. Full-height oak panelling, especially in its natural finish, remained very much out of fashion until the Gothic, Elizabethan and Jacobean revivals of the mid-nineteenth century. This was much encouraged by such publications as Joseph Nash's *Mansions of England in the Olden Time* (1859), which showed 'farthingaled' ladies and heavily booted gentlemen supping and conversing in old, panelled rooms, and by A.W.N. Pugin's championship of linenfold panelling in the interiors of the new Palace of Westminster.

Steam-powered cutting and planing machines could produce endless quantities of neat oak panelling for the more masculine rooms of High Victorian 'Gothic' houses, especially billiard rooms, libraries, dining rooms and halls (for instance, at Knightshayes Court, Devon, by William Burges). Victorian panelling often has a smoother finish as a result of this method of manufacture. It was very often finished with a heavy wax or varnish treatment which increased its yellow colour, or was stained to look 'old'. Arts and Crafts architects and clients favoured a return to painted panelling in the 'Queen Anne' style. In 1926 Norman Jewson preserved the wainscot installed in the Little Parlour at Owlpen Manor, Gloucestershire, installed in 1719, even though changes in floor level destroyed its correct proportions. In the 1890s Philip Webb designed beautiful new fielded panels painted in soft shades of green, blue and white for the main rooms at Standen, Sussex. One of the most enchanting tributes to an earlier fashion for carving fruit, flowers and animals on panelling can be seen at Tyntesfield, Somerset: in Matilda Blanche Gibbs's sitting room, finished in the 1860s, an unknown carver inserted meticulously accurate boxwood carvings of garden plants and flowers on the high dado that runs round the room, anticipating access to a splendid orchid house and conservatory (demolished in 1919)[17] (Figure 5.10).

Wooden panelling is easy to remove and replace. It can be reduced or extended by a skilled craftsman. Over the centuries much panelling has undergone such treatment, and in a conservation scheme it is essential to establish the original location and finish of any surviving panelling. Between 1900 and 1930 the restoration of many English manor houses by sensitive architects working in the Arts and Crafts tradition introduced huge quantities of panelling, both old and more recently made, into historic interiors in order to recreate a redolent sense of the past and provide a good and serviceable backdrop to comfortable furnishings. Such practices are evident at Great Chalfield Manor, Wiltshire, and Little Sodbury Manor, Gloucestershire, where the architect George Brakspear undertook sensitive

Figure 5.10 Dado and frieze with carved boxwood panels in Matilda Blanche Gibbs's room, Tyntesfield, Somerset, 1865–6. Courtesy of the National Trust.

restoration for purchasers of near-derelict medieval manor houses. At Barrington Court, Somerset, the National Trust acquired the shattered remains of a great Tudor house in 1906; for the next twenty years the tenant, Sir Henry Lyle (of Tate and Lyle fame), refitted the house with beautiful old panelling from many different locations all over England. At Berkeley Castle, Gloucestershire, the Great Hall was embellished in the 1920s with a post-and-panel screen from Glamorgan, and many other rooms with French and Flemish sixteenth-century panelling, all now looking convincingly at home after nearly ninety years.

From the 1930s much painted pine panelling was stripped, using caustic soda and other chemicals in order to achieve a lighter, more 'natural' look. The results have often been highly damaging to the timber when large quantities of chemical have not been washed out, and the exposure of knotted, grainy pine and deal is totally inappropriate in a historic setting. Recently, the prolific architectural salvage trade has continued the easy practice of 'moving rooms'.[18]

Doors and doorcases

Of all the architectural woodwork used to embellish the historic interior, the treatment of doors and doorcases often defined the quality and character of a room. Architects, clients and craftsmen paid particular attention to the materials, scale and design of these features, which might not be merely functional but could also express the significance and status of a particular space. This aspect was rarely developed in medieval houses – internal doors often simply replicated panelling used along the rest of the walls – but from the sixteenth century, when important houses began to include rooms devoted to more specific purposes, doors and doorways were given more elaborate decorative treatment. This can be seen very clearly in the construction of highly ornate interior 'porches' for great chambers, for instance at Montacute House, Somerset; Broughton Castle, Oxfordshire; and the Red Lodge, Bristol (Figure 5.11).

The door to the Great Parlour on the first floor at Ham House, Surrey, was made in 1638–9 by the joiner Thomas Carter with an imposing wooden doorcase painted to resemble white 'polished marble' with gilt enrichments. The door itself was panelled and grained to imitate walnut, with

Figure 5.11 Interior porch, 1598–1601, formerly in the Parlour, now in the library, Montacute House, Somerset. Courtesy of the National Trust.

complex architectural mouldings. It is larger in scale than the neighbouring door, which leads to lesser apartments. A similar treatment survives at Chatsworth, Derbyshire, where the oak door to the State Apartment at the head of the Great Staircase on the first floor has a dramatic alabaster doorcase, constructed in 1692.

With the introduction of apartments arranged in enfilade in later seventeenth-century Baroque houses, the doors opening through a series of rooms were given consistent treatment in terms of scale, although their decoration sometimes increased in richness with the significance of the rooms. The best oak, with large, fielded quarter-sawn panels, was used for most interior doors until the 1730s, when imported West Indian mahogany, the 'rich, red timber', was preferred for its colour, stability and figure. Either surrounded by equally fine mahogany or by pine painted a soft white or stone colour, these doors became a hallmark of Georgian interiors and form a marked contrast with the European tradition of treating doors in the same manner as wall panelling (Figure 5.12).

Figure 5.12 Mahogany door, Kedleston Hall, Derbyshire, c. 1765. Courtesy of the National Trust.

Even in a room as Francophile as the Music Room at Norfolk House, London, mahogany doors stand out in bold juxtaposition to the delicate white and gold *boiseries* that cover the rest of the walls. The Francophile Robert Adam promoted the use of decoratively painted doors in the European manner for fashionable interiors, for instance in the Etruscan Room at Osterley Park, Surrey, in 1775.[19]

During the middle decades of the eighteenth century, smart interior doorcases derived their style and ornament from classical architecture, with pronounced pediments and carved enrichments of egg-and-dart, bead-and-reel, laurel and acanthus leaves, festoons and masks. The great doorcase of the Saloon at Houghton Hall, Norfolk, carved in 1732, was singled out for admiration by Sir Thomas Robinson, who commented on the 'vast quantities of mahogany' used in the house: he estimated that the saloon door and doorcase cost £1000, but sixty more such doors were made for Houghton. In the 1760s the master carver and joiner John Hobcraft of London provided superb mahogany doors and doorcases for the main rooms at Corsham Court, Wiltshire, and Croome Court, Worcestershire. These had beautiful flame-figured panels and bright ormolu door furniture of the highest quality. Early protective finishes included beeswax, or rubbing with a thin flat oil varnish made from linseed, poppy seed or walnut oil, or natural resin varnishes. By 1800 French polish was frequently used to give a high gloss on mahogany doors, and many earlier doors were refinished in this way.

For lesser rooms in important houses and for simpler dwellings, doors and doorcases were made of painted pine with decoration appropriate to their situation: fielded panels for smarter rooms, flat panels and the simplest mouldings for less important spaces. Two-panel rather than six-panel doors were often used in smaller spaces on upper floors and in cottages, with colours ranging from white (expensive) to 'common' colours such as green, ochre, brown and dark red. During the Regency and Victorian periods, graining was frequently used as a finish for pine doors and other architectural woodwork. Architectural and builders' pattern books provided joiners with numerous designs and correct proportions.

By the nineteenth century a far wider range of timbers and finishes was available in London and other major cities for doors and interior joinery. Oak continued to be popular, especially for interiors in Gothic and Tudor revival styles, mahogany for standard rooms in the classical taste, and some exotic veneers such as satinwood or rosewood for drawing room doors, or painted pine with a huge range of decorative paint finishes.

Doors, like panelling, can be easily removed. Subdivision of historic interiors, changing fashions and safety requirements have all affected their retention and original surface decoration. It is important to assess their position and finish at the start of any conservation scheme. Evidence of 'cutting down' or enlarging can be established by looking carefully at the proportions of a door. Many mahogany doors have faded through long years of exposure to sunlight; they now appear a pale golden-brown with very dried surfaces but can be satisfactorily revived by a good joiner or cabinet-maker. Re-establishing the strong red colour of eighteenth-century doors, or the good rich dark brown of an oak door, can make a fundamental difference to the character of a historic room.

Architectural woodwork details

In addition to the major areas and features executed in wood, numerous details and fittings were provided by joiners and make subtle contributions to the integrity of a historic interior. Their loss or inexact replacement can be unnerving and unbalancing. This might involve, for instance, the replacement of an original dado rail with a modern and wholly inappropriate moulding of the wrong scale and profile. In eighteenth-century interiors, the moulding used for a dado rail echoed that used at the top of the skirting board and established a sense of full panelling around the lower part of a room or up a staircase. Window architraves, shutter boxes and skirtings were intended to match or blend successfully within a room or series of rooms (Figure 5.13). When windowsills were lowered in many houses after

Figure 5.13 Detail of shutter and architrave, c. 1768, Claydon House, Buckinghamshire. Only occasional repainting has ensured that the carved decoration remains crisp and clear. Courtesy of the National Trust.

1800, shutters and shutter boxes had to be extended and earlier panelling below the original aperture removed, often creating a sense of imbalance unless dado rails were also removed and taller skirtings inserted.

Because pine shutters were used very extensively from the eighteenth century and were subjected to considerable stresses of light, warping, water ingress and infestation, they have often been removed and replaced or screwed up. However, designs and instructions can be found for almost every type of shutter and architrave in the numerous pattern books published in the eighteenth and nineteenth centuries for this type of architectural woodwork, and evidence of lost elements may easily be discovered in other parts of a house. In the service building behind No. 1, Royal Crescent, Bath, a complete window and its surround of the late 1760s was found in a cupboard: the window was simply covered over when the owners of the main house no longer wished servants to see across the courtyard and into the main house. The restoration of Sir John Soane's elegant shutters and skirting boards at Moggerhanger House, Bedfordshire (1791–1811), enhanced the linearity and cool restraint of those remarkable interiors, previously shattered by decades of use as the County Sanatorium after 1919. Fitted furniture, such as kitchen dressers, buffet niches, linen cupboards and closets, has also suffered from changing fashion, excessive wear and tear, re-arrangement of rooms or the temptations of the architectural salvage trade, but again, sufficient examples survive to offer the possibility of creating replicas, especially for town houses. By noticing and recording every surviving detail during a survey and writing a conservation plan, much can be recovered and re-created, even in the most damaged of interiors.

Endnotes

1. John Evelyn, *Sylva, or a Discourse of Forest Trees* (1664), Book 1, Chapter 3.
2. Isaac Ware, *A Complete Body of Architecture* (1756), Book 1, Chap 21, pp. 77–78.
3. National Trust, *Kedleston Hall* (1998), p. 11.
4. William Salmon, *The London and Country Builder's Vade Mecum, or the Compleat and Universal Architect's Assistant* (London, 1748), p. 25.
5. C. Gilbert, J. Lomax and A. Wells-Cole, *Country House Floors 1660–1850*, Temple Newsam Country House Studies 3 (Leeds, 1987), p. 29.
6. T. Sheraton, *The Cabinet Dictionary* (London, 1803), p. 211.
7. P. Thornton and M. Tomlin, *The Furnishing and Decoration of Ham House* (Furniture History Society, London, 1980), p. 143.
8. Current thinking by the National Trust, which owns Belton House, is that this floor may be late Victorian, but evidence is inconclusive.
9. C. Morris (ed.), *The Illustrated Journeys of Celia Fiennes, c. 1682–c. 1712* (Macdonald & Co., 1982), p. 74.
10. *Oxford English Dictionary.*
11. For example, the dining room at Broughton Castle, Oxfordshire.
12. A. Wells-Cole, *Art and Decoration in Elizabethan and Jacobean England* (Yale University Press, 1997), pp. 169–200.
13. Morris, *Journeys of Celia Fiennes*, p. 140.

14. D. Esterly, *Grinling Gibbons and the Art of Carving* (Harry N. Abrams, 1998), pp. 202–204.
15. C. Rowell, 'Grinling Gibbons's carved room at Petworth: "the most superb monument of his skill" ', *Apollo*, 151, 458 (April 2000), 19–26.
16. D. Fitzgerald, *The Norfolk House Music Room* (Victoria and Albert Museum, London, 1973), pp. 26–29; Appendix B, pp. 51–52.
17. National Trust, *Tyntesfield* (2003), p. 25.
18. John Harris, *Moving Rooms, The Trade in Architectural Salvage* (Yale University Press, 2007).
19. Eileen Harris, *The Genius of Robert Adam: His interiors* (Yale University Press, 2001), pp. 176–77.

6 Metalwork and gilding

Lisa White

Introduction

Decorative metalwork and metal finishes have always made an important contribution to the historic interior. Before the Industrial Revolution in Britain, finely finished metal balustrades, locks, catches and hinges, as well as gilded surfaces, were expensive and usually the privileged possessions of the rich. But even basic strap hinges and locks wrought in iron by a local blacksmith could become a decorative feature on an internal door or shutter in a medieval or Tudor house (Figure 6.1). Because of the very nature of materials such as iron and brass, which are brittle and prone to corrosion, as well as centuries of use and changing fashions in design, much historic metalwork has been removed and replaced. Changes in the use and decoration of rooms has often involved the replacement of doors and their metal furniture; shutters have been screwed up and their metal pulls removed; original finishes have been lost beneath layers of later paint and detail obscured by a build-up of proprietary brass cleaners. In any conservation plan, careful attention needs to be given to surviving metalwork in the interior, as it may well help to explain other changes and developments within a house. Its rescue or replacement can make a major impact on an entire conservation scheme.

Although outside the scope of this chapter, reference should always be made to surviving historic ironwork in or from ecclesiastical buildings, from early medieval examples to magnificent Victorian pieces such as the screen from Hereford Cathedral, made in 1862, now conserved and displayed in the Victoria and Albert Museum. That museum also houses one of the greatest collections of decorative ironwork and brasswork, while the Museé Le Secq de Tournelles in Rouen houses a collection begun in 1870 of some of the finest French historic ironwork.

Interior finishes & fittings for historic building conservation, First Edition. Edited by Michael Forsyth & Lisa White. © 2012 Blackwell Publishing Ltd. Published 2012 by Blackwell Publishing Ltd.

Figure 6.1 Iron door furniture, c. 1530. The Vyne, Hampshire. Courtesy of the National Trust.

Staircases and balustrades

The largest and most conspicuous elements of decorative metalwork in historic interiors are staircase balustrades and balusters. However, these fittings were very rare and expensive until the mid- and later eighteenth century. An outstanding survivor is the balustrade of the famous Tulip Staircase in the Queen's House, Greenwich, designed by Inigo Jones in 1615 (Figure 6.2). Like exterior ironwork of the early seventeenth century, the balusters were painted bright blue to protect the metal from the damp environment near the Thames. The fame of the building and its designer, the novelty of the staircase's cantilever construction and the beauty of the ironwork all ensured the influence of this staircase in eighteenth-century Palladian buildings.

Oak and walnut were most widely used for the decorative as well as constructional elements of early and mid-seventeenth century staircases (see Chapter 5), and it was not until the 1680s that elaborate wrought iron appeared regularly in the interior.

Wrought ironwork is composed of bars of iron, heated and hammered into scrolling shapes which can be welded together to form balustrades,

Figure 6.2 Cast iron balustrade of the 'Tulip Staircase', Queen's House, Greenwich, designed by Inigo Jones in 1615. Courtesy of the National Maritime Museum.

gates and screens of almost any size. The work of the French ironsmith Jean Tijou in England between 1689 and 1700 for King William III and Queen Mary II at Hampton Court Palace, for the Duke of Devonshire at Chatsworth, and also at Burghley House, Drayton and Stonyhurst, established a taste for elaborate, floriate wrought iron gates, screens and balustrades in the French Baroque style, embellished with gilding. The style was disseminated through Tijou's publication of his *New Book of Drawings* (1693) and through aristocratic, ecclesiastical, corporate and civic patronage of native ironsmiths such as Robert Bakewell of Derby (chancel screen, All Saints Church, Derby; Radcliffe Camera, Oxford, 1744), Robert and John Davies (gates at Chirk Castle) and William Edney of Bristol (screen for St. Mary Redcliffe, Bristol, 1710). While much of their work was for exterior use, such as gates and screens for entrances to parks and gardens, interior examples, such as civic sword-rests for city churches, still exist in situ and provide a good indication of the quality and complexity of this hand-wrought material. Designs for ironwork balustrades in the style of Tijou were still being published in England in the late 1730s (Figure 6.3).

One of the loveliest examples of mid-eighteenth century wrought iron used for a staircase balustrade is at Claydon, Buckinghamshire, where an unidentified smith created a beautiful structure of S-shaped scrolls overlaid with trailing swags of gilt flowers, leaves and wheat ears, so delicately contrived that they rustle when a person ascends (Figure 6.4). In general,

Iron Pannelling for Stair Cases. Plate CLXXX.

Batty Langley Invent 1739. *Tho.ˢ Langley Sculp.*

Figure 6.3 Designs for iron staircase balustrades, published by Batty Langley in *The City and Country Builder's and Workman's Treasury of Designs*, 1739, Plate CLXXX. Photo: Lisa White.

it is fair to say that English staircase balustrades of the eighteenth century were more restrained than those designed and made in continental Europe.

Simple C- and S-shaped scrolls continued to be wrought in iron for staircases of the 1750s and 1760s: a range of patterns were published in W. and J. Welldon's *The Smith's Right Hand* (1765) and Ince and Mayhew's *Universal System of Household Furniture* (1762) (Figure 6.5). The simple repeating scrolls that create the balustrade of the two-story stone staircase at Woburn Abbey, Bedfordshire, are a good example; close examination reveals the variations in each scroll that distinguish hand-wrought work.

However it was the wide-scale introduction of cast, as opposed to wrought, iron that revolutionised its use in the interior. In 1756 Isaac Ware, in his *A Complete Body of Architecture*, described the qualities of both. He commented on the brittleness of cast iron:

that whatever is made of it, is liable to that accident, and often from the effects of air-holes will burst even at the fire.

This difference of cast iron and hammered, or as it is commonly called wrought iron, is very great in quality, and is not less in price; and in this last article the difference though great is very reasonable; the price of the cast iron being founded on nothing but that of ore and fuel, whereas the other depends upon a vast deal of labour; and it is made amends for by the intrinsic value: wrought iron which comes so much dearer, being always worth a certain price in any condition; whereas the merit of the other is principally in its form, its worth being when broke little or nothing.

Cast iron is however a very serviceable article to the builder, and a vast expense is saved in many cases by using it; in rails and balusters it makes a rich and massy appearance, when it has cost very little, and when wrought iron much less substantial would come to a vast sum. But on the other hand, there is a neatness and finished look in wrought iron that will never be seen in the cast; and it bears accidents vastly better.[1]

Although cast iron had been used for the railings around St Paul's Cathedral as early as 1714, and Abraham Darby began to use coke instead of charcoal for smelting in 1709, it was the development of larger manufactories during the Industrial Revolution in Britain that extended the use of cast iron universally. The Carron Iron Works in Scotland, established in 1759, and Darby's Coalbrookdale Works at Madeley, Shropshire, developed mass production of cast iron elements for all types of domestic use, including repetitive balusters for staircases. These became invaluable for the rapid urban building programmes of the later eighteenth century in

Figure 6.4 Wrought iron staircase balustrade, 1768–9, Claydon House, Buckinghamshire. Courtesy of the National Trust.

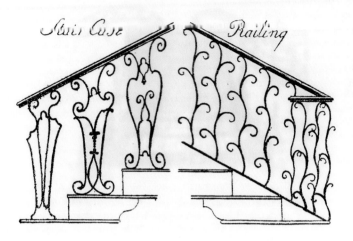

Figure 6.5 Designs for staircase railing, published in Ince and Mayhew, *The Universal System of Household Furniture*, Plate XCIII, London, 1762. Photo: Lisa White.

London, Bristol, Bath, Birmingham and many other towns and cities, where relatively inexpensive, light, precast decorative balusters could be used in any quantities. The city of Bath possesses perhaps the finest surviving in situ collection of such staircases (Figure 6.6).

Family connections and interest in the Carron Iron Works ensured the use of the material in many of Robert Adam's interiors, to great decorative effect, although the basic cast elements are simple, repetitive forms. One of the most delicate and sinuous balustrades was designed by Sir John Soane for Moggerhanger House, Bedfordshire, in 1806.

By the end of the Georgian period, numerous publications allowed build-ers and clients a huge choice of refined, neoclassical designs for cast iron staircase balusters, window balconies and lamp 'throws'. Interior metalwork was often painted in lead paints in a variety of colours that complemented the rest of the decoration of the interior: many Adam staircases used a bright blue, as at Osterley Park, Middlesex (c. 1766), light green or lead grey. William Chambers's beautiful iron staircases at Somerset house, London (c. 1775–1801), made by the London smith William Parmer, were painted a mid-blue. Bronze green was used for Henry Holland's elegant staircase and landing balustrades at Berrington Hall, Herefordshire, in 1784. Painted imitation of yellow bamboo work was applied to the cast iron staircase balusters of the Chinoiserie staircase at Brighton Pavilion, designed by John Nash in 1815. Black glossy paint was an introduction in the mid-nineteenth century. Careful paint analysis of all sections of painted balusters should always be undertaken to establish an original paint scheme, with careful searches for any gilding of highlights or specific decorative features.

Cast iron was often the favourite material for Victorian staircases, where styles became increasingly complex and heavy. L.N. Cottingham's *Smith*

Figure 6.6 Cast iron staircase balustrade, 'Fiesole' Villa, Bathwick Hill, Bathwick, 1846–8. Photo: James Davies.

and Founder's Director (1824) and Henry Shaw's *Examples of Ornamental Metalwork* (1836) illustrated many of the popular classical patterns using anthemions and paterae, while such foundries as Macfarlanes of Glasgow and Bayliss, Jones and Bayliss of Wolverhampton manufactured all types of cast iron railings for both internal and external use, in Great Britain and for export to the British colonies during the second half of the nineteenth century. Researching the numerous trade catalogues and pattern books of the period is always essential in re-establishing lost or heavily damaged ironwork of this period.

Architectural metal furniture

Although such details as door locks, bolts, hinges, handles and window catches may seem insignificant in any conservation project, correctness in design and scale can add immeasurably to the integrity of any historic scheme and should not be overlooked. Careful investigation of original evidence of fittings and of changes and replacements can all help to

Figure 6.7 Seventeenth-century iron door strap hinge, All Saints' Church, Kedleston, Derbyshire. Photo: Lisa White.

establish the historical record of a building's development. Sourcing correct replacements, either through architectural recycling emporia or reputable reproduction companies, can be a lengthy process but can lead to very satisfactory results. Fittings that are out of scale or fail to complement other architectural detail can have a jarring effect and should be avoided at all costs.

From earliest times until the seventeenth century, English door hinges, latches and handles were made of wrought iron, similar to those made right across Europe. Functional strap hinges were often transformed into decorative features by the addition of extra iron scrolls nailed to both external and internal doors (Figure 6.7).

Steel locks were made by specialist craftsmen and were expensive luxury items, only applied to significant doors and furniture, and as a result often superbly decorated. Again, many of the best surviving examples can be found in ecclesiastical buildings, especially English parish churches from the fourteenth century onwards, and the styles used were probably replicated in domestic examples, the majority of which have been lost through natural wastage, theft, demolition and changing taste. The expense of fitting doors with locks and keys is emphasised by the fact that they are listed in some early inventories of possessions.[2] Even in the eighteenth century, the selection of locks for specific doors was carefully considered and it is often possible to establish the long-lost purpose of rooms by the type of lock provided. Strong locks with complex mechanisms, even if plain, may well indicate a room that was used for the storage of valuable items, or an original door to the exterior.

Brass fittings for the domestic interior in England only started to be manufactured in large quantities from around 1700, so it is important to remember that most door hinges, handles and catches would have been made of iron before this date, unless expensive brass examples were imported from Flanders and the Low Countries. The English brass industry, born from the Elizabethan need for armaments in the later sixteenth century, developed slowly and was profoundly affected by the English Civil War (1642–8) and its aftermath. Brassfounders gradually developed expertise through Dutch involvement. By 1700 the raw materials of copper (from Cornwall, Wales and Northumberland), calamine (from Somerset and Nottinghamshire) and coal (from Wales, Staffordshire, Nottinghamshire and the Forest of Dean) could all be mined and transported to industrial centres for use, for instance in Bristol (Baptist Mills). The eighteenth century saw the great development of the brass industry in Birmingham and the West Midlands, producing everything from screws and thimbles to every type of ornamental fixture, weapon and 'toy' for home use and the export trade. Thus brass fittings became standardised in pattern and production and were distributed throughout the country by road and the canal system. By 1800, a house in Derbyshire might well have the same door handles as one in Devonshire. In major towns and cities, specialist retailers would stock ready-made goods and also have copies of the latest catalogues for inspection and choice. Many of these trade catalogues survive and can be consulted, but it is important to remember that patterns remained in production for up to twenty years.

Late seventeenth-century and early eighteenth-century brass rim locks for the internal doors of fine houses were often beautifully engraved with contemporary patterns in the naturalistic Dutch style and the crests and monograms of their owners. Examples survive at Dyrham Park, Gloucestershire, by John Wilkes of Birmingham (c. 1694), at Petworth House, Sussex, at Chatsworth, Derbyshire and at many more great Baroque houses (Figure 6.8). At Boughton House, Northamptonshire, the service and lesser rooms were fitted with iron locks whereas the grand rooms had fine brass locks and bolts.[3] John Wood, describing the increasing sophistication of house building and finishing in Bath in the 1720s, noted that whereas in former years even the best doors 'had only iron coverings varnished', now new buildings were furnished with 'the best sort of brass locks'.[4]

Rim locks, whether plain or embellished, iron or brass, continued in use throughout the period 1750–1900 for lesser doors made of pine, but mortice locks, set into the timber of the door itself, became more fashionable and widely used with the introduction of thicker mahogany doors for

Figure 6.8 Brass door lock by John Wilkes, Birmingham, c. 1690, Dyrham Park, Gloucestershire. Courtesy of the National Trust.

smart interiors. These were then finished with handsome brass or ormolu key escutcheons and ring handles, later superseded by round or oval knobs during the Regency and early Victorian periods. The cast and chased ormolu door furniture supplied by James Palmer, smith and brass founder to George III, for the mahogany doors made by John Hobcraft for Corsham Court, Wiltshire, in 1765, are beautiful examples of the Rococo style, incorporating little shells cast from natural specimens. Many more fine examples were made by Matthew Boulton's famous brassware manufactory at Soho in Birmingham, including those designed by Robert Adam for some of his most elaborate interiors.[5] Their delicate neoclassical patterns complement other designs used in the plasterwork and furniture of the interior. Brass versions were lacquered and ormolu ones were gilded, so that they remained bright and reflective and could be seen easily across a candle-lit room (a primitive form of fire-escape signage). Heavier mahogany doors also promoted the development of strong brass hinges, some designed as 'rising hinges' that allowed doors to close gently. Ring-pulls for window shutters were also neatly cast and finished, but have often suffered badly from neglect and the corrosive effect of a micro-environment between shutter and window glass over many years (Figure 6.9).

Figure 6.9 Ormolu shutter ring by Boulton and Fothergill, c. 1764, Kedleston Hall, Derbyshire. Courtesy of the National Trust.

During the nineteenth century the mass production of door furniture meant that every type of decorative fitting was available in styles that suited the overall decoration of a room, whether in the classical, 'French Revival', Renaissance Revival or Gothic style. For the latter, the Birmingham firm of Hardman and Sons manufactured hundreds of lock plates, door handles and grilles to the designs of A.W.N. Pugin, of robust yet delicate craftsmanship, for the numerous doors of the new Palace of Westminster, with subtle gradations of finish defining the various areas and purposes of the rooms to which they allowed access. Pugin and other Gothic Revivalists, including William Burges, also encouraged a revival of the use of iron or bronze door furniture for Gothic interiors, a practice followed by William Morris and other Arts and Crafts designers who rejected the brash brightness of Birmingham brasswares in the interior (Figure 6.10).

C.F.A Voysey favoured the use of copper door furniture. In many ordinary Victorian and Edwardian houses with painted doors, commercially produced brass and ceramic finger plates protected paintwork from staining and added to the proliferation of ornament to be found on door surfaces, and have been consistently removed by later generations.

Brass door furniture has been badly treated over the years by the use of proprietary abrasive cleaners and hard rubbing, which have removed original engraving and often left a residue of chemicals that clog decorative

Figure 6.10 Bronze door handle, 1889, designed by Henry Woodyer for the Dining Room, Tyntesfield, Somerset. Courtesy of the National Trust.

detail and can cause the metal to deteriorate. Originally, brass fittings were preserved by shellac lacquers, which in time will darken and deteriorate. Careful conservation is needed to remove old layers of dirt and lacquer before applying new acrylic-based lacquers or polishing with tarnish-inhibiting cloths to achieve long-term protection. Ormolu can be cleaned and, if necessary, re-gilded. Above all, keeping surfaces free of dust and moisture will ensure a degree of preservation.

Gilding

Applying gold leaf to different surfaces in the interior has long been a method of enhancing decoration and increasing radiance from the low levels of lighting that were available in the past (see Chapter 11). However, it was always an expensive practice, in terms of both materials and labour, and before the nineteenth century its use was restricted to the wealthiest families and institutions, often in rooms intended to look at their most dramatic at night. Thus the gilding of plaster ceilings in the eighteenth century, for instance, symbolised the great wealth of an owner who could afford not only the cost of gold leaf but also its cleaning, maintenance and the amount of light needed to dramatise its effect. During the nineteenth century more architectural gilding was added to earlier interiors to create splendid effects. In any conservation scheme, therefore, great care should be taken to investigate the physical and documentary evidence of architectural gilding to establish its origins.

Little architectural gilding appears to have been applied to interiors in Britain before 1700. The Balcony Room at Dyrham Park is an exception, where much of the original gilt highlighting of the architectural panelling survives.[6] The more regular use of oil gilding on architectural woodwork and plasterwork began in the 1730s, possibly through the influence of William Kent, who was aware of its widespread use in Italy.[7] Generally, gold leaf was applied using the oil gilding method in rooms that were as free of free of damp as possible (i.e. not halls or passageways) and were intended to be furnished with gilt seat furniture, tables and picture frames. Water gilding, which could be burnished brightly, was normally used for these furnishings.[8] The specialist craftsmen who gilded the moveable pieces of furniture may have been employed to gild the fixed timber decoration as well, and a team of plasterers would have included a gilder for major projects. Woodwork and plasterwork were prepared with sizes that could influence both the colour and the drying time of gilding: twenty-four-hour-drying size was usually considered best to produce a sufficient brilliance in oil gilding. Water gilding could be used for architectural features such as wooden curtain-cornices (often design en suite with bed-cornices) and for decorative borders to fabric hangings and wallpapers. In this process, the wooden surface would be coated with gesso (a mixture of whiting and size), on which fine detail could be carved or incised, and a ground colour applied which would condition the final appearance of the gold. Gold leaf would then be laid onto the moistened surface of the gesso. When dry, the surface could be burnished with agate tools to give a dazzling, hard metallic look (Figure 6.11).

Oil gilding and water gilding age differently and vary in their reaction to changes in environment, so the delicate relationships between the two finishes can often be lost or misread during restoration or conservation.

Surviving examples in houses of the first half of the eighteenth century show subtle uses of parcel gilding on the decorative carving of door-cases and window architraves in the most impressive rooms, whereas lavish full gilding was more popular in the nineteenth century. The exact location and amount of parcel, or partial, gilding of architectural elements was very carefully considered and arranged: the concave surfaces of fluted pilasters or columns, or the eggs and darts of a moulding, would be gilded to contrast with unhighlighted areas and create vivid effects. Different colours of gold leaf (using alloys of other metals) were carefully selected to vary the tonal effects: red, greenish bronze and paler yellow gold are mentioned in contemporary bills, instruction books and commentaries.[9]

The expense of such gilding is exemplified by the bills for work done at Canons, Middlesex, for the Earl of Chandos by the Italian *stuccatori* Bagutti and Artari: the plasterwork of the ceiling was valued at £250, its gilding at £155.[10] The surviving detailed account presented by Jean Cuenot for the carved and gilded drawing room for Norfolk House, London (1753–6), now

Figure 6.11 Examples of oil gilding and water gilding. The Building of Bath Collection (Bath Preservation Trust).

in the Victoria and Albert Museum, cites the cost of gilding the ceiling at £35.7s and the cornice and architrave at £28.5s.[11] Conservation of this room for redisplay in the British Galleries in 2000 provided a chance to investigate the history of its original gilding and subsequent treatment.

During the middle decades of the eighteenth century aristocratic taste favoured white-and-gold decoration for withdrawing rooms and music rooms (such as the one at Petworth House, Sussex, and Woburn Abbey, Bedfordshire) in a restrained French style, but this was soon superseded by the Adam brothers' introduction of more highly coloured architectural decoration which involved far less gilding (although more was added in nineteenth-century restorations). On very rare occasions, silver leaf was used for architectural decoration, despite its tendency to tarnish. In December 1775 Thomas Chippendale charged Edwin Lascelles £82.16s for '368ft very rich Antique Border'd Carved in wood and finished in Burnished Silver and varnished' for the Yellow Drawing Room at Harewood House.[12]

More widespread use of architectural gilding occurred in the nineteenth century, beginning with the lavish interiors created for George, Prince of Wales, later King George IV, at Carlton House, Windsor Castle and Buckingham Palace from 1800 to 1830, and subsequently in many aristo-cratic country houses and London houses: Lancaster House, Stafford House, London, and Chatsworth, Derbyshire, for the 6th Duke of Devonshire. However impressive, the lavish gilding employed by late Regency and Victorian decorators rarely had the delicacy of earlier schemes.

Oil gilding on architectural elements in the interior can last a long time, when well applied, but is subject to changes in humidity, contamination and inevitable deterioration. It is damaged by light and by heat, which can cause the surface to become cracked and crusty. Attempting to clean the surface by rubbing can cause more damage, and often the solution has been to apply another layer of gilding – and another. A cheap solution has sometimes been 'gold paint', actually made using bronze powder, which tarnishes and darkens with age. Professional conservators may be able to remove layers of over-gilding to reveal an original surface, but the process can be expensive and lengthy. Once again, careful examination of all the layers of decoration in an interior, and a search of other documentary evidence, will help to establish the age and significance of architectural gilding.

Further reading

Campbell, M., *Decorative Ironwork* (Victoria and Albert Museum, 1997).
Gentle, R. and Feild, R., *Domestic Metalwork 1640–1820* (Antique Collectors' Club, 1994).
Hayman, R., *Wrought Iron* (Shire Publications, 2000).

Endnotes

1. I. Ware, *A Complete Body of Architecture* (London, 1768), Book I, Chapter XXVI, p. 89.
2. 'An Inventory of the Goods and Chattles late of his Grace Ralph Duke of Montagu at his late Seat at Boughton in Northamptonshire taken March 25th 1709', in T. Murdoch, *Noble Households: Eighteenth century inventories of great English houses* (John Adamson, 2006), pp. 51–61.
3. 'On the great Stair case: Two Brass Locks, £1.0.0', *ibid.*, p. 53.
4. J. Wood, *An Essay Towards a Description of Bath* (1742–3), p. 25.
5. E. Harris, *The Genius of Robert Adam: His interiors* (Yale University Press, 2001).
6. Ian C. Bristow, *Architectural Colour in British Interiors* (Yale University Press, 1996), p. 49.
7. John Cornforth, *Early Georgian Interiors* (Yale University Press, 2004), pp. 158–59.
8. P. Mason and M. Gregory, *Of Gilding* (Arnold Wiggins & Son, 1989), pp. 5–11.
9. Cornforth, *Early Georgian Interiors*, pp. 122–29.
10. *Ibid.*, p. 126.
11. D. Fitzgerald, *The Norfolk House Music Room* (Victoria and Albert Museum, 1973), Appendix B, pp. 51–52.
12. C. Gilbert, *The Life and Work of Thomas Chippendale* (Macmillan, 1978), Vol. I, p. 209.

7 Chimneypieces

Lisa White

No article in a well-finished room is so essential. The eye is immediately cast upon it on entering, and the place of sitting down is naturally near it. By this means, it becomes the most eminent thing in the finishing of an apartment.

Isaac Ware (1756)[1]

Introduction: early chimneypieces

The earliest surviving decorative chimneypieces built into sophisticated interiors in Britain date mainly from the early sixteenth century. In medieval halls and hall-houses fires had been lit in a central hearth[2] and vented through smoke-louvres in the roof, before being moved to a side wall, enclosed above and at the sides, and accessing a chimney on an outer wall.[3] Much of the physical record of the luxurious interiors of abbots' and priors' lodgings in British monasteries was lost with their destruction or substantial alteration during the dissolution of the religious houses in the 1530s, but it is likely that chimneypieces for such rooms were as fine as other fittings for these interiors.[4]

In fifteenth- and sixteenth-century houses, chimneypieces had large apertures and hearths, with the masonry above supported by a substantial lintel of stone or timber. Often there was little or no decoration, although some rare survivors display carved stone decoration of the highest quality, similar to that on the architraves of doorways and in chantry chapels.[5] Many fireplaces were surrounded by continuous framed oak panelling that stretched across the top of the fireplace, sometimes without interruption, or with more distinguished panels immediately over the chimney, a style that lasted throughout the sixteenth and seventeenth centuries in provincial houses.[6]

Many early chimneypieces, whether in stone or timber, have fallen victim to architectural salvage and the antiques trade, or were simply removed when they fell out of fashion. At Acton Court, South Gloucestershire, two chimneypieces of 1500–1510, carved with animals and elegant heads in contemporary dress, were removed and thrown into the moat within thirty

Interior finishes & fittings for historic building conservation, First Edition. Edited by Michael Forsyth & Lisa White. © 2012 Blackwell Publishing Ltd. Published 2012 by Blackwell Publishing Ltd.

years of construction.[7] Others have been left in situ but with raised ornament that may have been cut back and keyed to take plaster.

From the 1550s, rich owners of secular houses (often profiteers from the
dissolution of the religious houses) began to accentuate chimneypieces in
important interiors, superimposing highly decorative overmantels that
incorporated sculptural figures, coats of arms, heraldic devices – symbols
of ownership and status – Christian and classical mythological figures and
creatures, Roman heroes, fruit, flowers, scenes and symbols, many adapted
from printed pattern sheets imported from the Netherlands, Flanders and
France.[8]

Materials for these much more sophisticated structures were local stones,
English alabaster, wood and stucco, the latter introduced by continental
craftsmen who employed and trained native plasterers to follow their
methods and patterns.[9] The materials and decoration can be compared
with those used on tombs and memorials in churches at the same time.[10]
They were often coloured, with occasional gilding to emphasise important
elements, and sometimes incorporated animals' skulls and horns as part of
heraldic decoration (Figure 7.1).[11]

Figure 7.1 The Chimneypiece in the Great Hall, Hardwick Hall, Derbyshire, c. 1601,
incorporating the coat of arms of Elizabeth, Countess of Shrewsbury. Courtesy of the
National Trust.

Unlike exterior decorative stonework, these interior pieces have been less subject to erosion and decay, though often subject to alteration, removal, replacement and repainting. Fine pale golden stone harmonised with the original light colour of oak panelling surrounding the chimneypieces, creating a fully integrated effect for the walls of a room. As oak panelling darkened over the years, such rooms now have a two-colour effect, very different from the original scheme. The Great Room of the Red Lodge, Bristol, c. 1577–85, is a good example.[12]

In Scotland during the late fifteenth, sixteenth and early seventeenth centuries, close cultural and political ties with France meant that chimneypieces were more heavily influenced by prevailing Franco-Italianate designs, using projecting canopies, with heraldic devices above in plasterwork.[13] These styles also became fashionable in England in the early 1620s and 1630s: a famous group of them have survived at the Little Castle at Bolsover, Derbyshire, decorated with coloured stones in the manner of Sebastiano Serlio (Figure 7.2).[14]

In the 1630s, Inigo Jones adapted contemporary French designs by Jean Barbet and Jean Cotelle for chimneypieces at Somerset House, London,

Figure 7.2 Chimneypiece in the Pillar Parlour, Bolsover Castle, c. 1620, using local stone and marbles. Courtesy of English Heritage.

and the Queen's House, Greenwich, for his French client, Queen Henrietta Maria.[15] Thus by 1640 many different materials were being used for the construction and decoration of chimneypieces. Their conservation, inevitably, requires a variety of skills. In particular, careful attention needs to be paid to assessing surviving surface ornament – paint, gilding – which may have suffered from removal or replacement.

Early chimney furniture

While the decoration of the fireplace surround developed dramatically between 1550 and 1650, fire fittings and furniture remained traditional: hearths were fairly large, open and adaptable for cooking in simpler houses, with an iron bar in the chimney to suspend cooking pots and other items over the fire or in the smoke. Great open fireplaces in kitchens continued in the medieval tradition. Firedogs or andirons supported bars which held faggots and logs in place, burning against a decorated cast iron fireback on the rear wall of the hearth.[16] A brass or ceramic curfew could be placed over embers to extinguish light or flames – an important piece of early fire prevention. Hearth equipment could be removed during summer months; the lime-rendered interior of the hearth would be cleaned and repainted regularly, and sometimes 'dressed' with fresh flowers and foliage.[17] Hearthstones were made of stone or brick. In addition to wood-burning grates, smaller iron baskets could burn coal (shipped from around Newcastle) and charcoal.

Seventeenth- and eighteenth-century developments

During the seventeenth century traditional fireplaces continued to be built in provincial houses, especially those with panelled rooms – parlours and best bedrooms, for example – where continuous panelling across the fireplace was both simple and effective. Panelling and chimney surround were either plain wood or were painted the same colour. This practice continued in North American colonial houses well into the third quarter of the eighteenth century.[18]

Developments included large bolection mouldings to trim the surround in wood or stone. From the 1670s onwards far more attention was paid to the finish of the chimneypiece, with a significant increase in the import of French, Italian and Spanish coloured marbles. Specialist marble suppliers occupied storehouses on the south side of the Thames at Southwark. Sir Thomas Leigh of Lyme Park, Cheshire, shopped in London for his chimneypieces in 1675, writing to his wife at home, 'I have been to look at some marble chimneypieces . . . I find there is a White Marble veyn'd and a delicate reddish marble full of white and coloured streakes. These are the two colours I intend to fix upon.'[19] As he shows, careful consideration was given to the appropriate colour of marbles for particular rooms, intended to complement the rest of the interior decoration. Of the surviving chimneypieces at Dyrham Park, Gloucestershire, that in the original state bedchamber on the *piano nobile* of Talman's east wing of the house (1698–1704) has tablet and slips of crimson and yellow Italian marbles, complementing the red and yellow velvet hangings of the state bed and chairs that stood in the room.[20] Thus a chimneypiece which survives in situ may provide clues for the original status, purpose or colour scheme of an interior even when all other evidence has gone.

Where Italian marbles were prohibitively expensive or unavailable, stonemasons used attractive local or native stones from Devon, Derbyshire and Connemara in Ireland, or decorators painted wooden mouldings in imitation of fancy stones and marbles.[21] One of the loveliest and costliest chimneypieces to survive from the 1670s is that in the closet of the state apartment at Ham House, Surrey: it is executed in delicate scagliola (Figure 7.3), which is also used on the windowsills executed by a Roman craftsman, Baldassare Artima.[22] In two other grand closets at Ham, for the Duke and Duchess of Lauderdale respectively, chimneypieces are set in the corners, locations frequently used for smaller closets and passage rooms in such houses.[23]

Very few chimneypieces of the straightforward bolection-moulded type had mantel shelves fitted above them at first, although these were often added later. From the 1680s sheets of mirror-glass were incorporated into

Figure 7.3 Chimneypiece in the Queen's Closet, Ham House, Surrey, c. 1674, decorated with *scagliola*. Courtesy of the National Trust.

panelling immediately above fireplaces to enhance the amount of light in the interior, and by the end of the century elaborate shelves and brackets to hold imported Chinese porcelain were crowded above the hearth, following designs by Daniel Marot (c. 1663–1752) for Queen Mary II and other aristocratic clients.[24]

By the later seventeenth century chimney apertures tended to be smaller and squarer in shape, still with open hearths and the traditional equipment of fireback, firedogs or andirons, which could become a significant decorative feature in their own right.[25] Smaller iron baskets for charcoal or coal could replace andirons and bars if desired, and the interior walls of the hearth would simply be lime-washed regularly in the traditional manner or, for smarter rooms, would be lined with ceramic tiles manufactured in increasing quantities in London (Lambeth), Bristol and Wincanton in the Dutch style.[26] During summer months when fires were not lit, the hearth might be filled with large Delftware vases for flowers and foliage, or might be covered with a decorative chimney-board which prevented soot, birds' nests and rain descending the chimney and harming precious floors and fabrics within a room.[27]

From 1700 to 1750 chimneypieces echoed the architectural styles prescribed for the rest of the fashionable interior, usually in the Palladian manner, adapting tabernacle frames, consoles and friezes from entablatures for windows and doorways.[28] Pattern books equipped both clients and craftsmen with hundreds of patterns and plenty of advice, and disseminated London style across England, Scotland, Wales, Ireland and the American colonies, often obliterating older regional distinctions. Designs were versatile and adaptable to the taste and wallet size of the individual, so that, for example, cheaper wooden versions could be substituted for more expensive stone or marble. They could also be adapted to deliver decoration regarded as appropriate to the purpose or status of each room in the house.

By the mid- eighteenth century it was normal to have elegantly decorated marble chimneypieces in the principal rooms of reception (that in the drawing room being the most flamboyant of all), while more modest examples furnished the best bedrooms and far simpler wooden versions in the upper rooms. William Chambers stated, 'Those of marble are the most costly, but they are also most elegant, and the only ones used in highly finished apartments.'[29] Nearly all these fashionable chimneypiece surrounds were attached to the fixed masonry of the chimney-breast using dowels and plaster. Their removal can be swift: hundreds have been stolen in overnight raids on vacant properties or sold for architectural salvage in recent decades. Sometimes when replacement has occurred, chimneypieces intended for grand rooms have been introduced into a room of much more modest character, often when houses have been converted into apartments or vice versa. Careful investigation is always required in any conservation plan to ascertain that the existing chimneypiece in a room corresponds in decoration as well as overall design and scale to the original purpose of the room.

In many grand houses in the earlier part of the eighteenth century, traditional overmantels displaying family heraldry and devices continued to be used, but increasingly these gave way to fashionable contemporary design in the classical taste, and by the 1750s and 1760s to some wonderful expressions of the Rococo, Chinoiserie and neo-Gothic styles, though these were usually reserved for specific rooms such as ladies' bedchambers or gentlemen's libraries. Complex designs of this sort were usually carved in pine and finished in gesso and paint, incorporating mirrors, candles branches and little brackets for ornamental porcelain.[30]

The necessity of applying particular themes or subjects to chimneypieces for specific rooms became a *sine qua non* of the genteel interior, often expressed through the use of correct classical orders and mythological subject matter: Bacchus for the dining room, Apollo for the saloon, Venus and Cupid for the bedchamber, Ceres for the breakfast room; Orpheus for the music room and so on (Figure 7.4).

Figure 7.4 Chimneypiece decorated with Bacchanalian symbols, Claydon House, carved by Luke Lightfoot, c. 1765. Courtesy of the National Trust.

Even when eighteenth-century rooms have changed their use and have been radically redecorated, an earlier chimneypiece may give clues to original purpose and decorative scheme. Coloured marbles used in chimneypieces were often matched in the tops of pier tables placed between the windows on the opposite side of the room.

Both Isaac Ware and William Chambers wrote extensively about chimneypieces in their architectural textbooks of the middle of the eighteenth century and any professional dealing with examples from this period would be well advised to read what they have to say very thoroughly.[31] Ware gives strenuous warnings against inappropriate ornament, the use of too many coloured marbles or the wrong proportions:

> Let those marbles, in their several kinds, be preferred whose ground is most pure, whose spots are best terminated, and whose veins run in the most agreeable manner; they should be light, and fantastically displayed; for a heavy variegation, or a vein running in a straight course, displease; where there is to be sculpture let the white be used, for nothing is more disadvantageous to a piece of carving than veins of another colour. They throw false lights and create confusion.

> For the lower parts, in general, no kind of marble is so well as the plain white; and the most beautiful of the coloured kinds should be disposed in columns and other ornaments, as freezes and pannels; and in this is to be shewn the great art of arranging them, so that they shall mutually set off one another.

> We would have the architect take care also to suit his colours to the subject; let him be as lavish of the lively tincts as he pleases in an elegant chimneypiece, but let him take care not to use too many of the gaudy colours on a tomb.

Ware also commented on suitable figure sculpture:

> Modern sculptors are full of nudities; but in a chimneypiece they would be abominable; they would shock the delicacy of our sex and should not be seen by the modesty of the other; they are therefore absolutely excluded from this service, and some drapery is always to be allowed . . . we banish anatomy from the parlour of the polite gentleman.

The importance attached to fine chimneypieces for the most formal rooms of the eighteenth-century house is underscored by the huge expense devoted to them. The best artists in the country were employed to produce magnificent sculptural surrounds incorporating fully three-dimensional figures and much, much more. In many instances these items were the most expensive elements of the interior and their purchase was carefully recorded in building accounts.[32] By the later nineteenth century they were being collected by museums and put on display as works of art in themselves, and they have become an integral part of the architectural salvage trade.[33] Where they have survived in great houses they still inform the visitor of the hierarchy and significance of the rooms they furnish (Figure 7.5).[34]

Amazingly, at Uppark, Sussex, despite the ferocity of the fire that took hold of the house in 1989, the beautiful chimneypieces commissioned by Sir Matthew Featherstonhaugh from the London statuary Thomas Carter in

Figure 7.5 Detail of marble tablet of the Chimneypiece in the Gallery, Croome Court, Worcestershire, c. 1765. Courtesy of the National Trust.

the 1750s for the principal rooms were relatively unscathed and have been conserved with minimal reconstruction.[35]

Firegrates and chimney furniture

In comparison to the expense and decoration lavished on the fireplace surround, chimney furniture of the early eighteenth century was still traditional: moveable fire baskets, firebacks and andirons still equipped the hearth, although the more fashionable were decorated with contemporary patterns.[36] Simpler houses and lesser rooms continued to be fitted with plainer, bolection-moulded surrounds. Also, many earlier houses, dating from the sixteenth and seventeenth centuries underwent extensive remodelling in the eighteenth century, but often retained earlier chimneypieces in lesser and service rooms, and on occasion earlier 'best' examples were moved to less important rooms, or even stored.[37]

After 1750 significant change in the fitting of hearths came as the mass production of cast iron grates developed in Shropshire at the Coalbrookdale works, and at the Carron Company works near Falkirk, Scotland.[38] These grates were cast in regular sizes for specific rooms (best rooms, bedchambers and garrets) and in their turn regularised the size of chimney hearths, especially in the new-built terraces, crescents and streets of Georgian Britain's developing cities, towns and holiday resorts (Figure 7.6).[39] They also standardised pattern across the country.

Their delicate neoclassical ornament was replicated in the marble and wood that surrounded them, with carved, inlaid, composition and ceramic ornaments, and in the slender mirror frames that surmounted them, effectively integrating them completely in the stylish interiors designed or influenced by Robert and James Adam.[40] As with earlier examples, much of the ornament used on these frames related to the purpose of a room and can again be used in identification of lost purpose or decorative schemes.

Figure 7.6 Cast iron firegrate, c. 1780; made in Coalbrookdale, Shropshire, showing the 'Iron Bridge' over the River Severn. The Building of Bath Collection (Bath Preservation Trust).

After 1760 more native stones and marbles were used, including beautiful specimens from Devonshire, Derbyshire, Scotland and Wales, sometimes in periods of shortages of imported materials – notably the French wars between 1793 and 1815 – or to advertise materials found on an owner's estate, or in an attempt to promote British industries.[41] The Derbyshire Blue John used at Kedleston Hall, and the Derbyshire pudding stone used for the 6th Duke of Devonshire's improvements and alterations at Chatsworth in the 1830s are fine examples (Figure 7.7). Replacing and repairing such pieces can present many problems as original quarries and mines have been worked out and closed.

Fire baskets did not go entirely out of fashion for fine rooms and were often still made in the best modern materials – polished steel and paktong, with elegant engraving and brass ornaments – distinguishing them from the more humdrum and commercial steel grates. In addition, free-standing stoves were being manufactured to provide efficient heating for garden rooms, conservatories, large halls and other spaces where open fires were unmanageable: the Governor of Virginia's great stove for the palace at Williamsburg is one of the finest.[42]

By 1800 the fitted grate and smart materials had been combined to create elegant register stoves for Regency interiors, while innovators and industrialists such as Count Rumford improved heat efficiency and smoke control for coal-burning hearths in increasingly large urban sites.

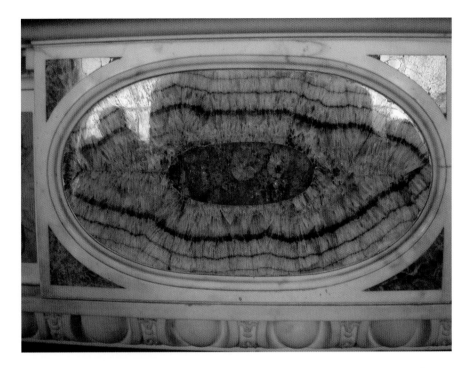

Figure 7.7 Detail of Derbyshire 'Blue-John' tablet in Chimneypiece, c. 1770, Kedleston Hall, Derbyshire. Courtesy of the National Trust.

Hullmandel's panorama of Bath published in 1825 gives some indication of the levels of pollution hanging over the city each morning, eating the very fabric of the houses.[43]

Inevitably, many free-standing fire baskets of the eighteenth century have disappeared from fireplaces, and have been replaced by Victorian or later fitted grates. Fitted hob-grates have been subject to the ravages of the architectural salvage trade, and to changing taste. When undertaking a conservation plan for a property, careful research is always required to ascertain the originality of the grate as well as of the chimneypiece itself (Figure 7.8).

Victorian style

The Victorians' delight in stylistic variety for their interiors and furnishing demanded an increasingly wide range of styles for chimneypieces. From the 1840s both surrounds and fitted grates were created in Rococo revival, Greek, Roman, Gothic, Tudor, Stuart and any other style to complement the eclectic interior.[44] Colour and a great range of materials were significant and ubiquitous. In the standard classical house, darker marbles and stones (sourced both in Britain and from all over Europe) were considered appropriate for more masculine rooms such as dining rooms and studies, while white Italian marble remained essential for fashionable drawing rooms.

Figure 7.8 Early nineteenth-century marble chimneypiece with cast iron grate in the Library at Wimpole Hall, Cambridgeshire. Courtesy of the National Trust.

As the scale of large Victorian country houses and public buildings increased, so too did the size of the chimneypieces they contained, so that some became monumental, built-in structures of great complexity, particularly when executed in the neo-Gothic style popular in the second half of the century.[45] Their numerous elements were often fixed together and to walls with iron cramps and bars, which can become victims of damp and corrosion. Their conservation, therefore, may be complex and expensive, comparable to the work required for large church memorials and other structures.

From the 1870s a fashionable revival of the idea of the 'inglenook' occurred, effectively extending the chimneypiece into forming an entire side of a room (Figure 7.9).[46] Details of the actual fireplace surround, grate and hearth were carefully designed as part of the whole structure, and the loss of them can damage seriously the architectural integrity of an interior.

Register stoves obscured the side walls of the hearth with shiny steel or brass, or the sides were fitted with hygienic patterned tiles from Minton and other factories. Overmantels became increasingly complex, often fitted

Figure 7.9 'Inglenook' fireplace in the Great Parlour at Wightwick Manor, Staffordshire, c. 1890. Courtesy of the National Trust.

with numerous small shelves or brackets to accommodate the dozens of ornaments that characterised Victorian homes, and mantel shelves covered and draped with fringed textiles that now seem to be extreme fire hazards. Many overmantels have been removed by subsequent generations as being too fussy, thus leaving the lower chimneypiece and grate looking awkward – and with their gaily coloured tiles painted over. This is not necessarily a new practice as such styles became deeply unfashionable after the First World War – or sometimes even earlier. In 1910 Lord and Lady Wraxall removed his father's magnificent neo-Gothic chimneypiece in the Drawing Room at Tyntesfield, Somerset, and substituted what they regarded as a more tasteful Italian Renaissance example: the former was found recently in a store beneath the chapel. Should it be reinstated?[47] Many complex decisions have to be made when reinstating Victorian chimneypieces for twenty-first-century owners.

By 1900, heating methods for British houses were starting to change. Central heating began to provide sufficient ambient heat throughout a house, obviating the back-breaking work of carrying coals and cleaning grates that had rendered the lives of housemaids so miserable for centuries. Eventually, gas and electricity completed the revolution, but they have not overcome the need, so ably expressed by Isaac Ware, for a fireplace to create a focal point, both socially and aesthetically, within the well-furnished room (Figure 7.10). In many modern houses, fireplaces and

Figure 7.10 Chimneypiece in the Larkspur Dressing Room at Standen, East Sussex, 1892–4, designed by Philip Webb in a restrained Arts and Crafts style. Courtesy of the National Trust.

chimneypieces are still introduced – not for warmth, but for their ability to create a sense of home. M.H. Baillie Scott wrote in 1906:

> In the house the fire is practically a substitute for the sun, and it bears the same relationship to the household as the sun does to the landscape . . . To live in a scientifically adjusted temperature with the fire relegated to the basement is to live in a grey and cheerless world; and so the house, however warm, without a fire may very reasonably be compared to a summer day without the sun. It is, therefore, no mere archaic affectation which leads us to cling to the open hearth and the blazing fire.[48]

Note: Original chimneypieces are fully protected in listed buildings of any Grade (I, II* or II), and Listed Building Consent is required for any alteration that might affect the character of such a listed building. Replacement or reinstatement would also require Listed Building Consent.

Further reading

Gilbert, Christopher, & Wells-Cole, Anthony, *The Fashionable Fireplace 1660–1840* (Temple Newsam House, 1985).
Kelly, Alison, *The Book of English Fireplaces* (Country Life, 1968).

West, Trudy, *The Fireplace in the Home* (David and Charles, 1976).
Wilhide, Elizabeth, *The Fireplace: A guide to period style for the heart of the home* (Little, Brown & Company, 1994).

Chimneypieces

Endnotes

1. Isaac Ware, *A Complete Body of Architecture* (1756).
2. Penshurst Place, Sussex, great hall, 1341; 'Bayleaf Famstead' from Chiddingstone, Kent, 1405–30, and the medieval cottage from Hangleton, Sussex, probably thirteenth century, both now reconstructed at The Weald and Downland Museum, Singleton, West Sussex.
3. Cotehele, Cornwall, the Great Hall, 1485–1539.
4. Muchelney Abbey, Somerset: the abbot's lodging of the early sixteenth century retains a fine fireplace with carved crouching lions as terminals to the roll-moulded overmantel.
5. Tattersall Castle, Lincolnshire, 1433–55; Hawkesbury, Gloucestershire: a surviving chimneypiece, probably from a Berkeley property in Wotton-under-Edge, Gloucestershire, with cusped arcading on the chamfered sides, late fifteenth century.
6. Chastleton House, Oxfordshire, the long gallery. Fixed panels and panelling developed from earlier, moveable textile hangings.
7. K. Rodwell and R. Bell, *Acton Court: The evolution of an early Tudor courtier's house* (English Heritage, 2004), pp. 252–54.
8. Anthony Wells-Cole, *Art and Decoration in Elizabethan and Jacobean England* (Yale University Press, 1997).
9. Geoffrey Beard, *Decorative Plasterwork in Great Britain* (Phaidon, 1975), pp. 23–33.
10. Margaret Whinney, *Sculpture in Britain 1530–1830* (Penguin, 1988).
11. Hardwick Hall, Derbyshire: the fireplace in the hall incorporates stags' antlers, heraldic symbols for Elizabeth, Countess of Shrewsbury ('Bess of Hardwick'), the builder of the house, 1590–99.
12. The Red Lodge, Bristol, built for Sir John Young, now a property of Bristol City Council, administered by Bristol Museums and Art Gallery; see also Apethorpe Hall, Northamptonshire, The Long Gallery.
13. Miles Glendinning, *A History of Scottish Architecture to the Present Day* (Edinburgh University Press, 1996).
14. Sebastiano Serlio, *Architettura* (1537–51), Book IV, Folio 8.
15. P.K. Thornton, *Interior Decoration in France, England and Holland in the Seventeenth Century* (Yale University Press, 1978), pp. 63–69.
16. A fine collection of seventeenth-century cast iron firebacks made in the Kent and Sussex Weald are displayed in the service passage at Petworth House, West Sussex, a property of the National Trust. See also the ironwork collections in the Victoria and Albert Museum, London.
17. Hannah Woolley, *The Queen-Like Closet, or Rich Cabinet* (1681); 'To dress up a chimney very fine for the Summer Time', William Hone, *The Every-Day Book*, 16 April 1826, p. 259.
18. For example, Stenton, Pennsylvania, the home of James Logan (1674–1751), a native of Bristol. Now administered by the Society of Colonial Dames of America.
19. National Trust, *Lyme Park* (1988), p. 33.
20. Now a property of the National Trust. The first-floor state bedroom is not open to the public.
21. Ian Bristow, *Interior House-Painting: Colours and technology, 1615–1840* (Paul Mellon Centre for Studies in British Art, 1996), Appendix C, pp. 188–200.

22. National Trust, *Ham House* (2000), p. 34.
23. See also examples at Dyrham Park, Chatsworth House.
24. D. Marot, *Nouveau Livre d'Apartomento* (1703), Plates 20, **27**.
25. e.g. Antechamber to the Queen's Bedchamber, Ham House, Surrey, c. 1670.
26. M. Archer, *Delftware: The tin-glazed earthenware of the British Isles* (Victoria and Albert Museum, 1997).
27. Victoria and Albert Museum, London, Museum Nos. W.35–1928, W.12–1994.
28. Elizabeth White, *Pictorial Dictionary of British Eighteenth Century Furniture Design: The printed sources* (Antique Collectors' Club, 1990), pp. 356–80.
29. William Chambers, *A Treatise on Civil Architecture* (1759), p. xx.
30. Crunden, Milton and Columbani, *The Chimney-Piece-Maker's Daily Assistant* (1766), Plate 29.
31. Isaac Ware, *A Complete Body of Architecture* (1756). W. Chambers, *Treatise on Civil Architecture* (1759).
32. e.g. the white statuary marble chimneypiece in the picture gallery at Corsham Court, Wiltshire, was provided by the sculptor Peter Scheemakers in 1763 at a cost of £325.
33. John Harris, *Moving Rooms* (Paul Mellon Centre for Studies in British Art, 2007).
34. Christopher Rowell and John Martin Robinson, *Uppark Restored* (National Trust, 1996).
35. *Ibid*.
36. C. Gilbert and A. Wells-Cole, *The Fashionable Fireplace, 1660–1840* (Temple Newsam House, 1985).
37. Croome Court, Worcestershire: the main rooms were extensively remodelled and the house re-cased in the 1750s, but earlier chimneypieces were preserved in the attic rooms.
38. Ironbridge Gorge Museum Trust, *Coalbrookdale* (1996); J. Donald and B. Watters, *Where Iron Runs Like Water! A new history of Carron Iron Works 1759–1982* (John Donald, 1998).
39. Bath Preservation Trust collections.
40. E. Harris, *The Genius of Robert Adam: His interiors* (Yale University Press, 2001).
41. C. Wainwright, *George Bullock, Cabinet-Maker* (John Murray/Blairman, 1988). George Bullock acquired the Mona Marble Works in Anglesey in 1806.
42. Graham Hood, *The Governor's Palace in Williamsburg, A Cultural Study* (Colonial Williamsburg Foundation, 1991).
43. Bath Preservation Trust collection, Huntingdon Chapel, Bath.
44. Charlotte Gere, *Nineteenth Century Decoration: The art of the interior* (Weidenfeld & Nicolson, 1989), Part 2, pp. 177–221.
45. For example, in the work of William Burges at Knightshayes Court, Tiverton, Devon, and Cardiff Castle.
46. e.g., Cragside, Northumberland; Wightwick Manor, Wolverhampton.
47. James Miller, *Fertile Fortune: The story of Tyntesfield* (National Trust, 2003), p. 150–52.
48. M.H. Baillie Scott, *Houses and Gardens* (London, 1906).

8 Wallpaper

Treve Rosoman

Introduction

Wallpaper is a commonly found decoration in old houses, but is something of a Cinderella subject. So often the first thing that an owner does in a newly acquired house or the first instruction that is given to the workmen is to remove all the old layers of paper; the common result may be the complete destruction of the building's interior decoration history. This applies as much to houses built before the Second World War as to houses built four hundred years ago.

The history of wallpaper is long; the earliest papers date to the mid-sixteenth century, but as a form of interior decoration wallpaper was common from the beginning of the eighteenth century. Paper was used not just for grand houses – in fact quite the reverse, in that some form of decorative paper was used in homes of a wide range of social classes especially as one gets closer to the twentieth century. The fact that the British government put a substantial tax on paper as early as 1710, which was not repealed until 1836, reveals the importance of such a seemingly inconsequential item as wallpaper.

This chapter will outline a brief history of wallpaper, and then look at the materials used in its manufacture, and how wallpaper was printed up to c. 1850. It will consider the influences on wallpaper design, how and where papers were hung in houses, and where one may find them even if they are not immediately obvious visually. Finally, it will offer some advice on dating and identifying patterns.

A brief history of wallpaper

The history of wallpaper, for all practical purposes, begins at the end of the seventeenth century with the discovery of the ability to glue sheets of paper together to create a roll of paper, or a 'piece' as it was called in 1700 and which is still a common trade term today.

Interior finishes & fittings for historic building conservation, First Edition. Edited by Michael Forsyth & Lisa White. © 2012 Blackwell Publishing Ltd. Published 2012 by Blackwell Publishing Ltd.

Wallpaper was block printed by hand onto hand-made paper until the mid-nineteenth century, when technical inventions and developments permitted the introduction of machines. The first development was continuous roll paper, then cylinder-printing by machine, after which improvements followed thick and fast: paper made from wood-pulp, engraved steel rollers for printing, and more and more complex methods of printing that speeded up production. Hand processes carried on in tandem, and by the early twentieth century designs made using small paint spray-guns were quite prevalent in the manufacture of large borders. In less than fifty years, wallpaper went from being entirely hand made to being produced in large new purpose-built factories; it changed from being a very London-based, quite expensive product to being a cheap everyday manufacture made predominantly in Lancashire, around Darwen, near Manchester. Hand-blocked paper continued to be made in London, and still is up to the present day.

Making hand-blocked wallpaper

From the earliest times in the seventeenth century, wallpaper was almost exclusively made in London by what were called 'paper-stainers' who sold direct to customers or sent goods out to customers in the country and colonies via agents.

Until about 1840 the paper used was a hand-made, rag-based product made by soaking cotton, linen and wool rags to make a pulp. Out of this a skilled tradesman, using a wire-bottomed mould measuring about 22 inches × 24 inches (55 cm × 60 cm), could make 1000 to 1200 sheets of paper in a day, in the process of which he would work his way through at least ten tons of pulp —or 'stuff', as it was called. The paper so made and used as eighteenth-century wallpaper is quite thick, not unlike modern cartridge paper. This paper was what is called 'laid paper', and when looked at through a strong light close parallel lines will be seen in it. A pattern could be woven into the mesh of the mould, which would create a watermark in the finished sheet. However, in this writer's experience is quite rare to find watermarked paper used as wallpaper.

Towards the end of the eighteenth century a finer paper was perfected, called 'wove paper'. This paper was made using a mould with a mesh that left no imprint of lines such as was found with 'laid paper'. Wove paper was principally produced for the burgeoning print trade as it was a very flat material perfect for taking fine line engravings. It was not commonly used for wallpaper until the early nineteenth century.

Once the paper sheets were produced, twelve of them were carefully glued together to make a length, or 'piece', that was about 12 yards long by 23 inches wide. These dimensions were set by the 1710 tax on wallpaper and were still much the same in the early twenty-first century in their metric equivalent (10.05 m × 52 cm). The tax was a duty levied by the Excise, and any evasion of money owed was punishable by death.

Hand block printing

Having made a 'piece' of paper, the next task was to print a pattern. Early papers were block printed; the blocks during the seventeenth and early eighteenth centuries were quite small, about 8 or 9 inches (20–22.5 cm) square, but by the 1730s they had become much more substantial. A typical block was made of strips of softwood glued together side by side, with another layer beneath laid crosswise so as to counteract any tendency to warp from the amount of water used to clean the block after use. On top of this block was placed a layer of a hard, grainless timber, such as a fruitwood or sycamore. This layer was carved away to create the pattern. A block was needed for each colour required in the finished design (Figure 8.1).

For at least a hundred years from 1730, blocks were about 23 inches (58 cm) wide – that is, the same width as the paper – but only a little over half the depth of the original sheet. The reason for this was that anything larger was too heavy to be lifted by one man. Carved fruitwood was excellent for making larger patterns, but for small dots brass pins were used; women, called 'pencillers', would draw in fine lines freehand; later, brass strip was inlaid into the block to create fine lines.

To print a paper, the block printer took a block from the store and checked it for damage, cracks, splits or warps. Any faults discovered were immediately repaired. The printer then grounded the paper with colour, using round brushes in such a way that no grain was left in the paint and it was perfectly smooth. Then the first block was prepared with colour.

Figure 8.1 Wallpaper woodblock, mid-eighteenth century. The Building of Bath Collection (Bath Preservation Trust).

Figure 8.2 Block Printing at Jeffrey & Co., Liverpool Road, Islington, London. A water-colour c. 1880, by Edith Capper. This shows a printer at work on what was almost the ultimate form of the table and very close to what is still used today by Cole & Sons. Courtesy of Temple Newsam House (Leeds Museums and Galleries).

Each block had a series of lines and pins along the side. One set of pins, called 'pin gauges', was used to position the block on the paper so that each successive block would run in a straight line along the length of the 'piece'. Other dots denoted each succeeding colour, so that the printer would know where to place the next block. (Modern newspapers have exactly the same lines and dots, and for the same reason.) These marks sat in the selvedge of the paper, and one side or the other would be trimmed off prior to hanging.

The block printer, by 1800, had an L-shaped printing table; the short side contained a box set with a blanket that was spread with colour, onto which the block was pressed (Figure 8.2). The printer, standing in the angle of the L, picked up the block and turned to set it down onto the grounded paper to print the first colour. He used a bar to increase pressure on the block, but this pressure had to be the exactly the same each time: if he pressed too hard the colour could spread out too much, and if he applied too little pressure it would not spread far enough. In the past such mistakes were very costly as the whole piece was wasted, and in the eighteenth century materials cost more than the labour; today, both cost much the same and this is still an expensive mistake. The printing of wallpaper is exacting and repetitive and takes about seven years to learn properly. After each application of the block, the paper is moved along and the pattern allowed to dry; when the whole length has been printed and dried the process is repeated for the next colour, and so on until the design is finished. Most eighteenth- and early nineteenth-century papers used only two or three colours plus the ground, so were relatively simple. To put this in context, the vast panoramic papers of the early nineteenth century, made in France by Zuber et Cie and others, could use as many as 1200 to 1500 blocks per design.

Flock wallpapers are a well-known type and have a long history; a patent was taken out in the late seventeenth century to make a paper that was covered with wool clippings to imitate fabric. Flock papers were made quite simply: instead of another colour being laid down, the colour was substituted by glue which was applied to the paper in exactly the same way. Then when the paper left the printing table it was put through a wide, cloth-bottomed trough. Either side of the trough stood apprentices, each armed with a stick, and the trough was filled with fine wool clippings. As the paper with its wet glue pattern went through the trough, the apprentices gently beat the cloth bottom, sending up a cloud of clippings that settled down onto the glued paper. It was then hung up to dry (Figure 8.3).

Figure 8.3 A rare French eighteenth-century flock wallpaper still hanging in its original setting. The paper was printed by the prominent Paris paper-stainer Reviellon in the 1770s. Drawing Room, Clandon, Surrey. Courtesy of the National Trust.

Designing wallpaper

Wallpaper designs were, to begin with, made in imitation of fabric designs. Needlework patterns such as blackwork were very popular in the early days as they were single-colour patterns quickly made using a ground colour – either an off-white or a pale buff – and a pattern outline in black. Such simple papers could be enlivened with stencilled colour very quickly dabbed onto the pattern. Crewelwork and chintz patterns were very popular as manufacturing processes improved in the early eighteenth century and more blocks were used to achieve multicoloured patterns. Floral patterns were great favourites – roses, sprigs of lilac, flowers on a trellis background, campanulas and so on. Abstract patterns were also surprisingly popular, although even these were often based on fabric precursors such as the oriental ikat or flame-stitch design – striking vertical zigzag patterns in reds, yellows and greens. Abstract, asymmetrical designs, often in shades of grey, were fashionable during the period 1790 to 1810 (Figure 8.4).

A favourite design for halls and stairwells was a pattern using either 'pillars-and-arches' or, a slight variant, 'gothick ruins'. By the early nineteenth century these patterns were being replaced by an almost endless variety of stone or marble finishes – in effect, a marbled hall.

Before the mid-nineteenth century almost nothing is known of early wallpaper designers apart from one man, Mathias Darly, and he is much better known as an engraver who provided plates for the cabinet maker Thomas Chippendale and others. He also produced a book of Chinoiserie designs in 1754.

The selling of wallpaper

English wallpapers of the eighteenth century were made for sale. Until mechanisation of the manufacture of wallpaper was introduced in the mid-nineteenth century, London-made wallpaper was widely exported to North America and Europe, even being smuggled into countries that Britain was at war with.

Wallpaper in the eighteenth century was usually sold direct by the manufacturers. Typically, their trade cards not only gave a list of products but also included small vignettes showing patterns and occasionally the interior of their shops; the cards doubled as both receipt and advertisement (see Figure 8.5).

Most customers were women, as it was they who commonly arranged for interior decorative schemes, though it was their husbands who paid. In London the majority of paper-stainers were located around St Paul's Churchyard – long the centre for the upholstery trade and also for publishing. The wallpaper-making paper-stainers combined both trades, using large quantities of paper and selling it people who were furnishing houses. They also went a stage further, buying waste paper from the publishing and print houses and turning it into papier mâché mirror frames, picture frames and similar goods.

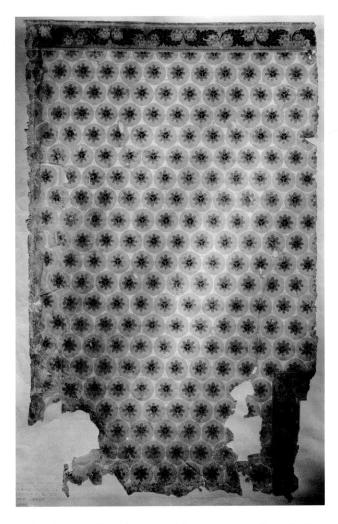

Figure 8.4 A colourful paper from the ground-floor rear room of a typical late eighteenth-century London terrace house. The orange and black combination became popular after the excavations of the Roman towns Pompeii and Herculaneum near Naples. Found at 47 Manchester Street, Marylebone, London (English Heritage).

By the early nineteenth century the trade had grown considerably, and as well as the manufacturers there were many who only sold wallpaper or were both sellers and paper-hangers.

The trade cards mentioned above sometimes gave quite detailed instructions as to how to hang paper, and similar instructions are attached to every roll of wallpaper sold today.

Where and how to hang wallpaper

Once the customer had bought the paper, they had probably also decided where it was to be hung. Halls and stairwells were generally hung with

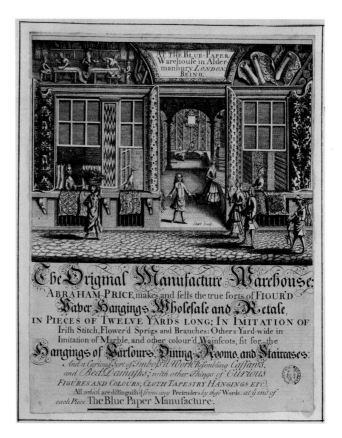

Figure 8.5 Trade card of Abraham Price's Blue Paper Warehouse, c. 1715. Note the range of papers illustrated and described, and also the small vignette in the top left showing paper being printed. Courtesy of the Bodleian Library, University of Oxford, Gough Collection.

papers of a pillar-and-arch pattern because these gave a greater sense of height to the room. Flock papers were considered proper for grand reception rooms – in town houses, usually on the first floor. Floral patterns were thought proper for bedrooms and ordinary living rooms, as long as they were 'not too gaudy' but were 'neat and plain'. Stripes were also found in bedrooms but are less common than florals.

While it was more usual to have a professional hang one's papers in London and large urban centres, those who lived in the country were certainly not above hanging the papers themselves or having some of their staff hang the papers for them. The usual method of hanging was to use a flour and water paste. Best practice was to hang the paper on a prepared ground of hessian or loose linen stretched over a battened wall. A lining paper was put over the canvas and then the top decorative layer applied above that. (It is not unusual to find many layers of wallpapers in old houses: the most that the present writer knows of is forty-seven layers, but fifteen to twenty is not at all uncommon.) As each new layer was put on, the paper would inevitably sag, but as it dried out it would become very taut. That

Figure 8.6 Printed wallpaper border, late eighteenth century, found in a house in Queen Square, Bath. The Building of Bath Collection (Bath Preservation Trust).

said, it was also common practice to hang paper directly onto the plaster – a very fine two-colour flock paper supplied by Thomas Chippendale to Sir William Robinson for his London house, in 1759, was hung directly onto the plastered walls – which only goes to show that there were no hard and fast rules, only a best practice. Until the mid-twentieth century, wallpaper was always hung with an overlap joint between each vertical strip; the butt-joint used today depends on straight-cut edges and very flat walls. Neither was the case in the past. The selvedge edge so important to the printing process was also forgiving of uneven walls as it allowed the paper-hanger some flexibility in putting one sheet up against the next. The selvedge was also not easy to remove in a perfect straight edge without a machine trimmer. The overlap joint also meant that it was very important to think out the method of hanging the paper before beginning; the hanger always started from the window, and great care was needed to make sure that the overlap joints would not create vertical shadows and so spoil the effect of the finished papered room.

Borders were a very common finish to the edges of wallpaper; they had the advantage of covering the marks of where the canvas had been nailed to the wall and leaving a neat finish (Figure 8.6). A variant was the fixing of a three-dimensional border, called a fillet. This could be made from papier-mâché, leather, lead, or carved wood and could edge the paper along the dado rail, sometimes following the outline of the door and fireplace although this was also a practice of wide variations.

A major change came about in the last years of the eighteenth century and the early nineteenth whereby the dado rail was removed and paper was hung from cornice to skirting board. This was a significant difference as it altered the proportions of a room and it essentially came about through a change in room use and decoration. It had always been the practice throughout the eighteenth century to arrange chairs around the room with their backs touching the dado rail; the rail protected the wall decoration and the chairs had no decoration to their backs – you don't pay for what you don't see, as it were. This formal arrangement declined as society itself became less formal and furniture was brought out into small conservation groups in the main living rooms. A simple outcome of this was that more wallpaper was required to cover larger areas of walls.

Papers can be found in many places in a house and are not always immediately obvious. Places that can often reveal paper are underneath dado rails and door architraves; these were often taken off during papering in order to make an easy straight line finish. Similarly underneath electric switches can be found small fragments that may not provide a pattern but will be excellent as colour guides. The insides of cupboards are also good places to find layers of old papers as they were not on public view and so were not worried about.

Dating and identifying wallpaper

A fundamental difference in wallpapers is between rag-based and wood-based paper. Rag paper is quite thick and has a distinct fibrous texture but, importantly, when it is torn it tears back at an angle, leaving a slanting surface – often called 'skinning' as it is so similar to when one tears skin from one's hand, for example. Wood, or cellulose, paper tears with a much more vertical line; it is a very acidic paper and with age becomes brittle and goes brown – a newspaper left in the sun for a while is the best example of this browning. Rag paper stays white but may be very grubby when taken off in an old building.

If one finds a rag-based paper the probability is that it is quite old. However, one must always bear in mind where the paper has been found. If, for example, it is in a grand fashionable house it may be a much more modern expensive hand-made wallpaper from a company such as Cole & Sons or Watts & Co. to name just two. If it is a William Morris pattern paper it might be a nineteenth-century original, an early twentieth-century version in a non-original colourway, a late twentieth-century hand-blocked design on machine-made paper from Sanderson's, or even a modern screen-printed paper. The pattern alone will not reveal the age.

There are a number of books now available that will reveal a great deal more about the history of wallpaper than there is space for here, especially as regards late nineteenth-century production methods. Identifying patterns is much more difficult, as the range of designs produced over the last three hundred years is so large that duplicates are rarely encountered. With small fragments one might only be able to deduce a probable pattern, but the larger the section of paper found, the easier it will be to determine the colours, the pattern-repeat, the paper's probable age and thus whether a similar design is available today or – and this applies to those working on important historic houses – whether it is possible to have a copy made.

Further reading

Entwisle, E., *A Literary History of Wallpaper* (Batsford, 1960).

Hoskins, L. (ed.), *The Papered Wall: The history, patterns and techniques of wallpaper* (Thames & Hudson, 1994; 2nd edn, 2005).

Nylander, R. (ed.), *Wallpaper in New England* (Society for the Preservation of New England Antiquities, 1986).

Oman, C. and Hamilton, J., *Wallpapers: A history and illustrated catalogue of the collection in the Victoria & Albert Museum* (Sotheby Publications/V&A Museum, 1982).

Rosoman, T., *London Wallpapers: Their manufacture and use 1690–1840* (English Heritage, 1992; 2nd enlarged edn, 2009).

Saunders, G., *Wallpaper in Interior Decoration* (V&A Publications, 2002).

9 Textiles

Annabel Westman

Introduction

Textiles have always played a crucial role in providing comfort and colour in the interior. They were also seen as a visible sign of wealth in the past, purchased as items of investment, with the choice of the rich silk velvets or more humble woollen cloths and linens reflecting the income of the owner. Today, however, while furnishing fabrics are still enjoyed for their variety and texture, they are rarely chosen for their status value. With the invention of man-made fibres and cheaper imports flooding the market during the twentieth century, not to mention the recent trend for minimalism, attitudes have changed. Rooms, for example, once named after the type or colour of the textile, are now more likely be referred to by the colour of the paint. Fabrics are no longer purchased to last several generations or to be used only on special occasions, with the result that they are no longer valued as items to be cared for. This current lack of understanding of the fragile nature of textiles has led to the degradation or disappearance of much of our historic textile wealth whose significance has, as a consequence, often been overlooked or misunderstood.

This chapter aims to redress the balance and convey the importance of textiles from the sixteenth century to the early twentieth century, explaining the variety of materials used, their design and colour, their application and the need for conservation. It will concentrate on the items that give a framework to the room, by providing a chronological survey of the different types of wall hangings, floor coverings and window treatment, rather than the individual upholstered pieces that can be moved easily or changed with the whims of fashion.

Comfort

It is useful when studying textiles, as with any industry, to have an understanding of the economic background and the technological developments that have transformed their use and manufacture over the years, both

Interior finishes & fittings for historic building conservation, First Edition. Edited by Michael Forsyth & Lisa White. © 2012 Blackwell Publishing Ltd. Published 2012 by Blackwell Publishing Ltd.

directly and indirectly. For example, the dissolution of the monasteries by Henry VIII, in 1539, led to huge amounts of wealth being released which the King and his favoured courtiers used to furnish new properties and make older dwellings more comfortable. The improved political stability in England in the second half of the century created the right conditions for building the great prodigy houses, such as Burghley, Longleat and Hardwick, giving ample opportunity for the creation of new schemes. Later in the seventeenth century, the revocation of the Edict of Nantes by Louis XIV, in 1685, which caused many Huguenot craftsmen (Protestants) to flee from religious persecution in France and settle in Britain, brought much-needed skills that improved all sections of the textile industry, including the latest fashions in upholstery. The Treaty of Utrecht, in 1713, gave Britain large colonial gains and exposure to trading opportunities around the world, which had a direct impact on the spread of disposable income, resources and design.

From the 1760s, huge technological improvements began directly to affect the textile industry, particularly the production of cotton in England, and the development of the power loom in 1785. From this period and throughout the nineteenth century, mechanisation of the industry gradually took over processes previously done by hand. One of the most important development was the invention of the Jacquard loom by Joseph Jacquard, in 1801. By the 1830s and 1840s, its use had transformed the industry, simplifying and speeding up the process of producing textiles with complex patterns, thus making them more affordable to the masses to decorate and provide comfort in their homes.

Colour

Until the early 1800s, dyes were based on vegetable sources, such as madder (red), indigo and woad (blue), and weld and quercitron (yellow) – the latter being available after 1783. They were vibrant in tone, and a typical sixteenth- or early seventeenth-interior would have canary yellows, emerald greens, sky blues, scarlets and crimsons jostling with one another in the tapestries, embroidered cloths and woven fabrics fashionable at the time. With the trend towards greater unity in furnishing schemes after the 1660s, colour still remained bright – a fact that is often hard for us to visualise today as so much has faded (Figure 9.1).

The dyeing industry underwent change in the early nineteenth century, with new processes and mineral dyes being introduced to supplement and replace the vegetable dyes. Experimentation blossomed with the interest in colour theory, and vivid creations were made with fabrics using contrasting and complementary tones. But in 1856 the industry was once again transformed, this time with the introduction of synthetic dyes (aniline dyes), following the extraction of the colour purple from coal tar. This discovery led to the rapid decline of natural dyes, despite the efforts of William Morris (1834–96), the highly influential English designer and craftsman, who tried to revive their use in the later nineteenth century.

Figure 9.1 Detail of crimson brocatelle wall hangings, c. 1870s, fitted into panels with a gilded fillet border in the Tyrconnell Room, Belton House, Lincolnshire. The section revealed under the painting shows the original colour contrasting with the faded material. Courtesy of the National Trust.

Wall hangings

A wide variety of different types of wall hanging were displayed, usually in the important rooms and bedrooms of the household. Only a few of the most expensive have survived, and these not always in their original position, which can give a distorted view of their use. In most cases, documentary evidence is all that remains to gain an insight into their design, colour and usage.

Tapestries

From the fourteenth century, tapestry was regarded as a major form of decorative art valued for the comfort it gave to a draughty interior, for its colour and pictorial interest and, above all, for its symbolic and powerful

Figure 9.2 The High Great Chamber, Hardwick Hall, Derbyshire – with a set of eight Flemish tapestries depicting the Story of Ulysses, c. 1560. Courtesy of the National Trust.

status. Tapestries, until the latter part of the sixteenth century, were only affordable by the very rich, and the rulers of Europe and wealthy land-owners vied with one another to get the latest designs from the looms of Flanders – notably Brussels – the centre of production in Europe. Henry VIII (1509–47), whose reign coincided with a golden age of tapestry produc-tion, was a keen collector and helped to stimulate the fashion in England. Subjects ranged from religious and mythological to hunting scenes and verdures, some with descriptions giving 'the circumstance of the matter' (Figure 9.2)

As demand grew, standards started to fall, leading to increased regula-tion by the Flemish guilds to maintain quality control. A ruling that became universal by 1544 was weaving the mark of the city and the master weaver on the edges of the tapestry. Despite this, by the end of the century a wide range was available, from the most expensive pieces enriched with metal thread and silk found in the palaces and grand houses, to coarsely woven or second-hand tapestries hung in the homes of less well-to-do families and even public houses.

Tapestries continued to be one of the most valuable and popular forms of wall hanging during the seventeenth century, found in the more important rooms and bedchambers of the household. Most tapestries used in England were Flemish in origin, but the rich also favoured the products of Mortlake (1619–1703), the most famous of the English tapestry manufactories. By the 1680s, however, Mortlake was losing ground to the Great Wardrobe (responsible for furnishing the royal palaces), and the smaller family-run factories based mainly in the Soho area of London

Figure 9.3 Detail of one of the tapestries by John Vanderbank dated 1691, set into the panelling in the Chapel Drawing Room, Belton House, Lincolnshire. Courtesy of the National Trust.

whose products, while largely provincial by comparison, were popular none the less.

Until the 1690s, tapestries were usually hung loosely down to the floor, or to the panelling below the dado level, edge to edge around a room including over the door, and suspended by hooks spaced at regular intervals just below the frieze (Figure 9.2). Most were purchased from merchants and adapted to fit an interior, but special orders became more common by the end of the century when tapestries started to be fixed to the wall behind mouldings. Queen Mary II was the first to commission John Vanderbank, master weaver at the Great Wardrobe from 1689 until his death in 1717, to make a set of 'Indian hangings' for her withdrawing chamber at Kensington Palace in 1690. Their design and novel method of display created a new fashion, and over fifty similar sets were made for English patrons. Only one set survives in situ, at Belton House in Lincolnshire, where the accounts record that it cost three times as much as any other type of wall hanging in the house (Figure 9.3).

Tapestries continued to be used in the main rooms of houses until the 1760s, with mythological themes, pastoral and verdure scenes, topical events and subjects such as the Seasons and the Four Continents remaining popular, but they were facing increasing competition from other materials, including leather and, notably after the 1730s, from wallpaper. In addition, the increasing number of paintings purchased on the Grand Tour, and the

Figure 9.4 The Tapestry Room at Osterley Park showing the set of French Gobelins tapestries designed by François Boucher, and an English carpet woven by Thomas Moore of Moorfields, 1775. Courtesy of the National Trust.

need to display them effectively, led to the gradual disappearance of tapestries in many grand reception rooms. While it had been a fashion in wealthy households during the seventeenth century to hang paintings or mirrors on tapestries, in the eighteenth century it was more accepted to display paintings on crimson or green woven fabrics, leaving tapestries to the bedrooms and dressing rooms. But even in these rooms they started to lose favour during the second half of the century, as the new fashion for lightness of texture and elegance of design meant that tapestries were either put in store, relegated to secondary bedrooms or destroyed. The most important exception to this general trend occurred in some of the houses where Robert Adam was involved as architect. At Osterley Park, for example, the owner and banker Robert Child was in the height of fashion when he chose to display French Gobelins tapestries, designed by François Boucher, in the Withdrawing Room (Figure 9.4). They were specially ordered to hang edge to edge, more like wallpaper, rather than singly in individual frames as in France.

The nineteenth century saw the revival of tapestry only in houses where there was an antiquarian approach to display, as at Hardwick Hall, Derbyshire during the 1820s and 1830s. It was not until the late 1870s that interest in the making of new tapestry was rekindled, first at the Windsor Tapestry Manufactory in 1878, and then by William Morris, who regarded tapestry as one of the noblest of the textile arts. His firm, Morris & Co., made tapestries to commission inspired by medieval designs until it closed in 1940.

Painted linen cloths

Linen hangings with painted or 'stayned' scenes to resemble tapestry were in common use during the sixteenth and early seventeenth centuries and found in many homes. They were relatively inexpensive – considerably cheaper than the tapestries with which they were often combined, their cost depending mainly on the quality of the linen. They were highly valued for their practical and decorative function, covering large expanses of wattle and daub or roughly finished surfaces. As wall finishes improved in the seventeenth century, particularly with the use of wainscot and plaster, and draughts were reduced, the use of painted cloths declined. Very few survive today, owing to their perishable nature and constant use, but some fine examples can still be seen in the Chapel at Hardwick Hall.

Embroidered hangings

Silk- and wool-embroidered hangings on a ground of silk and/or canvas were rare but they were highly valued, particularly in sixteenth- and seventeenth-century interiors with the vogue for canvas-stitch needlework, Florentine work and crewel-work embroidery. Large and small pieces were made, which added a feast of colour to the interior to create a rich and varied effect. There was a fashion for making 'slips' or motifs in colourful designs in tent or cross stitch on linen canvas, which were then applied to a silk background, such as the Oxburgh hangings in Oxburgh Hall, Norfolk. 'Patchwork' hangings made of different fabrics, sometimes cut from sumptuous cloths from the old monasteries, was another technique of which splendid examples survive at Hardwick Hall.

William Morris made a set of needlework hangings for the Red House in the 1860s, inspired by his study of seventeenth-century crewel work. They were exhibited in the 1862 exhibition and helped to raise the profile of embroidery, encouraging architects such as G.E. Street and M.H. Baillie Scott to produce designs.

Leather

Gilt leather hangings, often colourfully painted, made with calfskin, faced with tin foil, and embossed with patterns, were a popular alternative to tapestry or woven fabrics during the seventeenth and first half of the eighteenth centuries. The panels were chiefly produced in Holland and are often depicted in Flemish seventeenth-century paintings of merchants' houses. Original examples still survive in situ at Dyrham Park, near Bath, and Ham House, Surrey.

Woven hangings

Woven hangings of silk, wool or linen have always been popular throughout the centuries and right across the social divide as a deliberate tool to grade the importance of a room and to indicate status. Until the end of the seventeenth century, they were loosely hung like tapestries, sometimes with a little fullness, to give added luxury to the room whatever their type of cloth. Panels of fabrics of different colours, textures and designs were stitched or 'paned' together to give contrasting effects (Figure 9.5). Silk fabrics such as velvet, damask and taffeta were by far the most expensive, although any fabric with metal thread content would considerably increase the price.

Wool fabrics were the cheaper alternative and much more commonly used, although few survive today owing to general wear and tear and moth infestation. There were many different types – say, either plain or striped, dornix, fustian and kersey are all mentioned frequently in inventories. A Scotch 'plod' (plaid) room seems to have been popular in many houses during the later seventeenth and early eighteenth centuries, with wall hangings, bed and seat furniture to match, indicating the fashionable trend towards the integration of interiors with the same or similar-coloured textiles after the 1660s. Mention is occasionally made of different hangings for winter and summer, easily achievable when the hangings were either

Figure 9.5 Detail of the paned wall hangings of embroidered blue velvet and damask in the Queen's Antechamber, Ham House, Surrey, c. 1679. The damask (now yellow) is a later replacement. Courtesy of the National Trust.

loosely hung or attached with hooks and eyes, but with the desire for permanently fixing hangings after the 1700s, this fashion became less common.

With the decline in the use of tapestries, leather panels and painted cloths, woven fabrics enjoyed their greatest popularity in the eighteenth century. Silk damask was the most popular choice of silk, often with long pattern repeats, but cut silk velvets were a prestigious alternative among the wealthy until the 1750s, as can still be seen in the state reception rooms of Houghton Hall and Holkham Hall, Norfolk. Wool velvet, mixed silk and wool, or wool damask, brocatelle, mohair, camlet, cheney, and fabrics with printed or stamped (gaufraged) designs, were other alternatives used in principal rooms, mainly in crimson, green, blue and yellow. Only in the dining room were fabrics hangings frequently avoided owing to the widely held view that fabrics retained the smell of food.

Most patterned silk and wool fabrics were woven in narrow widths of between 460 and 610 mm (18 and 24 inches) (usually 535 mm, 21 inches), with plain fabrics sometimes slightly wider at around 760 mm (30 inches), the arrangement of the seams providing a visible and important articulation to the room. They were stretched on the walls against either plaster or plain softwood panelling with a backing of linen canvas or scrim and a layer of cartridge paper on top attached to battens. The tacks were hidden behind patterned braid or fillets made of carved wood, papier mâché or metal – often gilded (Figure 9.1).

The nineteenth century saw the increasing use of wallpaper in many rooms, although textiles remained fashionable in drawing rooms. Silk with borders, and striped silk from the 1780s to1830s, was popular, but silk damask remained the most commonly used fabric throughout the period, woven in modified eighteenth-century patterns.

Window curtains

While there was frequent mention of bed curtains in sixteenth- and seventeenth-century inventories, window curtains were rarely listed even in important rooms. When they were, their purpose was normally functional – a protection against draughts or sunlight. A single curtain could either be tacked to the frame and held open to one side, or suspended from rings, or tapes attached to rings, on iron rods supported by two hooks driven into the architrave or plaster at either side of the window. Single curtains were more usual than a pair, and warm woollen fabrics like say or serge were more frequently mentioned than silk taffetas or satins. When silk was used, it was often as a sun protection – white silk being the colour most preferred for this purpose – although very occasionally curtains were made to match the colour scheme of the room.

From the 1690s, however, curtains started to be treated more as an integral part of the furnishings. They became more decorative with the introduction of swagged valances and the 'draw-up' or 'festoon' curtain from France (Figure 9.6). These curtains had small rings sewn in three or

Figure 9.6 Engraved design for window curtains and furniture by Daniel Marot, c. 1700.

more vertical lines to the back of the curtains, through which cord was threaded to pull up the curtain to form swags. The fabrics used depended on the function of the room and the owner's status. Wool continued to be the most common, with camlet, haratean or moreen popular options for the majority of householders, but if silk was chosen for the grand bedchambers and reception rooms, taffetas of different weights, like lustring or sarcenet, or damasks in silk, wool, or a silk and wool mix, were the most likely choice. Cottons, such as dimity and printed chintzes, became popular alternatives from the 1760s.

While draw curtains on pulley rods, often with valances and cornices made to match, were popular until the 1730s, they were overtaken by the festoon curtain which became the most fashionable choice for the next fifty years or so. Another option was the 'drapery' curtain, introduced around the 1750s, which was pulled up by means of cord threaded through rings sewn diagonally to the back of the curtain, to frame both sides of the window. Both pull-up styles required a pair of cloakpins to take the cords, and evidence can often be seen in the sides of the window architraves showing where they were sited. Likewise, the bracket positions, supporting the cornice boxes and pulley laths onto which the curtains were tacked, can sometimes be identified either on the top of the architrave or in the plaster above.

The popularity of the pull-up styles, however, was eclipsed in the 1780s by the introduction of the 'French rod' curtain, which was ideally suited to the longer window extending to the floor. This new development consisted of two pulley rods which overlapped at the front, with two pulleys at one end and one at the other threaded through with a cord to open and close the curtains. The rods were usually hidden from view by a decorative valance, and the curtains were held open at the sides by large cloakpins or tassel tie-backs on hooks. They heralded a dramatic period in curtain styles, and the designers of the period, including Thomas Sheraton, George Smith, Rudolph Ackerman and James Barron, were full of advice about their importance and what styles should be adopted in individual rooms (Figure 9.7).

Between 1810 and 1830, there was a fashion for 'continuous drapery', particularly popular in drawing rooms, where the valances extended over two or more windows and were draped in creative swags and tails over cornice poles and boards – a style that was revived again at the end of the century (Figure 9.7). Combinations of different fabrics usually of two weights, such as silk and chintz, or silk and wool, in contrasting plain colours, lavishly trimmed, made up the curtain designs, which could cover the entire window wall. Elaborately painted or gilded cornices and poles, with decorative finials and other attached ornaments, completed the theatrical effect.

The French rod style of curtain remained popular throughout the century (and is still in use today in modern form). Around 1840, the 'lambrequin', a shaped stiffened pelmet with long sides framing the window, was introduced, but the Victorian era is chiefly known for its increasingly heavy drapery, with deep swags and folds fashionable from the 1850s and 1860s,

Figure 9.7 Design for window drapery by James Barrow, *Modern and Elegant Designs of Cabinet and Upholstery Furniture*, London, 1814.

often arranged to conceal the light from the upper windows. Patterned fabrics in strong colours in a variety of silks and wools, including damasks, merinos, reps and velvets, and heavily trimmed, became the vogue, with layered creations reaching a peak of complexity in the main reception rooms by the mid-1880s. Chintz was by now out of favour except for bedrooms.

There was a reaction against this profuse use of fabric by the reformist movement in the 1860s. Designers such as C.L. Eastlake, E.W. Godwin and Bruce Talbert called for window treatment to be more restrained and lighter fabrics such as cretonne were recommended. It was not until the end of the century, however, that simple draw curtains with plain, shaped or pleated valances were widely adopted as the style for the early twentieth century.

Blinds

The first patent for making blinds was taken out in 1692 by William Bayley, but it was not until the eighteenth century that they were in regular use. There were a number of different sorts available. The most popular were the spring blinds on tin-plate rollers (replaced by wood in the 1860s), despite plenty of evidence to suggest that they frequently went wrong. They were often fitted at the top of the inside frame of the lower sash window and made of linen (Holland) or wool (tammy), with green, blue and brown being frequently mentioned colours. Roller blinds with painted scenes were fashionable in the early to mid-nineteenth century. There were also 'unsprung' blinds pulled up by a continuous cord, Venetian blinds with wooden slats, often painted green, or painted wire gauze screens covering the lower half of the window.

Vertical pull-up blinds, like festoon curtains but with very little fullness, were also mentioned in eighteenth-century inventories, generally made of a light wool, or cotton after the 1770s. Permanently ruched festoon blinds with a scalloped base were a common feature of fashionable late nineteenth-century interiors. Light muslin draw curtains, plain or striped, were introduced in the early 1800s, forming an attractive addition to the new French rod curtains, but made of heavier lace from the 1840s, sometimes in two layers, reflecting the increasing complexity of curtain design at this period.

Floor coverings

By the end of the eighteenth century, most rooms had some type of floor covering but until this period it was not viewed as essential, and to our modern eyes floors would have looked very bare. When they were used, floor coverings would have added considerable warmth and colour to a room. There were several different types.

Hand-knotted carpets

Hand-knotted pile carpets were extremely rare in Britain before the sixteenth century. The first documentary evidence of their use in England was when Cardinal Wolsey ordered sixty carpets through the Venetian ambassador in 1518. Little is known of their design but they almost certainly varied in size and would have been intended to cover both the floor and table surfaces, a distinction that starts to be clarified in inventories by the end of the century.

An expensive and luxurious commodity, most wealthy households would only have had a small number. Until the early 1600s, they mainly came from Turkey and were known as 'Turkie carpetts', as distinct from carpets of 'Turkie worke', which were usually (but not always) of English or European origin and of which little is known. The popular designs were frequently illustrated in portraits of the period, and include 'Lottos', star and medallion Ushaks, and large and small pattern 'Holbeins'.

With the founding of the East India Company in 1600, costly carpets began also to be imported from Persia (Herat) and India (Mughal), with floral designs, coiling stems and palmette patterns. Of particular interest, although exceptionally rare, were the silk pile carpets of Isfahan from the Persian court of the Shah Abbas.

Carpets continued to be displayed on table or cupboard surfaces as well as on the floor until the early eighteenth century, but their use – notably those from Turkey – started to decline as the production of woven pile

Figure 9.8 The Saloon at Saltram House with blue damask hangings on the walls and an English carpet woven by Thomas Whitty at Axminster. Courtesy of the National Trust.

carpets from 1735, and specially commissioned hand-knotted carpets from the mid-1750s, got under way in Britain. The technique of hand-knotting had died out in England in the early 1700s, but the Royal Society of Arts in London organised a competition over three consecutive years from 1757, 'for the best Carpet in one Breadth after the Manner of Turkey Carpets'. The winners became the leading carpet manufacturers of the day: Claude Passavant (1755–61), Thomas Moore (Moorfields carpets 1756–93) and Thomas Whitty (Axminster carpets 1755–1835) (Figure 9.8). Most of the carpets were neoclassical in style, some specially designed to echo the ceiling in a room – a fashion that was expensive and only affordable by the very wealthy.

Thomas Whitty continued to produce hand-knotted carpets in the nineteenth century, adapting to the more eclectic tastes of the day, including Turkish, Chinese, Persian and French Empire designs.

During the Aesthetic Movement of the 1880s, Oriental carpets returned to popularity. At this time, William Morris began experimenting with the technique, inspired by his enthusiasm for floral Persian carpets. His 'Hammersmith Rugs' made at Morris & Co., as well as his production of woven carpets, were much admired, and other designers such as Walter Crane and C.F.C. Voysey became involved with the medium with considerable success.

Woven carpets

The eighteenth century saw considerable developments in the types of floor coverings on the market. One of the most important was the production of woven carpets, of which there were three main categories: ingrain carpets, commonly referred to as Kidderminster or Scotch, a reversible double-cloth without a pile that started production in Kidderminster in 1735, and quickly spread elsewhere; Wilton, a cut pile or 'velvet' carpet that began manufacture in Wilton about five years later; and Brussels, an uncut or looped pile carpet that was introduced at Wilton at the same time. Both Wilton and Brussels types were being made at Kidderminster by the mid-1750s. There was also a fourth group – tapestry woven carpets produced mainly in Aubusson in France but popular in England from about the 1780s.

These carpets were considerably less expensive than hand-knotted carpets and were already very popular by the 1750s, admired for their versatility of pattern, durability and distinctive texture (Figure 9.9). They were woven in narrow strips that could vary in width, but were usually 27 inches (686 mm) wide (an 'ell' in measurement), and which were sewn together and cut or 'planned' to fit the room. Designs were plain or patterned, with or without borders – the flexibility and variety of choice providing a distinct advantage over oriental carpets.

Very few eighteenth-century woven carpets survive but there are many inventory references and bills giving details of pattern and cost. Wilton and Brussels were more expensive than Kidderminster, which was generally used in bedrooms and passages by the second half of the eighteenth century. The carpets were generally obtained through the upholsterer or cabinetmaker, but by 1800 there were also specialist retailers with showrooms in London.

By the 1820s, fitted Wilton and Brussels carpets, often with hearthrugs to match, had become widespread and hand-knotted carpets were less exclusive. The patterns reflected the tastes of the period – heraldic and gothic designs, for example, being particularly popular after the 1830s. By the mid-nineteenth century, the industry had become mechanised and many complex designs with large bouquets of flowers, ferns and whorls were produced, which were only later tempered by the more controlled patterns of William Morris and the Arts and Crafts Movement after the 1870s.

_" OH! LISTEN TO THE VOICE OF LOVE .

Figure 9.9 Satirical print by James Gillray, published by Hannah Humphrey, London, 1799, showing typical woven strip-carpet of the period. Private Collection.

Needlework carpets

Needlework carpets, worked mainly in tent stitch and cross stitch, enjoyed great popularity around the 1720s–1760s. They were often made in the home with the help of professional 'pattern drawers'. A number survive, mainly with floral designs, which show their remarkable virtuosity. The technique enjoyed a revival, although the designs were considerably simpler, when Berlin wool work became a popular pastime among the leisured middle classes in the 1830s–1860s.

Painted floorcloths

In the early eighteenth century, painted floorcloths or 'painted carpets' were introduced, and by the end of the century they had become particularly popular in areas of the house that experienced hard wear. They were seen as a status symbol and were frequently shown to advantage in entrance halls, imitating geometric chequered patterns and marble pavements. In the early nineteenth century they were frequently placed in dining rooms under the buffet, and sometimes placed between the carpet and the wall.

In 1863 linoleum was patented, which provided a more hardwearing surface, but painted floorcloths continued in production until 1914.

Matting

Thick rush matting, sewn together in narrow plaited strips and planned to the room, was widely used in sixteenth- and seventeenth-century wealthy households and was by far the most common form of floor covering, if the floor were covered at all. Rush matting is frequently depicted in the portraits of the period under Turkey carpets. After the 1660s smaller, individual mats began to be introduced which were finely woven in plain or brightly coloured patterns and referred to in inventories as 'Portugal', 'Barbary', 'Dutch' or 'Africa' mats, according to their place of origin. They were prestigious items and frequently placed under the grand beds of the period.

In the eighteenth century, apart from bedside mats, matting declined in use except in areas such as halls and passages that endured heavy wear. However, there was a revival during the Regency period, and again at the end of nineteenth and the early twentieth century, when mats in bright colours were enjoyed, particularly in bedrooms.

Conservation

Textiles start to deteriorate from the moment they are made, and maintaining the right environmental conditions in terms of light, humidity and temperature is essential to their survival. They are particularly sensitive to the ultraviolet radiation in daylight that causes colours to fade and the fibre structure to deteriorate. Light damage cannot be reversed.

Much of our textile wealth has been preserved in the past by traditional housekeeping skills. Case curtains were supplied for expensive wall hangings, including some tapestries that were originally only put on display for special occasions. Case covers were provided for furniture, and carpets were protected with coverings of baize or drugget, laid over areas liable to hard wear. Blinds were drawn against sunlight, and when the family was not in residence the house was 'put to bed' by shrouding the interior furnishings with dust sheets and closing the shutters.

During the first half of the twentieth century, many housekeeping practices were ignored or forgotten partly owing to the reduction in staffing levels of many large houses. As a result, huge damage was done to textiles – a danger that has been heightened with the increasing numbers of houses open to the public, leading to longer hours of exposure to light and atmospheric pollution. Since the 1970s, however, a gradual understanding of the importance of textile conservation and the scientific effect of adverse conditions has developed. Many windows of historic houses are now fitted with ultraviolet filters and light levels are reduced with the increasing use of blinds. Many housekeeping skills have returned – although there is still much to be done – which has at least arrested some of the decay so that future generations can continue to enjoy our rich textile heritage.

Glossary

Brocatelle: a complex weave with similar patterns to a damask, often made with a combination of silk and linen.

Camlet: a plain weave, mainly woollen cloth woven in different widths and qualities. It could be treated with different finishes to give added lustre.

Chintz: a printed cotton, sometimes glazed.

Cretonne: a term used for a variety of heavy unglazed cottons or linens with printed designs either hand-blocked or machine-printed.

Cross stitch: a small diagonal stitch worked left to right and crossed back diagonally from right to left.

Crewel work: an embroidery worked in crewel wool, a loosely twisted two-ply yarn.

Damask: a reversible fabric made of silk, wool, linen, cotton or a mix of fibres, the pattern created by two different weave structures.

Dimity: a stout cotton cloth of different qualities, often with a figured or striped pattern, and usually white.

Drugget: a coarse woollen fabric of various colours, similar to felt, and used to protect carpets or as a floor covering on its own.

Florentine embroidery: (similar to Hungarian point, Bargello work, flame or Irish stitch) worked with an upright stitch used to create a flame-like pattern usually in various colours.

Harateen: a worsted material, related to moreen and camlet, often with a wavy pattern.

Lustring: a lightweight taffeta.

Merino: a woollen cloth made using wool from the merino sheep.

Moreen: a worsted cloth with a waved or stamped pattern, similar to harateen.

Muslin: a fine cotton, plain or striped.

Plaid: a cloth with a pattern of intersecting stripes.

Rep: a plain weave in silk or wool with a ribbed appearance.

Sarcenet: a thin silk of plain or sometimes twill weave.

Satin: usually a silk fabric with a smooth lustrous surface.

Say: a fine woollen cloth of twill weave; a type of serge.

Serge: a twilled woollen cloth of many different qualities.

Taffeta: a plain silk with a ribbed appearance and a high-lustre finish.

Tent stitch: sometimes called petit point, it is a small diagonal stitch or a half cross stitch.

Verdure: a tapestry consisting mainly of landscape scenes and foliage.

Further reading

Campbell, Thomas P., *Tapestry in the Renaissance* (Metropolitan Museum of Art, 2002).

Campbell, Thomas P. (ed.), *Tapestry in the Baroque* (Metropolitan Museum of Art, 2007).

Fowler, John and Cornforth, John, *English Decoration in the 18th Century* (Barrie & Jenkins, 1974).

Gere, Charlotte, *Nineteenth-Century Decoration: The art of the interior* (Weidenfeld & Nicolson, 1989).

Gilbert, Christopher, Lomax, James and Wells-Cole, Anthony, *Country House Floors 1660–1850* (Leeds City Art Galleries, 1987).

Montgomery, Florence, *Textiles in America 1650–1870* (Norton, 1984).

Saumarez Smith, Charles, *Eighteenth-Century Decoration* (Weidenfeld & Nicolson, 1993).

Schoeser, Mary and Rufey, Celia, *English and American Textiles from 1790 to the Present* (Thames and Hudson, 1989).

Sherrill, Sarah, *Carpets and Rugs of Europe and America* (Abbeville, 1996).

Thornton, Peter, *Seventeenth-Century Interior Decoration in England, France and Holland* (Yale, 1979).

Thornton, Peter, *Authentic Décor, The Domestic Interior 1620–1920* (Weidenfeld & Nicolson, 1984).

10 Ceramic and glass

Lisa White

Since earliest times ceramics have been used in the interior for both hygienic and decorative purposes. They have been subject to intense wear and, despite their robustness, have undergone replacement and alteration. On occasions, decorative tiles have been lifted or removed from their original positions to be displayed as 'antiques', or have even been re-laid in different positions – for instance, in gardens or garden buildings. Any survey of a historic interior should take into account where they may have been used, and a careful search made for any surviving evidence. This chapter is intended to give an overview of the use of ceramic and glass finishes in the historic interior.

Early floor tiles

From the Roman period ceramic floors were used in British interiors in the form of thin bricks and tiles. From the thirteenth century floors were made of regularly shaped earthenware tiles laid over a mortar screed of lime, sand and grit which would secure the tiles and prevent their fracturing through movement or excessive pressure. Decorative patterns were created by pressing wooden stamps into the wet clay tiles, and pouring coloured pipe clay into the indented shape; the whole tile would then be fired in a kiln. Colours were restricted to a range of earth tones – green, yellow, brown and red – set against the natural colour of the clay body. Elaborate arrangements of different patterned tiles created beautiful floors, incorporating heraldic, mythological, religious and naturalistic symbols which complemented colourful wall paintings, carved stone, painted woodwork and textiles. Today their worn surfaces often give little indication of their original bright colour.

Evidence from medieval monastic foundations shows that decorative clay tiles were used extensively for the floors of churches, refectories and other important interiors, including, for instance, that of the first-floor library of Lichfield Cathedral, Staffordshire, which is still in situ. The Benedictine

Interior finishes & fittings for historic building conservation, First Edition. Edited by Michael Forsyth & Lisa White. © 2012 Blackwell Publishing Ltd. Published 2012 by Blackwell Publishing Ltd.

Figure 10.1 Earthenware floor tiles at Titchfield Abbey, Hampshire c.1400. Courtesy of English Heritage.

Priory at Great Malvern, Worcestershire, was a major centre for the production of decorative tiles which were distributed over a wide area, having good supplies of fine clay from the Severn Vale nearby. Other early centres of production were in London, Coventry and Bristol, but manufacture could be established wherever good supplies of clay were available (Figure 10.1).

Great secular interiors of the medieval and early Tudor period were also fitted with elegant and colourful tiled floors, for instance in the royal palaces at Westminster and Winchester and at Clarendon Palace, near Salisbury. A tile kiln was discovered there together with the remains of beautiful tile pavements of c. 1250, decorated with dragons, gryphons and interlace patterns (now in the British Museum, London).[1] Cities with extensive trading links with other parts of Europe imported decorative floor tiles: in Bristol, one of England's richest commercial cities, the floor of the early sixteenth-century Poyntz Chapel of St Mark's Church (now the Lord Mayor's Chapel) is made of highly coloured Spanish tiles interspersed with English heraldic examples. In the 1520s Cardinal Wolsey imported tiles for The More, his house in Hertfordshire. Flemish paving tiles in patterns of green and yellow were imported through London in c. 1535 for Hampton Court Palace, Surrey, at a cost of five pence per hundred. Most remarkably, a beautiful floor of Flemish-made maiolica tiles in the Italian fashion, by Guido da Savino (who had emigrated from Castel Durante to Antwerp), survives at The Vyne, Hampshire, although the original location of these tiles is unclear (Figure 10.2).[2]

Figure 10.2 Flemish tiles, early sixteenth century, The Vyne, Hampshire. Courtesy of the National Trust.

Major archaeological research at Acton Court in South Gloucestershire in the 1980s revealed substantial use of fine polychrome floor tiles dating from the late fifteenth and early sixteenth centuries, while the cloister walk on the north side of the Privy Garden at Thornbury Castle, South Gloucestershire (before 1521), was also tiled.[3] From the medieval period until the early nineteenth century, locally made bricks or plain clay tiles provided a simpler form of ceramic floor for more modest homes. These were both warm and relatively easy to keep clean.

Tin-glazed earthenware or Delft tiles

During the seventeenth and eighteenth centuries many fashionable houses were paved with stone for halls, staircase halls and passages, often in contrasting colours and patterns in the continental European style; such floors were more classical, architectural and durable than the somewhat old-fashioned and softer clay tiles. However, at the same time a taste

Figure 10.3 English tin-glazed earthenware tile, made in London, c. 1750. Private Collection.

developed for another type of ceramic decoration in the interior which was to become immensely popular. In the sixteenth century the manufacture of tin-glazed earthenware tiles developed in Holland and within a few decades they were being imported into Britain in huge quantities. Dutch émigrés set up tin-glaze potteries in Norwich and London, and soon their production was imitated in Lambeth, near London, in Bristol, Wincanton and Liverpool, and at the Delftfield Pottery in Glasgow. Three of these centres were leading mercantile cities, and the tiles produced there were exported to British colonies in America and the West Indies. In the early eighteenth century their decoration followed imported Dutch examples – Bible stories (often taken from contemporary engravings), classical mythology, rustic figures, birds, animals, flowers, ships and endless variations of patterns from Chinese export porcelain (Figure 10.3).[4]

Later in the century more recognisably English subjects, such as picturesque landscape scenes and topography, appeared on tiles and other tin-glazed 'useful wares', and borders became more distinctive. Cobalt blue patterns on the white tin-glazed surface of the tile were by far the most numerous, but other colours were also introduced in the eighteenth century, such as manganese red/purple, copper-sulphate green and antimony yellow. The Bristol potteries developed a very delicate decoration of two shades of white, known as *bianco sopra bianco*, which echoed lace patterns in contemporary dress. After 1756 production speeded up with the introduction of transfer-printing, although much detail continued to be finished by hand. These tiles were intended for vertical surface decoration, where the pictures could be 'read', and were not usually robust enough to be used on floors.

Some tiles were produced to form pictorial panels in their own right, but most were intended primarily for practical use, where their glazed surfaces could be regularly washed. They were used to line fireplaces (see Chapter 7), 'buffets' or niches intended for serving water or wine, basin-niches, garden rooms (e.g. at Hampton Court, Surrey), apothecaries' shops, surgeries and the dairies of country houses. Excellent examples of the latter survive at Uppark, and Goodwood in West Sussex, at Blaise Castle, Bristol, and at Woburn, Bedfordshire. At Dyrham Park, Gloucestershire, decorative tiles from the early eighteenth-century dairy were 'recycled' into a new, larger dairy in the 1840s and surrounded with plain white examples to show them to advantage.

Eighteenth-century tin-glazed earthenware tiles have rarely been out of fashion and replicas are still manufactured today. Because of their popularity they have become collectors' items and victims of architectural salvage. Thousands have been prised out of eighteenth-century fireplaces, buffet niches and garden buildings for sale as individual antiques. Others have been thrown away as fashions changed. Sometimes inappropriate tiles (in date or scale) have been reintroduced into replaced chimneypieces. In any conservation plan it is essential to analyse carefully what tiles may have been used in a historic interior and when, and to consider whether replacement is acceptable (Figure 10.4).

Victorian tiles

From the 1830s the taste for decorating interiors in the neo-Gothic and 'Old English' styles prompted a new demand for ceramic tiles with medieval patterns. A.W.N. Pugin designed and Herbert Minton manufactured encaustic tiles with Gothic patterns for the Palace of Westminster and for many of Pugin's new churches in the 1840s and 1850s.[5] At the same time, Victorian concerns for hygiene within the home, and especially in close-packed urban housing, encouraged the use of durable, modestly priced, washable ceramics in the interior. From the 1850s more surfaces were covered with plain and decorative tiles than ever before. The firms of Maw & Co., Craven Dunnill, Godwin, Doulton, Pilkington, Burmantofts and many more produced wall and floor tiles for every type of building – hospitals and slaughterhouses, factories, department stores, schools, hotels, museums, railway stations and public houses.

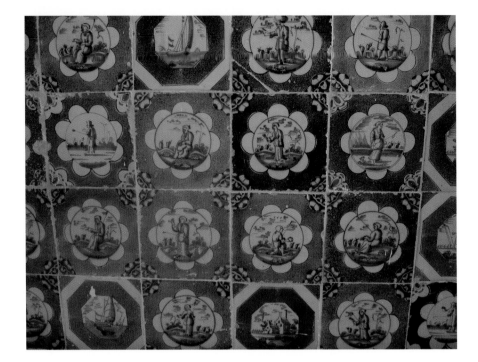

Figure 10.4 Eighteenth-century English 'Delftware' tiles fitted as a splash-panel for a twentieth-century bathroom at Barrington Court, Somerset. Courtesy of the National Trust.

In the domestic interior tiles were provided for kitchens, larders, pantries, service passages, bathrooms, toilets, smoking rooms, halls, stairways, nurseries and conservatories, and for fireplaces in each room. Even entire chimneypieces could be manufactured in glazed tiles (Figure 10.5).[6]

Commercial artists produced designs in every possible style, from neo-Gothic to French Revival, Aesthetic Movement and Arts and Crafts. Colours could be vivid, and patterns far more complex than those of the previous century. Their rich colours and high glazes complemented the sumptuous textiles and bold wallpapers of Victorian houses. William Morris employed the Dutch firm Ravestyn of Utrecht to produce 'Delft' tiles in eighteenth-century patterns, as well as commissioning others from William de Morgan for the Arts and Crafts interiors carried out by Morris & Co. Transfer-printing and mass production in the Potteries region around Stoke-on-Trent ensured low prices for many 'art' tiles for middle-class, mid-Victorian homes whether in Britain or anywhere in the British trading world – by now including Australia and India.

Despite their utilitarian connotations, tile floors were created for many distinguished and luxurious houses in the Victorian period. Among splendid survivors is the hall floor at Wimpole Hall, Cambridgeshire, made at the Benthall works of Maw & Co., Broseley, Shropshire, in 1880. The design incorporates the owner's monogram and motto, and the threshold to the former Ante-Chapel suitably bears the Latin inscription, 'Salve!' The floor

Figure 10.5 The tiled larder at Wightwick Manor, Staffordshire, c. 1890. Courtesy of the National Trust.

in the main entrance passage, called The Cloister, at Tyntesfield, Somerset is laid with Minton tiles of exceptional quality, bordered with elaborate polychrome patterns. With a target of 150 000 visitors per year to the property, the National Trust faces the problem of protecting these beautiful tiles from the damage of so many feet. One possible solution is the use of 'mouse-mat' fabric which can be printed with photographic images of the original floor (Figure 10.6).

Antique tiles were also recycled in some Victorian houses: at Dumfries house, Ayrshire, the Dutch tiles that line the chimneypieces in the main rooms look convincingly original at first glance. In fact, they were inserted by the architect Robert Weir Schultz (1860–1951) for the 3rd Marquess of Bute in 1898–9 during the extension and alteration of the house.[7]

After World War I changing tastes in interior decoration towards simpler schemes and lighter colours meant that Victorian ceramic tiles went dramatically out of fashion. Some were simply painted over or covered up, but far more were hacked off walls and thrown away. The introduction of plumbing and heating has also caused many Victorian tiled floors to be treated very badly, on the assumption that floors would then be covered

131

Figure 10.6 The Cloister, Tyntesfield, Somerset, laid with Minton tiles, c. 1870. Courtesy of the National Trust.

with fitted carpet. Fine tiles designed by famous Victorians are now collectors' items in their own right and are prey to removal in the same way as eighteenth-century Delft tiles are. Surfaces have been badly worn over the years, and incorrect methods of cleaning have been used frequently, so that much damage and degeneration has taken place. However, with careful conservation, the rich polychromy of many Victorian interiors can be restored if original tiles are still in place.

Glass

The history and significance of stained glass in ecclesiastical buildings is extensively discussed in many publications and cannot, for conciseness, be included in this chapter.[8] However, it is important to remember the role of painted, stained and reflective glass in historic domestic interiors. In the past it received more attention for its decorative quality than is often the case now.

Stained glass was often a medium in which to record family ownership and achievement in a historic property, thus adapting for secular purposes an art that was widely recognised in abbeys, cathedrals and churches. In country houses at the centre of great estates, chapels fulfilled a dual function in recording family history in tombs, memorials and glass windows, as well as providing space for worship. Surviving stained glass in such rooms can be a vital record of either continuous or varied ownership from the sixteenth century onwards.[9]

In other important rooms, heraldic glass reinforced statements of ownership, especially in halls, staircases and great chambers during the sixteenth and seventeenth centuries where it was incorporated into mullioned windows with leaded lights (Figure 10.7).

Figure 10.7 Heraldic glass in the Great Hall, Montacute House, Somerset, sixteenth century. Courtesy of the National Trust.

The introduction of sash windows in the later seventeenth and early eighteenth century more or less ended the use or reuse of smaller panes of heraldic or other stained glass in fashionable classical houses, unless it was preserved for particular dynastic reasons. However, a group of mid-eighteenth-century antiquarians, including Horace Walpole, identified the picturesque qualities of antique stained glass and effectively created a market for it, at a time when much was being removed from English parish churches and was also available for sale in continental Europe. In 1737 William Stukeley recorded in Stamford:

> the churchwardens of St Martin's took away all the painted glass of that church, and put up plain glass in the stead . . . Thus these incurious and thoughtless people demolish these most admirable ornaments . . . glaziers commonly broke it all in pieces and sold it for old glass. Sometimes I heard of it before execution done, and purchased the pieces . . . and put up great quantitys at my house on Barnwell.

Glaziers working on churches received more money for the lead cames than for the glass, but already a substantial amount of antique examples from English and continental churches were to be found in dealers' shops in London.[10]

In the Great Parlour, Library and other rooms at Strawberry Hill in the 1770s, Horace Walpole inserted antique stained glass in the upper lights of windows, leaving the lower lights clear to allow unimpeded views of picturesque landscapes beyond the house. This became a regular, 'Romantic' treatment from the later eighteenth century and during the nineteenth century, for instance at Fonthill, Wiltshire (1796–1816) for William Beckford, and at Lord Grosvenor's Gothic fantasy, Eaton Hall, Cheshire, designed by William Porden from 1804–12 and in the 1820s (remodelled in the 1840s and 1870s and demolished in 1963) (Figure 10.8).[11]

It is important to remember this arrangement of coloured glass when tackling conservation projects to avoid leaping to conclusions about the disappearance of decorative glass from lower lights when it never existed. Stained glass is very easily removed and can be repositioned easily: it is essential to follow documentary evidence to establish original, secondary and later installations of the material in a historic interior.

After 1800 the fashion for installing antique glass developed rapidly, assisted by the vast quantities available following the destruction of religious foundations in Europe. The broker John Christopher Hampp (1750–1825) of Norwich purchased antique glass not only from dealers but even directly from the churches, especially in Rouen. The great country house chapel at Ashridge, Hertfordshire, was filled with Renaissance glass from Germany, possibly procured by Hampp and which was eventually removed to the Victoria and Albert Museum.[12]

Modern glass was made to complement antique pieces, for instance that by James Pearson and by the firm of Egintons of Birmingham for Beckford at Fonthill Abbey, Wiltshire. Sir Walter Scott commissioned new heraldic glass for his Armoury and staircase at Abbotsford, which was intended to

Figure 10.8 Heraldic glass in the upper lights of a window, early nineteenth century, Baddesley Clinton, Oxfordshire. Courtesy of the National Trust.

'cut a very lightsome and gay figure and will throw a beautiful light upon the room'. At Uppark, Sussex, Sir Harry Fetherstonhaugh took Humphry Repton's advice and installed classical glass panels in the Servery to the Dining Room. These were taken from sketches of the Elgin Marbles done by Repton's son John Adey Repton, and executed by William Doyle in 1813. In the centre is a small late sixteenth-century roundel of Flemish glass depicting a banqueting scene. The panels were intended to be lit from behind by Argand lamps to create a magical effect (Figure 10.9).[13]

At Brighton Pavilion in the 1820s the firm of Crace and Sons inserted painted glass ceiling panels with delicate Chinoiserie ornament in the low lights of the first floor South galleries to provide borrowed light in an otherwise windowless space. In the ostentatiously grand Music Room, decorative glass oculi were back-lit with gas lamps.

Using coloured glass had passed from being an antiquarian pastime into the mainstream of interior finishes. Where specially commissioned glass was too expensive or inappropriate, similar effects could be achieved with painted transparent window blinds as suggested in Edward Orme's *An Essay on Transparent Prints* (1807). This is also significant in any analysis of original decoration, as surviving fittings for blinds may not necessarily indicate sun-blinds; they may have been decorative. A watercolour of c. 1820 of the Little Parlour at Renishaw Hall, Derbyshire, the home of the Sitwell family, shows a semi-transparent window blind half-drawn over standard

Figure 10.9 Coloured glass window back-lit by Argand lamps, designed by Humphry Repton, 1812–13, The Servery, Uppark, Sussex. Courtesy of the National Trust.

Georgian sashes, an attempt to unite the earlier decoration of the house with 'modern' Gothic wallpaper and antique seat furniture.[14]

Commercial production of large sheets of plate glass from the 1830s, the abolition of the government taxes on glass in 1845 and on windows in 1851, and cheaper methods of manufacturing coloured, transfer-printed, acid-etched and pattern-rolled glass in large quantities all promoted a greater use of the material as a significant decorative feature in the Victorian and early twentieth-century domestic interior, especially for windows and internal doors.

The leading practitioners provided glass for ecclesiastical, domestic, public, professional and commercial interiors: Thomas Willement (1786–1871), C.E. Kempe (1837–1907), John Hardman & Co. of Birmingham (established 1838), Powell & Sons of Whitefriars, London, and Morris & Co., the latter using designs by Rossetti and Burne-Jones. Some of these companies, such as Hardmans of Birmingham, remain in production today and have conservation workshops; the archives of others have been preserved

Figure 10.10 Coloured glass in upper lights at Wightwick Manor, Staffordshire, 1887–8, by C.E. Kempe to designs from William Morris's *Earthly Paradise*. Courtesy of the National Trust.

and can be consulted. Many Victorian country houses and public buildings have survived with good examples of artistic furnishing glass still in situ, in a wide variety of styles from full-blown Gothic (Palace of Westminster) to Arts and Crafts (Wightwick Manor), Elizabethan Revival and Art Nouveau. Beautiful examples have also been rescued for display in museums (Figure 10.10).

In addition to the finest work produced by these firms for individual and institutional clients, even modest Victorian families were able to afford slips of decorative patterned glass, further adding to the intensity of surface ornament in such interiors. Very often these simpler, cheaper pieces have fallen victim to damage, brittleness caused by age and exposure, changing taste and the conversion of houses into flats and apartments. Public houses and theatres, once the homes of riotous Victorian glass, have suffered particularly badly, although the Crown Liquor Bar in Victoria Street, Belfast, Northern Ireland, one of the National Trust's more surprising properties, is a superb example of survival and restoration in 1991.[15]

The Modern Movement of the twentieth century continued to use glass as a significant decorative interior finish and the tradition for coloured glass in front doors, interior doors and furniture lasted in modest and traditional

Figure 10.11 Coloured window glass in the landing window at 'Mendips', Liverpool, 1931. Courtesy of the National Trust.

homes until World War II – for example at 'Mr Straw's House', Blyth Grove, Worksop, Nottinghamshire (a typical terrace house built in 1905 and unchanged since the 1930s), and in 'Mendips', Menlove Avenue, Liverpool, built in 1931, the childhood home of John Lennon (Figure 10.11).[16]

One of the most refined twentieth-century interiors which acts as a homage to glass is that of St Matthew's Church, Millbrook, Jersey, designed by René Lalique (1860–1945) in 1934. Here, a designer most known for his decorative objects for the secular interior returned to an ancient use of one of the loveliest materials for the finishing of this wonderful church.

Figurative etched glass is characteristic of the finest Art Deco interiors, as at Liverpool's Philharmonic Hall (1936–9), by Herbert J. Rowse, with its glazed doors and first-floor windows by Hector Whistler.

Mirror glass

Reflective glass only came to form a truly fixed element in the finishing of interiors in the late seventeenth century as the technology for making larger sheets of glass developed in Europe and England, but it remained hugely expensive and therefore a luxury largely confined to royal and aristocratic interiors. Louis XIV's statement of absolute power in the reflective surfaces of the Galerie des Glaces at Versailles is one of the most famous uses of mirror glass in the Baroque period. A plainer but nevertheless important use of mirror glass in an architectural rather than a furnishing role survives in the State Apartment at Chatsworth, Derbyshire, where Gerreit Jensen supplied the 1st Duke of Devonshire with 'glass for the door of the Great Chamber' in 1688, described by Celia Fiennes in 1697: 'at the end of the dineing room is a large doore all of Looking-glass, in great panels all diamond cut, this is just opposite to the doors that runs into the drawing roome and bed chamber and closet, so it shows the rooms to look all double'.[17] Jensen's door does indeed contrive to trick the visitor into believing that a second enfilade of rooms exists – one of the first theatrical uses of mirror glass in an interior in Britain.

In 1664 the Worshipful Company of Glass-Sellers and Looking-Glass Makers was incorporated and controlled the production of glass manufacture in the City of London. The 2nd Duke of Buckingham was also instrumental in establishing the production of mirror glass at Vauxhall: by 1700 the factory advertised 'rough plates from the smallest sizes to those of six foot in length, and proportionable breadth, at reasonable rates'.[18] Most glass was made by the 'broad' process, which involved blowing, cutting and opening out the resulting tube and laying it flat before cooling (Figure 10.12).

Attempts to manufacture glass sheets by casting were not particularly successful in England before 1773, when the British Cast Plate Glass Manufacturers were established. From then on much larger sheets were available for mirror glass.

Figure 10.12 Sample of eighteenth-century mercury-silvered mirror glass. The Building of Bath Collection (Bath Preservation Trust).

The *Dictionarum Polygraphicum* of 1735 gives a full account of finishing processes whereby glass plates were ground and polished, bevelled and silvered. The latter process is described thus:

> A thin blotting paper is spread on a table, and sprinkled with fine chalk; and then a fine *lamina* or leaf tin, called *foil*, is laid over the paper; upon this *mercury* is poured, which is equally distributed over the leaf with a hare's foot or cotton. Over the leaf is laid a clean paper, and over that the glass plate.

> The glass plate is press'd down with the right hand, and the paper is drawn gently out with the left; which being done, the plate is covered with a thicker paper, and loaden with a greater weight, that the superfluous *mercury* may be driven out, and the *tin* adhere more closely to the glass.

Silvering was dangerous, and a major health hazard.

Mirror glass borders could be finished by bevelling, engraving or decorating with *verre-églomisé*, a process in which gold leaf is applied to the back of clear glass, engraved and filled with black or other colours in decorative patterns. Because of its expense, mirror glass was often returned to manufacturers for resilvering and reuse. Occasionally, such recycled pieces can be found in mirrors dating from the mid-eighteenth century.

The most expensive mirror glass made in Britain was used for 'pier glasses', framed sheets of glass fitted to the piers of masonry between windows in the main reception rooms of fashionable houses, above a table which supported candelabra, and thus the set acted as a night-time lighting system (see Chapter 11). This was a convention that lasted through to the nineteenth century, when dropped sills and the introduction of full-length French windows prompted furnishers to extend mirror glass below the table top.

One of the most extravagant uses of decorative glass in an eighteenth-century interior must have been in the Drawing Room of Northumberland House, Charing Cross, London. This was designed by Robert Adam for the Duke and Duchess of Northumberland in 1773; the walls were to be entirely lined with sheets of French mirror glass and plate glass, backed with red foil to imitate porphyry, from dado to ceiling cornice – one of the most complex, colourful and costly installations of the period. It was dismantled when Northumberland House was demolished in 1874 and stored at Syon House, Middlesex, until parts were sold to the architectural dealer Bert Crowther of Syon Lodge, who rented out sections for parties. In 1953 the Victoria and Albert Museum acquired the remains and a single section is displayed in the British Galleries after sensitive conservation.[19] Another of Adam's clients, the actor David Garrick, also commissioned sparkling mirror and coloured glass decoration for the interior of the Theatre Royal in Drury Lane in 1775.

By the early nineteenth century British manufacture of large cast sheets of mirror glass, whether in flat, concave or convex shapes, opened up greater possibilities for its use in the interior. Sir John Soane (1753–1837) ingeniously incorporated such pieces into his conjoined houses, 12 and 13, Lincolns Inn Fields, London, in 1812–13 to create dramatic effects of light and reflection in his dining room and library on the ground floor, where daylight was considerably restricted by the narrowness of the site.[20]

Fitting mirror glass safely into such interiors was carefully considered. In the dining room at Uppark, Humphry Repton designed new alcove recesses for the display of Sir Harry Fetherstonhaugh's magnificent plate. The opposing alcoves were fitted with mirror glass to create reflective vistas across the room, and Repton advised Sir Harry in 1812, 'remember not to confine it too tight or it will break – put lead or woollen cloth near the edges'.[21]

The designer George Smith published a design in 1808 for a drawing room recess which 'is made into a window, having the Glass of one entire plate, without any sash-bars; a plate of mirror glass slides within the wall, which is at night to be drawn over the window'.[22] Internal sliding mirror-glass window shutters were also used in the Duke of Wellington's Waterloo Gallery (1818–19) at Apsley House, London, where at night they reflected the ceremonial plate on the dinner table and the Duke's great collection of paintings.

By the mid-nineteenth century large sheets of mirror glass had become an essential element in interior decoration, particularly for overmantels of drawing room chimneypieces, and were affordable not just by the super-rich but by the professional and 'middle classes'. This is demonstrated by the inclusion of hundreds of designs in mid-Victorian pattern books.[23] Silvering processes became faster and cheaper after 1840 with the development of a new method of depositing true silver in a thin film on glass, rather than the older process of using a tin and mercury amalgam, which gave the finished product a brilliant but harder-looking surface prone to tarnishing when exposed to humidity. The harsh metallic effect of modern mirror glass did not appeal to the designers and creators of Arts and Crafts interiors from the 1870s onwards, and less of the material is to be found in such interiors, but for by far the largest number of Victorian and Edwardian domestic interiors, substantial areas of mirror glass had become a standard feature. Replacing old mirror glass when it has been broken or removed is often problematical. Old glass is fragile and in short supply, even for furniture restorers and conservators, while new glass lacks historic character, colour and movement. In any conservation scheme, reusing even fragmentary amounts of mirror glass may assist in creating convincing replacements.

Further reading

Archer, Michael, *Delftware: The tin-glazed earthenware of the British Isles* (Victoria and Albert Museum, London, 1977).

Britton, Frank, *English Delftware in the Bristol Collection* (Sotheby Publications, London, 1982).

Graves, Alun, *Tiles and Tilework of Europe* (Victoria and Albert Museum, London, 2002).

Tait, H. (ed.), *5000 Years of Glass* (British Museum, London, 1991).

Van Lemman, Hans, *Architectural Ceramics* (Shire Publications, 2002).

Van Lemman, Hans, *Victorian Tiles* (Shire Publications, 2000).

Endnotes

1. T.B. Beaumont James and A.M. Robinson, *Clarendon Palace: The history and archaeology of a medieval palace and hunting lodge near Salisbury, Wiltshire* (Society of Antiquaries of London, 1988). Elizabeth S. Eames, *Catalogue of Medieval Lead-Glazed Tiles in the Department of Medieval and Later Antiquities in the British Museum, Volume 1*. Text and Catalogue (BMP, 1980). British Museum, Department of Prehistory and Europe, Museum No. 1006.49.
2. Maurice Howard and Edward Wilson, *The Vyne: A Tudor house revealed* (National Trust, 2003).
3. Kirsty Rodewell and Robert Bell, *Acton Court: The evolution of an early Tudor courtier's house* (English Heritage, 2004).
4. Michael Archer, *Delftware: The tin-glazed earthenware of the British Isles* (Victoria and Albert Museum, 1977). Frank Britton, *English Delftware in the Bristol Collection* (Sotheby Publications, 1982).
5. Pattern books survive at the Minton Museum, Stoke-on-Trent, Staffordshire.
6. Cf. Jackfield Tile Museum, Ironbridge Gorge Museum, Shropshire.
7. Christie's London, *Dumfries House: A Chippendale commission*, vol. II, 13 July 2007, Lots 568–70. (The sale was cancelled owing to the rescue of the house and contents by the Great Steward of Scotland's Dumfries House Trust.)
8. F. Mehlman, *Phaidon Guide to Glass* (Phaidon, 1982); H. Tait (ed.), *5000 Years of Glass* (British Museum, 1991).
9. A. Ricketts, *The English Country House Chapel: Building a Protestant tradition* (Spire, 2007).
10. Clive Wainwright, *The Romantic Interior: The British collector at home, 1750–1850* (Yale, 1989), pp. 88–89.
11. John Cornforth, *English Interiors 1790–1848* (Barrie & Jenkins, 1978), pp. 47–49.
12. Wainwright, *The Romantic Interior*, pp. 66–67.
13. Christopher Rowell, *Uppark*, (The National Trust, 1995), p. 48.
14. Cornforth, *English Interiors*, p. 72.
15. M. Girouard, *Victorian Pubs* (Studio Vista, 1975).
16. Purchased by his widow Yoko Ono and presented to the National Trust in 2003.
17. C. Morris (ed.), *The Illustrated Journeys of Celia Fiennes c. 1682–c. 1712* (Macdonald & Co., 1982), p. 106.
18. *The Post Man*, February 13, 1700.
19. Eileen Harris, *The Genius of Robert Adam: His interiors* (Yale University Press, 2001), pp. 95–103.
20. S. Palmer, *The Soanes at Home: Domestic life at Lincolns Inn Fields* (John Soanes Museum, 1998).
21. M. Meade-Fetherstonehaugh and O. Waner, *Uppark and Its People* (George Allen & Unwin, 1964), p. 78.
22. George Smith, *A Collection of Designs for Household Furniture* (1808), Plates 152, 153, pp. 30, 31.
23. E. Joy, E. *Pictorial Dictionary of British Nineteenth Century Furniture Design* (Antique Collectors' Club, 1977), pp. 374–82.

11 The impact of historic lighting

Lisa White

Introduction

'Light, God's eldest daughter, is a principal beauty in a building,' wrote the preacher and divine Dr Thomas Fuller (1608–61) in 1642.[1] He was referring, primarily, to the planning of windows and room use in daytime, but his words must also apply to this chapter which considers the quality of domestic lighting before electricity, and its effect on the interior and contents. By asking the question, 'By what light was this, or this, intended to be seen when it was first made?' our perception of many things will be altered.

When a historic interior is to be studied with its conservation in mind, an essential exercise must be to study its lighting history over the years. The existence of original materials or lighting systems before 1850 may be difficult to establish, as little evidence may remain prior to the installation of 'fixed' supplies (gas and electricity). This chapter therefore provides an overview of historic lighting and its impact on the domestic interior. Understanding what went before will have a profound influence on what lighting should be introduced in the future, to complement the interior.

A very great deal has been written on historic interiors and their furnishing, but they have seldom been interpreted in relation to artificial light. But first, how was artificial light achieved? How did it affect usage and activity in the household?

Providing artificial light

Attempting to provide artificial light has often been the cause of disastrous fires, including that at Windsor Castle on 20 November 1992, a conflagration caused by an electric light placed too close to a curtain. Lack of attention could be fatal (Figure 11.1).

Robert Southey, in his *Letters from England*, published in London in 1807 under the nom de plume of Don Manuel de Espriella, commented on the dangers in English homes when servants were careless:

Interior finishes & fittings for historic building conservation, First Edition. Edited by Michael Forsyth & Lisa White. © 2012 Blackwell Publishing Ltd. Published 2012 by Blackwell Publishing Ltd.

Figure 11.1 Engraving after William Hogarth, 'The Politician', published in London, 1775, showing the risks of reading by candlelight. Private collection.

> . . . for nothing but candles are used to give light for domestic purposes, and accidents happen from a candle which could not happen from a lamp [i.e. an enclosed oil lamp]. The accumulation of furniture in an English house is so much fuel in readiness: all the floors are boarded, all the bedsteads are of wood, all the beds have curtains. I have heard of a gentleman who set the tail of his shirt on fire as he was stepping into bed, the flames caught the curtains, and the house was consumed. You may easily suppose this adventure obtained for him the name of The Comet.[2]

In fact, the fire itself, when not out of control, provided one of the main sources of light as well as warmth for much of Europe for thousands of years. In the 1830s the gifted amateur artist Mary Ellen Best illustrated the cosy and productive glow of a coal-burning grate in a Yorkshire cottage.[3] It recalls James Fennimore Cooper's description, in *The Pioneers*, published in 1823, of Dr Grant's house outside Templeton: 'The bright blaze from the hearth rendered the light from the candle Louisa produced, unnecessary, for the scanty furniture of the room was easily seen and examined by the former.'[4] Incidentally, Southey struck a warning note about coal fires, for the coals, he said, 'frequently exploded into the room'.[5] Enclosed wood-burning stoves, widely used in the rest of Europe, were regarded as much safer, if not illuminating or visually comforting.

For many centuries, the standard domestic lighting in the European interior comprised a combination of firelight, oil lamps and candles. Oil lamps had altered little from biblical times, with squat bodies and spouts which held the wicks, using whatever oil was most easily available and economical – olive and nut oil in southern Europe, rapeseed or colza oil further north. For the poorest sections of European and early North American communities, especially those living near the coasts, fish oil was also used for lighting as well as nutrition and was one of the few artificial lighting materials not to be taxed. Oil lamps produced a faint, localised yellow glow, they required constant attention and, unless enclosed by semi-opaque horn or expensive glass shades, they would go out in any draught.

The humble candle was equally unsatisfactory by our standards. In English the word applied to two types, which are clearly differentiated in French – the *chandelle* and the *bougie*. The first is made of wick dipped in tallow – that is, rendered animal fat; the smelliest was pig or goose fat, the better sort mutton or beef. Tallow candles sputtered, burnt unevenly and fast, gave a feeble yellow light and impregnated everything with a smell of stale food – it must have been like living permanently in a burger bar. Tallow candles were usually made at home or procured from the tallow chandlers, who in London exercised a monopoly in the trade through their livery company. Tallow candles were the cheapest and most regularly used in every household.

Rush-lights were also made from tallow, where the thin pithy shaft of a green rush was dipped in animal fat and held in a small clamp or pincer (Figure 11.2). Rush-lights also needed constant attention as the rush burnt down, and gave, if anything, an even feebler light than tallow candles – although William Cobbett maintained that you could read as well by a rushlight as by a tallow candle, writing that 'My grandmother, who lived to be pretty nearly ninety, never, I believe, burnt a candle in her house in her life.'[6] Making tallow candles or rush-lights depended on a supply of animals for the fat. It is worth remembering that labourers, even rural ones, lived largely on a vegetable diet in the seventeenth and eighteenth centuries; meat was a luxury, and so was the fat – but one bullock could supply an average family's needs of tallow for about a year.

Thus for the serving, labouring and manufacturing classes of society – by far the largest part of the population – artificial light was virtually non-existent before the Industrial Revolution. Nearly all work, especially skilled manufacture and craftsmanship, took place during daylight hours. Repetitive tasks that needed little or no light – prayer, sleep or sin, were for the dark. William Hogarth's illustration of the Death of the Earl in the series of paintings depicting Marriage à la Mode of 1743 makes the point. In fact, in many of his paintings and engravings Hogarth used the motif of the extinguished, or nearly extinguished, candle to underline the moral message of his stories.[7]

Figure 11.2 Pincer or clamp for a rushlight, iron and timber, late eighteenth century. Private Collection.

By the eighteenth century candles and lamp oils were also being processed from spermaceti – oil from the head cavity of the sperm whale. About a ton came from each whale and was purified along with the rest of the whale in an industry that we now regard with distaste. Spermaceti oil produced hard, white candles which were more expensive than tallow ones. Eventually, after about 1870, paraffin wax candles replaced tallow versions as the basic type used in many domestic households.

The better sort of candle was the *bougie*, made of moulded or rolled beeswax around a cotton wick. Wax candles were luxury items, more expensive than tallow, sweeter-smelling, and regarded as suitable for the elegant interiors of genteel society.

By the early eighteenth century beeswax candles, like other luxuries, were subject to government taxes (2d per pound) and, in London, a monopoly by the Wax Chandlers' Company. Wax candles were approximately three times as expensive as tallow candles and twice as expensive as spermaceti.

Because of their expense, wax candles were stored safely by the housekeeper in cupboards or candles boxes and their use was considered care-

Figure 11.3 Coloured engraving, 'The Suspicious Husband', published 1768. The light emitted by a smoking candle in the chamber stick barely illuminates the scene beyond the faces of the lady and her servant. Private collection.

fully. New candles were issued for the best rooms, the stumps recycled in lesser rooms, and nothing was ever wasted.

The light produced by a single eighteenth-century wax candle was similar to that produced by one hundredth of a modern sixty-watt light bulb – a paltry amount by modern standards (Figure 11.3). 'I am glad', says Lady Middleton to Lucy, in Jane Austen's *Sense and Sensibility*, 'you are not going to finish poor little Annamaria's basket this evening, for I am sure it must hurt your eyes to work filigree by candlelight.'[8] Mrs Delany contented herself with large-scale cross-stitch for a needlework carpet for her evening work. As a result of such poor light levels, great ingenuity was devoted to maximising the power of a single candle, and much information about wealth and social status could be given through a display of light.

For the wealthy and leisured classes, the evening was the time for entertainment. Dinner, the main meal of the day, took place during the afternoon by natural light, when preparation of food could take place in kitchens 'below stairs'. After dinner, ladies would withdraw for tea – outside in the summer, and indoors in the winter, when servants would bring candles for the withdrawing room and other rooms of entertainment – music room, ballroom, saloon and, of course, the bedchamber. Then the usual activities would begin – parade, intrigue, conversation, gossip, flirting, music, dancing, cards – all of which could continue until the early hours. Moonlight would sometimes guide guests on their way home.

So it was in these rooms of the fashionable house that particular attention was paid to their contents and decoration by night-light, as it was to the costly and sumptuous costumes of those who paraded in them. An immense English court dress or Mantua of 1740–45, which is now in the Victoria and Albert Museum, is one of the most dramatic examples of power dressing that has survived.[9] It is embroidered in silver thread on a rich red silk ground to catch flickering candlelight at different angles, causing advance, recess, brilliance, shadow, movement, stillness – Baroque features at their highest expression. No wonder the architect William Kent is recorded as designing women's dresses; these were, in effect, architectural elements within the illuminated room.

Men's costume, even for déshabillé, could be just as dramatic. Using gold or silver thread, dramatic effects could be achieved through subtle weaves of main and sub-patterns as in the wonderful 'bizarre' silks produced by the Spitalfields silk weavers in the first decades of the eighteenth century. Add to this jewellery, cut steel buttons and buckles, hairdressing and all the rest – intended for the rich to deliver their most powerful messages by night-light. No wonder preparations were likened to dressing for battle.

Managing artificial light

The spaces through which these glittering pillars of pampered humanity moved could be very large, and to light them effectively was a major challenge to architects and craftsmen. The blaze of light for Louis XIV's ball held on his return to Paris after the Siege of Strasburg in 1682 was a truly remarkable spectacle. Thousands of candles in rock-crystal chandeliers and candle branches thrusting out from the walls shed light and dripped wax onto the assembled company. The Galerie des Glaces at Versailles, designed by Jules Hardouin-Mansart and created between 1678 and 1684, with entire walls of reflective mirror glass, silver furniture and rock-crystal chandeliers, was not only a masterful stage set but sent the political message that the awesome power of the Sun King appeared no dimmer when his natural counterpart had set in the western sky.

The dramatic effects that could be achieved with artificial lighting were undoubtedly studied by many great architects and interior designers from Mansart and his colleague Charles Le Brun at Versailles, to Jean Le Pautre, Daniel Marot, William Kent and later Robert and James Adam, Sir William Chambers and Sir John Soane.

The scale of lighting for great parties was often contrasted in eighteenth-century letters with that used for family evenings. George III's visit to Bulstrode in 1772 caused Mrs Delany to comment that the Dowager Duchess of Portland 'had the house lighted up in the most magnificent

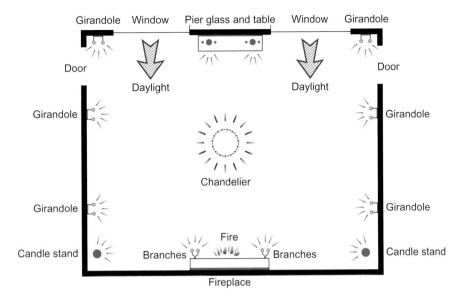

Figure 11.4 Candle-lighting plan for an eighteenth century interior.

manner: the chandelier in the Great Hall was not lighted before for twenty years'.[10] Sir Thomas Robinson, describing Sir Robert Walpole's entertainment of the Duke of Lorraine at Houghton in 1734, counted candles: 'They dined in the Hall which was lighted by 130 wax candles, and the saloon with fifty, the whole expense in that article being computed at £15 per night.'[11] As with all things in the rigid hierarchy of eighteenth-century British society, the niceties of rank were distinguished by the number of candles lit for a visitor.

Where to place artificial light to maximum advantage and minimum physical hindrance was carefully considered, and we will now deal briefly with the main places in which lights came to be placed in a conventional way in the later seventeenth and eighteenth centuries in the main rooms of entertainment (Figure 11.4). Ceilings, walls, the chimneypiece and some key floor spaces could all be utilised for lighting equipment – provided, always, that they were accessible to servants or others to trim or replenish candles or lamps, and were not out of human reach.

Chandeliers were the single most effective way of lighting with large numbers of candles in one spot without using up floor space – but also the most expensive. The logistics of lighting them quickly, and keeping them well trimmed for an entire evening, are largely forgotten now. As a rule they were not hung as high as when they are fitted for electric light, and moved up and down on a cantilever system with a pulling ring at the very bottom.

Different numbers of candles could provide varying light levels according to types of entertainment, expense, and the demands of the rest of the room's decoration. In 1756 the architect Isaac Ware discussed lighting requirements of rooms with different wall treatments. Dense textile hangings required more lighting than pale, flat, more reflective paint.[12]

Household accounts and shopkeepers' bills for the eighteenth century show that candles were supplied in different lengths to burn for specific periods according to the expected length of a party – four- or six-hour lengths were fairly standard. Summer and winter requirements would, of course, be different.

Among the great survivors in England are the marvellous rock-crystal chandeliers of the late seventeenth century, including one at Hampton Court Palace which crashed to the floor during the fire in 1986 and which was painstakingly re-assembled. Equally fine are the five or so great silver chandeliers of the same period, including one which is now in the De Witt Wallace Gallery at Colonial Williamsburg, Virginia, and one made in 1694 for William Cavendish, 1st Duke of Devonshire, and now at Chatsworth, Derbyshire, which still has its baize-lined oak storage case. These are the grandest and most expensive pieces of lighting equipment, reserved for the greatest and wealthiest in society.

Less expensive but often equally impressive are the numerous large brass chandeliers made for churches, halls and assembly rooms throughout the later seventeenth and eighteenth centuries.

Wooden chandeliers were perfectly suited to the fluent compositions of the Rococo carvers. In 1762 Thomas Chippendale commented in the third edition of *The Gentleman and Cabinet-Maker's Director* that 'Chandeliers are generally made of glass, and sometimes of brass, but if neatly done in wood and gilt in burnish'd gold, would look better and come much cheaper'.[13]

As Chippendale indicated, glass was fast becoming the preferred material for chandeliers. In the 1730s York Assembly Rooms had eight chandeliers carrying fourteen candles each. Developing techniques during the Industrial Revolution allowed the production of curvaceous glass branches, elaborately shaped drip pans and festoons of stars and pendant drops. They had reached the height of fashion by the 1770s – for instance, in those provided by Thomas Parker for Bath's Assembly Rooms, and later by Perry and Company for the Prince Regent at Carlton House and Brighton Pavilion (Figure 11.5). These stunning cascades of glass have remained an essential part of status decoration in palaces, great houses, hotels and even sumptuous flats ever since, adapted in the nineteenth and twentieth centuries for oil, gas and finally electricity.

Apart from ceilings, walls were obviously able to provide space for lighting equipment. Branches or small sconces could hold single candles or multiples (Figure 11.6). At their simplest, tin or brass plates with candle cups provided basic wall lights for ordinary rooms. Finely wrought in silver or silver-gilt, they could announce the status of a noble owner; particularly fine examples of the 1680s are at Knole in Kent, made for the 6th Earl of Dorset. In the Rococo period these sconces became the perfect vehicles for virtuoso carvers such as Matthias Lock and James Pascall, who supplied the gallery at Temple Newsam with huge carved and gilt sconces in the 1760s.[14]

Adding mirror glass to a sconce creates a 'girandole' (named after a seventeenth-century Italian firework). Those executed by John Linnell after

Figure 11.5 The Ballroom of the Assembly Rooms, Bath, designed by John Wood the Younger, opened in 1771, with glass chandeliers provided by William Parker of Fleet Street, London. Courtesy of the National Trust.

Figure 11.6 Engraving after William Hogarth, 'The Laughing Audience', 1733, showing fixed candle branches on the theatre walls. Private collection.

designs by Robert Adam for the Gallery at Osterley Park House, Middlesex, in 1770 are of carved and gilded pine with brass candle branches. The quality of gilding makes a huge difference to the reflective quality of these pieces when new: red bole beneath the gold produces a warm, rich tone, while yellow bole produces a sharper, paler colour. Two or three layers of gold leaf increase the density of the final effect; burnishing some parts and leaving others matt creates movement and depth.

Later eighteenth-century girandoles benefited from the Industrial Revolution as methods of bending and cutting glass became cheaper and more commonplace; convex or cut glass in a girandole, according to Hepplewhite, 'might have a very pretty effect in a well-furnished room'.[15]

Corner candle stands, identifiable by their height, could illuminate the places that other candles could not reach – such as those designed by Robert Adam, based on the classical tripod form, for the Antechamber to the State Bedchamber at the banker Robert Child's house at Osterley Park (see Figure 9.4). The walls of this room were hung entirely with Gobelins tapestry of such a dense pattern and colour that there is no reflective quality on the walls whatsoever. Perfume burners on the mantelpiece added to the claustrophobic effect of this room, which was undoubtedly intended to be seen at its most ravishing at night.

More entertaining are Thomas Sheraton's designs for corner candle-stands published in his Encyclopaedia of 1804–1806, in currently fashion-able Gothic and Chinese tastes – the latter complete with fishbowl and fish, intended to produce a novel effect with the candlelight diffused through the water.[16]

On every surface, of course, candlesticks, candelabra or lamps could be arranged to provide sufficient, localised light. Very often single candlesticks can be seen close together in contemporary illustrations. Games tables, pianos, music stands and desks could all be fitted with extra branches, some perhaps safer than others. Candlesticks, or chamber-sticks, were put out on the hall table last thing at night, for members of the household to light their way to bed.

Most important, in terms of all later seventeenth- and eighteenth-century lighting equipment and room arrangement, was the use of large areas of reflective glass to enhance the poor quality of candlelight. From the 1640s in France, and the 1660s in England, fashionable new-built houses were arranged on the apartment plan, with suites of interconnecting rooms ranged along the length of a façade, their windows placed regularly to admit daylight from the same side into all rooms, as for example in the State Apartment at Chatsworth in the 1680s. At night, light from the same side of the room was provided by candles placed on tables against the piers or blocks of masonry between the windows.

The large mirrors hung on the piers ('pier-glasses') above the tables became, in effect, the 'night-time windows' reflecting and increasing the candlelight and throwing it across the room (Figure 11.7). This system had important implications for the hanging of pictures – where the most impor-tant should go so as to catch the advantage of artificial light as well as daylight. The arrangement became standard by the end of the seventeenth

Figure 11.7 A pier glass supplied to Erddig, near Wrexham, Clwyd, in 1723 by John Belchier of London, with a giltwood pier table supplied in 1726. Placed between the windows, these two pieces of furniture formed a principal source of reflected light in the night-time interior. Courtesy of the National Trust.

century, and was used throughout the eighteenth and early nineteenth centuries until the fashion for bay windows destroyed the convention.

At their grandest, these pier-glasses and tables, sometimes accompanied by additional stands, were among the most expensive pieces of furniture commissioned for the 'state apartments' of palaces and great houses. At their simplest, the devices of candlestick, table and mirror could double the light in any interior.

Marquetry, silvering and full gilding of the candlestands, pier frame and pier table created a highly reflective surface and added immensely to the full drama of the artificially lit interior. Tables and glasses intended for rooms used more during daylight hours were not gilded to the same extent – this would have been regarded as a waste of money and 'improper' in terms of eighteenth-century taste. The gilt pieces were for show in the drawing room at night, which should, according to Sheraton in 1794, 'concentrate the elegance of the whole house, and is the highest display of the richness of furniture'.[17] If they look over elaborate to twenty-first-century eyes, it is because we fail to understand the messages they were intended to send.

A lot of the time we simply miss them altogether, as we shuffle through country houses on the drugget, occasionally bumping into these awkwardly placed tables permanently fixed to the walls between the windows. If, on the other hand, we take up the position of the honoured guest of previous centuries, standing before the fireplace on the opposite wall, then the full significance of the pier lighting system is apparent: great zones of luxurious damask tumble down between highly carved and gilded decoration, brilliant with reflected light.

As technology developed in the eighteenth century, so the sheets of glass became larger and larger – for instance, in the great glasses designed by Robert Adam in 1771 for the Picture Gallery at Corsham Court in Wiltshire, or in the Drawing Room at Syon House near London. The gilt frame may have become less prominent, but was still essential. In 1774 Chambers commented, when designing Lord Melbourne's house in Piccadilly, 'Glasses without gilding are large black spots that kill the effect of everything about them.'[18]

The most dramatic use of reflective glass all over the walls in the later eighteenth century must have been Robert Adam's scheme for the Drawing Room at Northumberland House at Charing Cross of 1773. The glass panels, mounted in gilt frames, were backed with red gilt foil to create a dazzling effect. Part of it can still be seen at the Victoria and Albert Museum, but once again the original impact of this remarkable room is largely lost to us now.[19]

Apart from the window wall, sources for candlelight were fixed above the fireplace – either standing on the mantelshelf itself, or on attached 'branches' of carved wood or gilt wire. In Chippendale's design, plate 182 of the third edition of the *Director* (1762), the chimney-glass is crowned by an eagle.[20] This is the attribute of Jupiter, and is the only living creature said to be able to look at the fiery magnificence of his master – thus the symbol of light itself – a classical allusion that would not have been missed by an educated eighteenth-century onlooker.

Chippendale and other eighteenth-century designers also included many patterns for practical and attractive lighting for halls, staircases and passages. These could be lit by oil or candle and were usually protected against draughts by glass shades. Their survival rate has been mixed as they were so often swept away by the advent of gas and electricity.[21] Very fine examples dating from 1772 have survived in the staircase hall and passage at Osterley Park, Middlesex, designed by Robert Adam and probably made by Matthew Boulton's factory, the Soho Works in Birmingham.

The impact of artificial light

We will now explore the way in which designers, craftsmen and clients used their knowledge of artificial light when producing or using all sorts of objects – especially those in parts of the house intended to be seen at their best at night. This understanding went far beyond merely using reflective surfaces in proximity to the light source itself – for instance, in a candlestick or mirror glass.

We have already seen how light was considered for its effect on clothes.

At Knole, in Kent, bed hangings dating from the early seventeenth century in the Spangle Bedchamber also have small gilt metal sequins stitched to the fabric panels to catch the dim light (Figure 11.8). The inner hangings of the magnificent eighteenth-century state bed at Calke Abbey, Derbyshire, found after over two hundred years of storage, is embroidered with silk and metal threads on a dark blue ground, obviously designed to make maximum impact by night-light. In fact nearly all objects intended for the bedchamber were designed with candlelight in mind.

In the middle ages, when loose tapestry hangings adorned the walls of a bedchamber, the gold and silver thread in them twinkled when the hangings moved in the draught, and the figures in them, often nearly life-sized, almost came alive.[22]

Existing fragments of Baroque patterns for furnishing textiles, identifiable by their bold outlines and dramatic contrasts of colour, remind us of the need for strength in designs intended to be seen in dim light, and we should be wary of criticising them now for being too showy. If you take the great sofas at Kedleston in Derbyshire, carved by John Linnell in 1759 as part of Nathaniel Curzon's triumphantly patriotic decoration, these pieces

Figure 11.8 Detail of a bed valance, late sixteenth or early seventeenth century, now at Knole, Kent. The satin panel is decorated with appliqué strapwork patterns and small gilt sequins intended to reflect candlelight. Courtesy of the National Trust.

of furniture might seem grossly over-decorated when looked at in daylight or under full electric light. When seen under more subtle lighting, they are truly amazing – and indeed cease to be furniture, and approach erotica.

Not only gold can excite: in the later seventeenth and eighteenth centuries the exotic, glossy surfaces of lacquer were almost as alluring. John Stalker and Henry Parker, in their *Treatise of Japanning and Varnishing* asked, 'What can be more surprizing than to have our chambers overlaid with varnish more glossy and reflecting than polished marble? No amorous nymph need entertain a dialogue with her glass, or Narcissus retire to a fountain to admire his charming countenance, when the whole house is one entire speculum.'[23] The recording of so many lacquer cabinets in seventeenth- and eighteenth-century bedrooms and closets – intended to be seen most enchantingly at night – is therefore no coincidence.

Obvious examples are to be found in door furniture, invariably made from reflective metal so as to be visible across a room as well as being attractive and providing security. Clock dials were carefully designed and decorated to be well legible at night, when attempting to handle tinder-boxes might not be practicable.

Gilt book bindings, with gilt titles on the spines of volumes, ensured that their subject matter could be more easily read by candlelight (Figure 11.9). The use of gilding on such practical objects as tea cups and saucers might also not just have been for decoration, when we remember that tea was often taken after dinner, which would imply by candlelight during winter months. The bold patterns and colour of blue-and-white Chinese export porcelain of the seventeenth and eighteenth centuries retain their strength when seen by low light levels. Hundreds of other examples may be quoted, from the simple clarity of playing cards to gilt names on decanters for the evening table.

Whenever you come across an object made before c. 1830, and you think it too strongly patterned or brightly gilded, stop and ask yourself, 'How was this object first intended to be seen? By poor night light?' It may explain a lot.

The impact of technological change

However, major changes in artificial light began during the Industrial Revolution and were soon to cause a similar revolution in the domestic interior. These changes were heralded in 1784 by Émile Argand's eponymous lamp. Better refining of spermaceti and colza oils, the use of Argand's and later other systems of glass tubes, which improved air flows, and pumps to regulate the flow of oil meant that new oil lamps were preferred to candles for many parts of the house. One Argand lamp could provide the equivalent amount of light to ten wax candles. The bright, white light they gave enabled many more activities to take place during the evening with only one or two lamps instead of many candles. Family and friends could gather round a large table in the drawing room or library to read, sew, sketch, write or play.

Figure 11.9 Detail of a book binding showing the effect of candlelight upon the gilded lettering and decoration. Private collection.

Such brilliance was not always appreciated. In *The Woman in White*, published in 1860, Wilkie Collins created the poignant mood of the drawing room during the evening:

> We sat silent in the places we had chosen – Mrs Vesey still sleeping, Miss Fairlie still playing, Miss Halcombe still reading – till the light failed us. By this time the moon had stolen round to the terrace, and soft, mysterious rays of light were slanting already across the lower end of the room. The change from the twilight obscurity was so beautiful that we banished the lamps, by common consent, when the servant brought them in, and kept the large room unlighted, except by the glimmer of the two candles at the piano.[24]

Brighter artificial light may also have influenced changes to colour schemes. Yellow, which had previously lost all quality by candlelight, could now be used as a drawing room colour for walls and upholstery, without turning to a dull mud, when lit by brighter Argand lamps.[25] On the downside, these lamps still required constant cleaning to avoid smoking that would pollute both the air and delicate objects within a room.

Figure 11.10 Coloured engraving, 'Dos a Dos or Rumpti-iddity ido: Natural accidents in practising Quadrille Dancing', published by S.W. Fores, London, 1817. The print shows gas lights in the form of spouting dragon masks, and flaming burners fixed to the musicians' gallery. Private collection.

Many improvements and different versions of the Argand lamp were developed during the nineteenth century and remained an essential piece of domestic equipment well into the middle of the twentieth century, until the arrival of the National Grid provided nearly all homes in Britain with electricity.

More brightness was to come (Figure 11.10). Gas was used by the pioneer William Murdoch to light the outside of Matthew Boulton's Soho Works in 1802 and Ackermann's Library in London in 1813, and by 1823 some forty thousand gas lamps lit 215 miles of London's streets. The upper windows of the Music Room in Brighton Pavilion were back-lit by gas lamps as early as 1822, causing a sensation – indeed, the lighting of the whole of the king's fantasy house by the sea was more spectacular than it is now. In fact, three different types of artificial light might be used at once for a glittering evening.

Although relatively cheap, the heat, smell, noise, condensation and unreliability of coal gas caused some to remain suspicious. In Pugin's beautiful new interior of the House of Lords completed in the 1850s, the Peers voted to continue with candles rather than risk immolation by gas lamp. Prince Albert, on the other hand, was much keener on modern technology and had gas installed at Windsor in the 1850s. In many Victorian homes, gas was used to light service areas, staircases and passages, but not necessarily installed in sitting rooms or bedchambers, where the corrosive effect of the coal gas could cause substantial damage to furnishing fabrics and wallpapers, and might be a risk to health. In 1874 Sir William Holburne's town house in Bath contained gas light fittings for the domestic quarters in the basement, the staircase and landings, but not in the dining room, withdrawing rooms and bedchambers.[26] Despite such drawbacks, the great period for domestic gas lighting, delivered through iron pipes to all relevant parts of the house, was from about 1840 to the end of the century. Marvellous examples of gas chandeliers were displayed at the Great Exhibition of 1851, including one over 5 metres in height by Cornelis and Baker of Philadelphia.[27]

Electricity was soon to follow, with Edison's pioneering achievements in 1879, and Joseph Swan's amazing contemporaneous electrification of the newly built Cragside (1869–85) in Northumberland by Norman Shaw for Lord Armstrong – the first English country house to be fitted with electricity from the start (Figure 11.11).

Figure 11.11 The Staircase at Cragside, Northumberland, designed by Norman Shaw for Lord Armstrong 1869–85, and fitted with electric light by Joseph Swan, 1879. Carved wooden lions hold poles for the light fittings. Courtesy of the National Trust.

There were teething troubles, as Swan described in a local newspaper:

It was a delightful experience for both of us when the gallery was first lit up. The speed of the dynamo had not been quite rightly adjusted to produce the strength of current in the lamps that they required. The speed was too fast and the current too strong. Consequently the lamps were far above their normal brightness but the effect was splendid and never to be forgotten.[28]

During the later 1880s and 1890s many country houses were adapted to electric lighting, which at first was less satisfactory than gas in providing sufficiently strong light. Tyntesfield, in Somerset, was originally fitted with gas lighting, but by 1890 a new electricity supply was installed with its own engine house in the grounds for Anthony Gibbs, who spent his first night as owner of the house testing 'all the new-fangled electric lights'.[29] At Arundel Castle, Sussex, a temporary electricity supply was provided in 1878, and a permanent one in 1891; recent refurbishment has included an impressive refitting of the original lamps. A beautiful and very complete set of electric lamps for an English domestic interior can still be seen at Standen, in East Sussex, designed by Philip Webb and built between 1892 and 1894, where the original electric light fittings designed by John Pearson and W.A.S. Benson, with opalescent glass shades made by Powell of Whitefriars, are still in working order (Figure 11.12).

One of the most dramatic changes resulting from the advent of electric light was caused by new positions. Light bulbs suspended from high up on the walls or from the ceiling ensured that artificial light fell downwards on the objects and decoration of the room, in contrast to the centuries-old upward thrust of light from candles and lamps. As electric light became standardised, it may have caused designers to change their colour palette, for paler colours and more subtle patterns could work by the new bright light. C.R. Ashbee and C.F.A. Voysey designed with electricity in mind, while William Morris, with his darker tones and bold patterns, still thought in candle terms, maintaining that indigo was the only blue dye to behave satisfactorily by candlelight.

If there is one image worth remembering from the pre-electric age, it must be the view of a Boston tea party painted by Henry Sargent in 1821, now in the Museum of Fine Arts, Boston. Light and sound seem to flow from a further room, catching the features and composed elegance of the fashionable people and details of the furniture and ornaments. What we have gained in practicality and power since this picture was painted, we have perhaps lost in subtlety and loveliness.

Conclusion

When preparing a conservation plan for a property, it is imperative to establish early in the process what artificial light originally existed in a building, and how it might have changed. Physical and documentary evidence should provide many answers.

The next step should be to create a lighting plan and decide on individual requirements for each room. At Arundel Castle, Sussex, a new lighting

Figure 11.12 Electric light fitting designed by the architect Philip Webb and made by John Pearson of the Guild of Handicraft for the Drawing Room at Standen, East Sussex, 1892–4. The lights were made of repoussé copper with patterns of sunflowers. Powell of Whitefriars supplied the glass twists that decorate the flex and the opalescent fluted shade. Courtesy of the National Trust.

system in the chapel provides three 'levels' of electric light: 'Victorian', which recreates the permanent installation of 1891; 'Praying', which respects the continuing use of the room; and 'Cleaning', which uses the brightest level. Early planning of a lighting system will establish where and how wiring may be required, and may save time and expense later in a programme.

Further reading

Dillon, M., *Artificial Sunshine* (National Trust, 2002).

Moss, R.W., *Lighting for Historic Buildings: A guide to selecting reproductions* (Preservation Press, John Wiley & Sons, 1988).

Temple Newsam House Studies, No. 4, *Country House Lighting 1660–1890* (Leeds City Art Galleries, 1992).

Endnotes

1. Rev. Dr Thomas Fuller, *The Sacred and the Profane State* (London, 1642).
2. Robert Southey, *Letters from England; by Don Manuel Alvarez Espriella, Translated from the Spanish* (London, 1807), Letter XXII.
3. Caroline Davidson, *The World of Mary Ellen Best* (London, 1985), Plate 59.
4. James Fennimore Cooper, *The Pioneers* (1823), Chapter XII.
5. Southey, *Letters from England*, Letter XXII.
6. William Cobbet, *Cottage Economy* (1821).
7. William Hogarth, *Marriage à la Mode* (London, 1745), Plate V.
8. Jane Austen, *Sense and Sensibility* (1811).
9. Victoria and Albert Museum, Department of Furniture Textiles and Fashion, Museum No. T227 & a – 1970.
10. Lady Llanover (ed.), *The Autobiography and Correspondence of Mary Granville, Mrs Delaney* (1861–62), Series II, Vol. 1.
11. Sir Thomas Robinson, *Historic Manuscripts Commission*, XV (1731), Appendix, Pt V.
12. Isaac Ware, *A Complete Body of Architecture* (London, 1756).
13. Thomas Chippendale, *The Gentleman and Cabinet-Maker's Director*, 3rd edn (1762), Plates CLIV, CLV.
14. Elizabeth White, *Pictorial Dictionary of British Eighteenth Century Furniture Design: The printed sources* (Antique Collectors' Club, 1990), Part V, pp. 381–97.
15. A. Hepplewhite, & Co., *The Cabinet-Maker and Upholsterer's Guide* (1788), Plate 113.
16. Thomas Sheraton, *Encyclopaedia* (1804–06), Plate XX.
17. Thomas Sheraton, *The Cabinet Dictionary* (1803), p. xx.
18. W . Chambers, *A Treatise of Architecture* (1759).
19. Victoria and Albert Museum, Museum No. W.31:1–66–1955.
20. Chippendale, *The Gentleman and Cabinet-Maker's Director*, Plate CLXXXII.
21. *Ibid.*, Plates CLII, CLIII.
22. T. Campbell, *European Tapestry Production and Patronage, 1400–1600*, Metropolitan Museum of Art, New York Helibrunn Timeline of Art History (website www.metmuseum.org/toah/).
23. John Stalker and George Parker, *A Treatise of Japanning and Varnishing* (London, 1688), Preface, p. xv.
24. Wilkie Collins, *The Woman in White* (1859–60, Penguin Classics, 1974), p.81.
25. James Barron, *Modern and Elegant Designs of Cabinet and Upholstery Furniture* (London, 1814), illustrates a drawing room with yellow walls.
26. Inventory of Sir Thomas William Holburne, Bart, April 1874.
27. Illustrated London News, *Illustrated Catalogue of the Great Exhibition* (London, 1851).
28. *Newcastle Daily Journal*, 1900.
29. The National Trust, *Tyntesfield* (2003), p. 9.

12 Paint colour and paintwork

Patrick Baty

Sixteen years ago, perhaps rather harshly, this author reviewed a book that claimed to be about traditional paints. The main argument of the author of that book was that most of the constituents of the 'classic' paints of the past came from environmentally friendly sources, which, 'unlike modern plastic paints', actually worked, and 'presented softer, more subtle colours than readily available nowadays'. Salmon eggs, peanut oil and ultraviolet [sic] were cited as being typical constituents, while the reality of such heavy metals as lead, arsenic, mercury, cobalt, copper, manganese and cadmium was carefully forgotten. The word 'natural' was employed frequently and used as shorthand for 'old-fashioned', 'harmless' and 'good'. It was constantly juxtaposed with 'modern', which is synthetic and therefore 'bad'.

Unfortunately these erroneous sentiments prevail, and when combined with increasing awareness of environmental issues the situation becomes even more confused. Market forces have muddied the waters by turning attention to the visual properties of 'traditional' paints, while at the same time stressing their 'green' credentials. As a result, the question of which paint to use on the surfaces of a historic building has become a sensitive one. Some earlier warnings on the labelling and marketing of paints have been met with a heavy-handed response from big business, but this chapter will attempt to steer the prospective user through some of the options and give the lie to various myths.

Conservation projects

Historic buildings come in many different forms, and the approach taken will depend on several factors; the key ones being:

- Is it conservation repair or simply decoration?
- Is the building listed – Grade I, II* or II?
- What time and money is available?

Interior finishes & fittings for historic building conservation, First Edition. Edited by Michael Forsyth & Lisa White. © 2012 Blackwell Publishing Ltd. Published 2012 by Blackwell Publishing Ltd.

Figure 12.1 Kew Palace, Richmond, Middlesex, royal home of George III and members of his family.

In a house associated with a historical figure and now open to the public, a more academic approach may be relevant. Here the aim is usually to present a sequence of rooms as they were at an earlier stage. An analysis of the paint layers may help to understand what colours were applied originally so as to replicate these in a similar type of paint. Such buildings will usually be listed Grade I or II* (Figure 12.1). Of course, paint analysis or full repair is not necessarily obligatory when dealing with a listed building. However, a decorative scheme using colours and finishes that are considered appropriate might be required by the statutory authority to avoid changing the character of the building significantly. To state the obvious, the first thing to consider when redecorating a listed building is what the aim of the exercise is. All too often projects proceed without consideration of the real purpose, and with no more than basic research. When reinstating a scheme that previously existed, it may be important to consider using a paint that resembles an earlier type. Aside from correct colour, the texture and finish are significant. However, this is easier said than done; unless paints are being specially produced for a large-scale conservation project, even what appears to be a traditional and therefore, perhaps, 'appropriate' product may not be quite that.

Traditional paint

Before reaching for the tin that has 'traditional' on its label, or one produced in a 'traditional' manner, it is worth remembering what traditional paint was. Prior to the last quarter of the nineteenth century, there were three basic types of paint:

- oil paint – generally based on lead carbonate ground in linseed oil
- water-based soft distemper – chalk and water lightly bound with an animal glue size
- water-based limewash – slaked lime thinned with water to the consistency of milk.

Of these, the last was mainly employed on external surfaces or on the interior walls of vernacular buildings and will not be considered further in this chapter.

With a few modifications these paints continued to be used, largely in their traditional form, until World War II. Lead paint probably reached its zenith in the early 1930s with the introduction of two British Standards, BS 261 and BS 262, which laid down the percentage of lead that paints had to contain 'for the finished paint to exhibit all the well-known and desirable characteristics of White Lead'.[1]

The main concern was for the protective qualities of the paint, while nowadays the following visual characteristics of lead are most prized (Figure 12.2):

- texture and the retention of brush marks, requiring application to ensure that this feature works with the decoration
- variable finish, with some areas displaying different sheen levels
- unique ageing characteristics, in particular, the phenomenon of 'pentimento', which is the gradual increase in the refractive index of the oil with which it is mixed, causing white paint to become more translucent over time
- the almost metallic patina seen on old lead painted surfaces.

After World War II the character of oil paint changed. The near perfect mix, produced by the partial saponification of the linseed oil by the lead, was initially replaced by other less efficient products that were based on non-hazardous white pigments. However, with the introduction of other binders, longer-lasting paints are now produced to cope with the more demanding needs of exterior joinery. None of these new paints has the appearance of a genuine lead paint. Since 1992, as a result of a European Community Directive, the use of lead in decorative paints has been severely restricted. Several companies continued to offer lead paint for use in Grade I or II* listed buildings, but few of their products contained the high proportions of lead carbonate required by the two British Standards of the 1930s. Further changes are now taking place, with all manufactured coatings from 2010 having to comply with the new limits on volatile organic compounds (VOCs),[2] and this may eventually restrict the continued use of lead in paint. As a result of these restrictions, conventional solvent-based paints – gloss, eggshell and flat oil, which tend to lie significantly above the 2010 VOC limits – will either need to be reformulated, or will no longer be available. However, extensive research and trials were carried out by the paint manufacturers, and most released their 2010-compliant products ahead of time.

Figure 12.2 Thorpe Hall, Peterborough, Cambridgeshire: traditional lead paint.

These and further Directives – from health and safety (including working conditions) to transport, air pollution and waste – have produced a culture of environmental correctness and compliance, where compliance itself can be used as a commercial tool.[3] Big paint manufacturers vie to meet 'green' credentials. It seems that it will not be possible to adjust the few available lead paints while ensuring that they meet the standards demanded by BS 261 and BS 262, though it is likely that lead paints will be available until further Directives are passed.

If lead were finally to disappear, there would be no oil paint that could legitimately be termed 'traditional' in the context of architectural painting in the UK. Several varieties of paint on the market have a linseed oil binder, but the lighter-coloured ones are primarily based on the pigment titanium dioxide and, as such, were virtually unknown before the 1960s and certainly prior to the 1930s. Dark colours are produced by grinding iron oxides with linseed oil, but these too lack the vital lead component to match the quality of earlier lead-based paints. There is a Swedish tradition of *Falun* red, used on wooden cottages and barns, but to refer to such paints as 'traditional' in a British context is misleading in all but a few cases of vernacular decoration.

Advocates of linseed oil paints often preach with a selective zeal, full of negative references to 'the petrochemical industry' or to 'plastic' or 'synthetic' paints. Modern paints are said to be not 'breathable' and to have a proven record for causing damage to the underlying substrate of the building as a whole. This perceived but mythical need for all surfaces to breathe contradicts all the architectural elements that have clearly been painted on a regular basis for over two hundred years. One wonders when the remarkably sound tripartite windows of a building of the 1770s had last been able to breathe under their fifty-two decorative schemes.[4] Indeed, the same might apply to the plaster walls of countless eighteenth- and nineteenth-century houses that have been painted since they were built.

More insidious is the frequent usurpation of the benefits of lead paint – references to the pre-World War II use of linseed oil paints as a natural and effective means of protecting wood, while failing to mention lead itself. The beneficial properties of zinc oxide, as the white pigment component, is mentioned by some manufacturers, seemingly oblivious of the technical literature of the early twentieth century, when even that advocate of zinc paint, J. Cruikshank Smith, had to admit that it was poorly opaque and had a slow drying time.[5] Forty years later it was appreciated that the hardening effect of zinc on oil tended to produce a non-elastic, brittle film that might lead to premature breakdown. The ideal, it was acknowledged, seemed to be in admixture with white lead.[6] A careful study of the early texts could prevent this constant re-invention of the wheel.

In spite of the characteristics of recent linseed oil paints, devotees will insist that theirs is a 'traditional' product while disparaging emulsion paint as 'modern'. The colouring matter employed in these paints is 'pigment' – as in 'pigment rich', or in the claim that a higher proportion of 'pigment' has been used than in ordinary paints – while in conventional paint the material is termed a 'stainer'. The majority of linseed oil paints on sale in the UK are manufactured in continental Europe – Germany and Sweden being well represented, having been concerned with green issues for many years. However, time and distance must be considered before specifying and purchasing such European products. A locally manufactured paint makes more sense, and the prospect of a six-week delay between consignments would stretch the patience of many a project manager.

There is no doubt that a properly made linseed oil paint handles beautifully under the brush and produces a finish with many of the visual characteristics of lead paint, perfect for the recreation of an early eighteenth-century scheme in a panelled room. However, the specifier should think twice before embarking on the repainting of exterior joinery, as this requires the complete removal of all existing coatings before application. It would be a brave specifier who explains to his client that all fifty-two existing schemes will have to be stripped before adopting a (lead-free) blend of titanium dioxide and linseed oil.

Care when specifying

Although there may still be a place for lead paint in the more demanding of academic conservation projects, we should be aware of developments in the USA. In March 2000, partly inspired by the recent settlement with the tobacco industry, Santa Clara County in California filed a suit against the manufacturers of lead paint. This class-action lawsuit was brought on behalf of all public bodies that expended funds to cope with a public health hazard that is considered particularly dangerous to children. It asserted that the manufacturers produced and disseminated a toxic product for many years after they knew it was hazardous, and that the manufacturers conspired to mislead the government and the public about the hidden dangers of lead in paint.[7] Many other countries, cities and public bodies later joined in the suit, so it is perhaps understandable that specifiers are now hesitant about lead paint.[8]

Lead as an exterior paint

In view of the pronounced chalking effect of white lead paint when exposed to the elements, especially if actually adulterated with chalk as it often was, it is likely that the painting of exterior surfaces was carried out at frequent intervals. An account of 1774 informs us that in 'The third year the gloss is done . . . in the fourth if you rub the painting with your fingers, it will come off like so much dust'.[9] James Crease, a colourman, writing in the early years of the nineteenth century, seems to confirm this, when he recommended that 'rails, gates &c to be done once in three years at least'.[10]

Having examined countless painted surfaces, the author's observations confirm that external paint was applied at fairly regular and frequent intervals. A simple calculation can be applied to the exterior paint of a building. If the age of the building is divided by the number of paint layers on it, one will come up with a very rough idea of the repainting cycle (provided, of course, that all the paint survives). With this in mind, a random selection was taken of twenty buildings that were erected between 1742 and 1874, all of which still retained their complete layers of paint.[11] It was found that the repainting cycle varied between once every 4.4 and once every 9 years, averaging at 7.2 years. Compared with good-quality modern paint, there seems nothing particularly remarkable in that, and certainly short of the ten to fifteen years claimed by some manufacturers of linseed oil paint.

It is true that, because of the tendency of lead paint to chalk with age, a modern gloss paint initially looks brash by comparison. However, developments in resin technology have resulted in durable semi-gloss paints for exterior use. A modern *exterior*-graded paint, which combines properties of flexibility with a degree of permeability to moisture vapour, is more than likely to surpass the performance of a lead paint, without the drawbacks.

All too often, when reading an account of the redecoration of a historic building, we learn that 'paint scrapes' were made, or that lead paint, distemper, or something like 'milk paint' has been used.[12] This is usually regarded as sufficient to justify the use of modern paint, and it would seem churlish to probe further.

However, the plot thickens as several of those who seek to perpetuate a mythical rose-tinted past – sometimes described as 'Copper-Kettledom'

– have become uncomfortably aware of the knowledge and analytical techniques now available. Not be outdone, their latest ploy is to employ paint analysis to disregard the findings and then to suggest that their finished scheme was based on research.

As an example, at a Grade I Baroque church, analysis established that – unusually – the first scheme had been applied in an oil paint.[13] This was restored with an apparently traditional distemper that came from a tin and was of a type unknown before the early 1960s. The colour incidentally was chosen from a colour card of so-called historical colours, and bore little relation to that first used in the church. When asked for an explanation, the person responsible for the choice of paint and colour claimed to be too busy to supply the supporting evidence.

For some, there will be the philosophical – or shall we say the 'feel-good' – factor of using a paint that is marginally closer to the original material than a frankly modern one. However, as shown above, this argument cannot be fully sustained.

Some years ago we analysed the paint in the house lived in by the composer Georg Friedrich Handel in London in the early eighteenth century. Having established what colours had been applied during Handel's occupancy, the painting specification was prepared. For reasons of cost, availability, health and safety, and time, lead paint was out of the question. The problem was to find a modern paint for the panelling that would suggest the traditional material. Several trials failed to find one that met all the requirements, and so a modern, solvent-based eggshell was applied over a coarsely applied acrylic undercoat. The texture was suitable and, although it will not age in the same way as lead paint, the associated maintenance problems will be avoided.

Distemper

As regards water-based paint for interior plasterwork, the term 'distemper' is well known. However, this is a generic term encompassing several different coatings, and there is really only one type that is of relevance to historic buildings. 'Soft distemper', as it is more accurately called, is excellent for coating decorative plasterwork or ceilings. Washed, finely ground chalk, known as 'whiting', forms the main constituent, loosely bound with a water-soluble glue size usually made from animal bones, horns or skin, often nowadays under the name of 'rabbit skin glue'. Because of the animal glue content, it has a very limited shelf life, even if refrigerated. By definition, therefore, a true soft distemper cannot be bought, even in a tin. Soft distemper is applied by brush and can be removed with a wet sponge when dirty or in need of recoating. Its great advantage is that when applied to decorative plaster ceilings, for example, the detail is not lost as the previous coat of paint must be removed before redecoration. An emulsion paint, on the other hand, would be added as yet another disfiguring layer that would eventually require removal. As well as its permeability to moisture vapour, which makes it an option in areas inclined to mild damp, soft distemper has the added bonus of being inexpensive. It is easily made and applied, and can be laid on quickly by an experienced decorator. However, it is not durable, and is neither washable nor suitable for areas of heavy traffic, hence its name of *soft distemper*. As a result, in the nineteenth century various binders were added to increase its resilience. These additives varied in type and efficiency, and often had a profound effect on the technical properties of the paint.

Among the most common sorts of 'improved' distempers were the primitive emulsions known as 'oil-bound distemper', 'casein-bound distemper' or, more properly, 'water paint'.[14] Note here the use of the word 'emulsion' to indicate a mixture of two liquids that normally cannot be combined, such as oil and water. It may come as a shock to learn of the very fine line between a bound distemper, or water paint, and an emulsion paint, as found on the shelves of many builders' merchants.

These early emulsion paints were generally supplied in a stiff paste, which was thinned with water to a brushable consistency for application. On evaporation of the water, the paint dried to a porous film, with the glue – often in the form of casein – acting as a temporary binder during the drying of the oil, which finally hardened the film so that it became moderately wipe-able.

The current trend for labelling or referring to these primitive emulsion paints as 'distemper' is storing a problem for the future. They are frequently specified on the premise that the substrate can breathe under a historically appropriate and pleasing matt coating. Unfortunately, these early emulsions had a number of weaknesses. Certainly they had a matt finish, and some did have a degree of permeability to moisture; however, they did not have the key advantage of soft distemper – its reversibility.

When the Paint Research Association made comparisons between a typical trade emulsion paint and a water paint that was being sold as a distemper, it was found that there was scarcely any difference in the moisture vapour permeability of the two systems.[15] However, as the 'improved' distempers cannot readily be removed, further coatings tended to be applied on top, and then within two or three schemes of redecoration, problems could occur. The strength of the bond of water paint is less than that of oil paint, and though the coating has some resistance to water, it is nonetheless absorbent. The liquid in a new coat of paint applied on top will soften it to some extent and cause it to swell. Water paint, moreover, is applied in thicker and heavier coats than oil paint. In drying, the paint contracts strongly, and in doing so exerts a considerable pull on the underlying film, weakening the grip of any parts that are not firmly attached to the surface.[16]

A substantial strain is placed on the bond of the old coating. Two, three or even more coats can be safely applied on occasion, but there comes a time when the weight and stress are too great, and cracking and flaking takes place at the weakest points in the system.[17] Local repair and making good is of no help, and total removal back to a sound base is the only way to address the problem.

Unfortunately, it is not possible to lay down any rule or even give any indication of when failure is likely to take place, and the appearance of the old finish is not necessarily a reliable guide to its stability. Much depends on the quality of the old coating and the number of coats on the surface. The atmospheric conditions to which the finish has been exposed may influence its behaviour; in a room subject to condensation, for instance, the repeated wetting and drying of the surface will progressively weaken the binder of the water paint.

Is it worth taking the risk merely for the appeal of using a product with an esoteric or rose-tinted name on the label? Surely the decoration and protection of the historic fabric is worth more than allowing manipulation by the marketing man.

This is by no means a blanket recommendation for the use of modern paint in the redecoration of historic buildings. What is urged is the considered use of paint that meets all the technical and aesthetic requirements, shorn of hype, ignorance and whimsy. Use a linseed oil paint based on zinc or titanium, if you wish, but understand why you are doing so, what it is, and what it is not. On important conservation projects, whatever is done should be carefully documented and an explanation given in a guide book, if there is one.

Endnotes

1. From British Standards 262, quoted in *White Lead Paints: Why, when and how specified* (London, White Lead Publicity Bureau, 1934).
2. VOCs are organic chemical compounds that evaporate readily and enter the atmosphere. In the presence of sunlight they can create ground-level ozone and photochemical smogs, which can contribute to the pollution of the atmosphere. The official name of the legislation released by the European Union is EU Directive 2004/42/EC. Within UK legislation, this EU Directive has been introduced under the name 'The Volatile organic Compounds in Paints, Varnishes and Vehicle Refinishing Products Regulations 2005'.
3. J. Jotischky, 'Coatings, regulations and environment reviewed' 11 *Surface Coatings International*. Part B; Coatings Transactions, Vol. 84, B1-90, January 2001.
4. Patrick Baty, 'Home House, 20 Portman Square, London W.1. A Report on the First Scheme following an Examination of the Paint on Various Surfaces' (1998), p. 13 (unpublished). It is interesting to observe that the redecoration cycle was just over four years. Does this tell us more about the durability of the paint or the powers of the Portman Estate?
5. J. Cruickshank Smith, *Oxide of Zinc: Its nature, properties and uses* (Trade Papers Publishing Co. Ltd, 1909), pp. 39–40.
6. A.E. Hurst, *Painting and Decorating* (Charles Griffin & Company Ltd, 1949), p. 65.
7. Office of the County Counsel, Santa Clara County.
8. Similar actions have since been dropped by the states of Ohio and Rhode Island.
9. Francis Armstrong, *An Account of a Newly Invented Beautiful Green Paint* (1774), p. 7.
10. James Crease, *Hints for the Preservation of Wood Work Exposed to the Weather* (1808), p. 15.
11. By definition, the more recent layers on all the samples were in non-lead paints.

12. The belief that milk saw widespread use as an ingredient in paint is based on a recipe published at the time of the French Revolution when materials for painting were in short supply. This was published in translation in 1801 and disseminated widely. Antoine Alexis Cadet-de-Vaux, 'Memoir on a Method of Painting with Milk', *The Repertory of Arts & Manufactures*, Vol. XV (1801), pp. 411–21.

13. A significant statement in itself, when most other churches of the period that have been examined were first painted in a water-based soft distemper. This was originally in a wealthy parish.

14. These reached their heyday in the mid-twentieth century and are best remembered under such brand names as Walpamur and Duresco.

15. Patrick Baty, 'Oil Bound Water Paint v. Non-Vinyl Emulsion Paint: Vapour Permeability Testing at PRA', *Traditional Paint News*, 1, 3 (October 1997), 49–50.

16. J.G.E. Holloway, *The Modern Painter and Decorator*, 5th edn, Vol. 1 (Caxton Publishing Company Ltd, 1961), 134.

17. *Ibid.*

13 Recreating historic schemes of interior decoration

James Finlay

With any historic building, research is the foundation for all reinstated and resurrected schemes of interior decoration. With buildings displayed to the public, as with National Trust properties, the visitor often just sees the modest tip of an iceberg. But, cleverly deployed, research can deepen an appreciation of a house, and an understanding of the processes of curatorship and conservation, and greatly enrich a visitor's experience as he or she journeys round a house.

Historic houses have unrivalled value for displaying artefacts and collections within a sympathetic environment, and have the potential to offer a richer experience for the viewing public than the more didactic confines of a museum. Human stories can be interwoven; interpretations can be made both more intense and more subtle, and a genuine fascination can be built up incrementally by gently encouraging responses as well as absorption of hard facts. Indeed, the benefits are so multi-directional that sometimes the significance of the bigger picture can be overlooked, or easy gains missed.

Research

Research can be as varied as the types of buildings, but there are broadly similar categories for every project, each covering many disciplines and needing to be adapted to the available financial and evidential resources. The reasoning behind a reinstatement of interiors is rarely straightforward. In the case of a house or property open to the public, it has to knit into a general presentation policy, and the collated research has to be thoroughly cross-referenced to provide the most relevant information for the job in

Interior finishes & fittings for historic building conservation, First Edition. Edited by Michael Forsyth & Lisa White. © 2012 Blackwell Publishing Ltd. Published 2012 by Blackwell Publishing Ltd.

hand.[1] The project should allow for devising displays of some of this research material, which can perhaps include explanations of the ways in which it was found. Abandoning the research to filing cabinets and hard-drives once the reinstatement project is finished is missing a trick. It can greatly enhance and enliven a room's presentation, perhaps drawing out ways in which the aesthetics of a room were affected by social class, aspirations, finances, technology and taste, or more simply by focusing on an artefact, or a particular aspect of the research project. This research-led approach is just an example of many different ways of presenting historic interiors that have emerged over the last century or so, paralleling the increasing sensitivity to a building's creators, location, workmanship and evolution shown by conservators dealing with its structure.

Sometimes the presentation and conservation options appear dauntingly convoluted, so it is good to be reminded of Sir Bernard Feilden's 'seven degrees of intervention', as they have direct relevance to the study and rehabilitation of historic decorative schemes:[2]

- prevention of deterioration
- preservation of the existing state
- consolidation of the fabric
- restoration
- rehabilitation
- reproduction
- reconstruction.

All reconsidered schemes need to be founded on the prevention of deterioration and consolidation of the fabric; otherwise the duty of care will be undermined. The building's roof must be watertight, the stairs safe, the electrics up-to-date, and all its fabric covered by sensible maintenance schedules.

The preservation of the existing state is relevant to the 'stopped clock' or 'conserve as found' approach and has gained currency as a fail-safe, easily specified tactic for the display of rooms in historic houses, or even a complete house. Calke Abbey, Derbyshire, now a property of the National Trust, is just such an example (Figure 13.1).

Repairs to the fabric have to be carried out sensitively and invisibly in order to agree with a ruthless 'no change' policy. This inevitably ossifies, and lends importance to, the last owner's taste or to the tired decline of a once-great building. It also panders to our contemporary and romanticised view of a culture or a decorative scheme gone to seed, or just charmingly quirky. At best, the 'conserve as found' approach preserves a rich undercurrent of clues and patina for us and future generations to analyse and interpret. At worst, it can warp our appreciation of a house and its collection, and the care that was taken over its creation and assembly.

The more obvious types of intervention – restoration, rehabilitation, reproduction and reconstruction – tend to be at the fore when recreating old or lost schemes of interior decoration. They suggest the need to rescue or remake elements in a scheme which were covered up by later work, or ruined by the corrosive effects of light, damp, dirt and wear, or dispersed

Figure 13.1 The Schoolroom at Calke Abbey, Derbyshire, Reference: 3960. Courtesy of the National Trust.

through auction rooms or wills, or even stolen. The research for constructional intervention and changes to surface decoration based on precedent has to be very carefully prepared, thought through, managed and recorded. The research needs a co-ordinator who has an overview of the project, to ensure that all the disciplines are able to contribute and collaborate: this will often include art, architectural and social historians, archaeologists, conservators, materials analysts, curators, structural engineers, and also specialists in such areas as historic upholstery, furniture and domestic technology. Where thorough investigations are needed, they can be usually be broken down into three principal areas (but can take many forms and emphases, depending on the significance and idiosyncrasies of the individual building or room under study):

- site research
- archival research
- contextual research.

Site research consists of a series of tests, analyses and investigations that can be used to unpick the layers of previous decorative schemes that survive in a room. Often the clues are extremely fragile or elusive, and the site research should come very early in a project. Any prior, well-meaning modifications, even to apparently minor details such as electric wiring, can put valuable evidence at risk.

First is an architectural assessment, which involves the examination of a room with the aim of establishing the date of its creation, the principal materials used and its evolution. This might include a measured survey and recording of significant features, and observations including:

- the room's plan and situation relevant to adjacent rooms, and what this suggests for its creation, and original and subsequent use
- comparison of existing floor plans with previous ones, where available
- joinery panels, mouldings, decorative plasterwork, architectural furniture, fittings and scars of lost fittings
- windows – styles of glazing, mouldings, shutters, fittings for blinds, curtains and any related external fittings
- fragments of former textiles, carpets, wallpapers which may be concealed – for instance beneath flooring or behind a fitted bookcase
- flooring – looking for clues of installation or adaptation in order to help date a room
- services, including bell systems, vents, gas pipes, electric cabling or heating, again looking for clues of installation or adaptation.

The search for evidence of the various painted surfaces in a room can reveal much about the way a room was decorated and treated. Samples of paint, back to and including the substrate, may be removed from surfaces and examined using microscopic analysis to determine the progression of the painted schemes. Properly interpreted, findings from the different painted elements can be integrated to enable the description of original schemes, highlight missing links and reveal architectural changes. Further scientific tests may be advisable to reveal the medium and pigments used in a particular paint layer. Not only does this help to build up a recipe for a particular paint, but also the identification of certain pigments may even date a scheme: for instance, the use of French ultramarine (an artificial version of the prized and extremely expensive true ultramarine extracted from lapis lazuli) would suggest paint no older than the 1840s.

Such analysis should form an essential record if paints have become friable, or if stripping is needed to reveal carved work lost through clogging, or if there is any other risk to the breadth and quality of the available paint evidence. There are three practical processes to the analysis: the first involves an appraisal of the room or building, ideally based on an earlier architectural assessment, and an agreed proposal for the analysis; the second is the choice of sample locations and the taking of samples; and the third is the sample analysis itself, with writing-up of the findings.

The value of paint analysis lies in the way in which it is presented and communicated, and how the evidence is recorded. Microscopic analysis of decorative paints is a relatively recent discipline, and its value for the future will be as much about what its sampling has preserved for further research as what it can reveal today. So thorough recording should not just depend on a carefully written account but should also ensure the preservation of the detached samples. This will require a coordinated approach to archiv-

Figure 13.2 A fragment of late nineteenth-century wallpaper found behind a light switch on a bedroom wall at Sudbury Hall, Derbyshire. All other surfaces had been stripped. Photo: James Finlay.

ing the primary evidence that has been detached from surfaces. It is still wise practice to keep paint evidence intact in situ, especially if any quantity of clues are partially lost or damaged, with a filed record to indicate the location and significance of the preserved paint history. An even safer way of recording and preserving evidence for the long term is to annotate in a discreet place alongside the sample.

Architectural location analysis can reveal much by the observation of less obvious clues: crucial paint or wallpaper samples or other remnants from a previous scheme may have been masked by later fixtures or fittings, perhaps within a niche that has been blocked up, a fitted cupboard, a link to an adjoining room, or other places that may have been spared the attention lavished elsewhere (Figure 13.2). Decorators have usually prioritised preparation work – more effort goes into making good at eye level and in areas prone to wear and tear. Therefore the best paint histories will often be found higher than 2 metres, or in less accessible or visible places. Also, complex surfaces are usually rich in surviving paint evidence because they are awkward to rub down and prepare for new surfaces; good examples are enriched mouldings or the junctions between a field and some raised work.

Other low-tech methods may also help when looking for visible clues: for example, a raking light source might help establish significant details concealed beneath later layers, such as stencilling or other applied patterns or designs, the tell-tale of wallpaper joints, or crucial fragments of a patterned wallpaper. Be alert for constructional inconsistencies: not just subtle differences between one door's mouldings and the next, but the invasive repair or dry-lining of a wall that might have covered over the historic plane and lost adjoining details to a skirting or a cornice. A raking light survey might reveal scars from a blocked-in door or window, an altered chimneypiece or lost raised plasterwork on a ceiling.

Existing polychrome work, such as mural painting, *trompe l'oeil* and stencilling, however deteriorated, can be surveyed using high-tech methods, using both infrared and ultraviolet light sources. Both these non-invasive inspection methods have differing advantages, and may be able to pick out substrate repairs, retouching work, underdrawing, or other details so damaged that they may be unreadable in normal daylight conditions. Such information can be photographed for the record, and may inform further investigations or sampling work.

Painted schemes can also be revealed by exposing paint layers using mechanical scrapes or chemical stripping. This should be seen as essential if any accurate understanding of colour values is to be made, or to see a patterned or *trompe l'oeil* scheme. It is a complicated process, and requires many tests to determine the safest solvents and best stripping methods, but at its most successful it enables windows to be opened onto a particular paint layer that has already been identified as important – whether a plain colour or a fancy marbling scheme – so it can be seen and appreciated under the correct fall of light. It should be possible to make a credible assessment, rather than relying on reports solely from microscopy. The conservator or analyst who prepares the 'window' will be able to advise on the variation in colour or tone that might be expected from a paint's original appearance, depending on the deterioration of the pigment and binder.

Decorative paint evidence is often the most robust physical guide to the superficial appearance of previous schemes of decoration. While it can deteriorate in time, it is not nearly as fragile as textile evidence (encompassing upholstery through to floor coverings), which is usually an equally important constituent of any scheme. Paint evidence often remains locked into its strata for many centuries, and with care and planning can survive successive redecorations.

Finally, conservation trials may reveal fixed in situ elements as the key survivors of a critical or original decorative scheme, and need cleaning or repair. These could include gilded mouldings, grained joinery, mahogany doors, oak floorboards, a stone pavement or a marble chimneypiece. A stone relief may need cleaning, or over-paint may need to be removed from *scagliola*. Precious relics are not always obvious, and often the apparently most mundane survival of a plain decorator's paint forms the rarest and most evocative link with an otherwise lost scheme. The making good and cleaning of sample areas will establish early benchmarks for a renewed scheme, and enable conservators to prepare advice, estimates and timings for their work.

Archival research

Archives can provide the facts on which to build and arrange research, and can be accessed in various places: a local record office, national or other archives such as the National Monuments Record, and letters, drawings or photographs that may still be held at the property or in the collections of friends or relatives of a property's family. Professions or businesses that once had dealings with a property are also useful targets for research, as their papers may be accessible and provide another slant. A house's previous owners may have employed an external agent: for instance, wallpapers may have been purchased from Cowtan's, or furniture from Gillows, both of whom have archives. As so many archives and catalogues can now be researched through the internet, the first place to try a UK-based query is usually the National Archives website, which reaches into all local record offices.

Depending on the available archives, such research can be rewarding and provide immense insights into the evolution of a building and its decorative history. Even apparently straightforward inventories are often rich sources of information, but the most exciting gains can be unexpected – material costs, details of suppliers, and incidental social facts that flesh out a dry story. The researcher needs to be focused and methodical, but not so focused that the bigger picture is missed, or a parallel story overlooked.

The archive trail can include:

- bills and accounts
- inventories
- census returns
- images; drawings, paintings and photographs
- maps and aerial photographs, to pinpoint large building projects or alterations
- auction catalogues
- letters and diaries of the property's owners
- letters and diaries of their friends, relatives and visitors
- surveys.

Contextual research

Experience and acquired knowledge always provide the best context for research; but every scheme requires subtleties and variations that will involve further reading and study to enable it to be placed firmly within its background of time and taste. Complementary work may look at other contemporary schemes by the same designer or architect, or at other work commissioned by the same client. It may perhaps include a broader study and understanding of contemporary taste such as colour theory, archaeological and antiquarian fascinations, or reading about style-setters such as Vredeman de Vries, Palladio, William Kent, the Adam brothers, A.W.N.

Pugin, C. L. Eastlake, J. C. Loudon, Robert Kerr, Walsh Porter, Edith Wharton, Nancy Lancaster, John Fowler and so on. An appraisal of contemporary decorating techniques, via trade manuals, pattern books, and manufacturers' and suppliers' records, is also helpful in building up a practical background of what was achievable and sought-after in furniture-making, upholstery and house-painting. Clues can also be drawn from paintings, drawings and photographs of similar schemes. References may be found in diaries and correspondence reporting on the actual subject of the research project, or of a very similar one. Finally, wherever possible, an academic study should place a scheme of decoration in its historic context, and develop links and themes with the contemporary political, scientific and social worlds. For example:

- How did the Unitarian beliefs of the Greg family in the early nineteenth century affect the look of their new home adjoining Quarry Bank Mill, Cheshire?
- How did wars slow down or influence the spread of ideas in Europe?
- What was the effect of political unrest or economic recessions?
- How did technological advances affect the palette available for dyes and pigments, the transport of construction materials round the country, or the manufacture and cost of wallpaper?
- How were building projects and schemes of decoration funded?

Threads of such an understanding can feed valuably into more practically focused research, and give the final result greater grounding and depth.

Interpreting research

Interpretation feeds off research and grows alongside wider concerns for the display and presentation of a property, often contained in a Conservation Plan. But it pays to be pragmatic, as findings from both archival and in situ research might reveal an unexpectedly rich or unusual scheme, highlight another phase in the owner's or building's story, or suggest another method of presentation. The order of attack is negotiable, but it is usually best to start with archival work, as this forms the framework on which all other research is built. Certain projects may also require conservation trials, which in themselves can be useful touchstones for the first appearance of the recreated scheme; and if any repair is needed urgently, this, and any essential materials analysis, must take precedence.

A comprehensive research paper must be underpinned by clear communication and the use of clearly understood nomenclature. Understanding the classical orders, Gothic styles (as codified by Revivalists in the nineteenth century) and the development of the main European styles of architecture should be the foundation for any research into an architectural scheme of decoration.[3] Just as it is impossible to provide a critique of a piece of music without knowing the notes, it is likewise impossible to judge and assess a work of architecture without knowing the building blocks, and the evolution and accumulation of details. Reasoned accounts of decorative schemes depend on getting into the mindsets of those who created them. However, mention of dosserets, dado-rails, rustication or nogging could be confusing and off-putting to the lay reader, and well-annotated photographs or line drawings are a useful support to a written report.

Even when the aims of a scheme's re-creation are straightforward, the journey to its realisation is usually complicated by the sheer number of elements and choices that need consideration, and by the constraints of the budget. Below are some typical concerns that can affect the final look of a reinstated scheme. Almost all revolve around the tension between what is known to be correct for the scheme, and how these perceived truths have to be compromised to accommodate the best methods of interpretation and the practicalities of the project:

- **Usage.** If a room is open to the public, or used by the public, how does this square with what is known about the historical layout chosen for the room? What about wear and tear on surface finishes such as paints, fabrics or carpets originally designed for light domestic use?
- **Sourcing new or replacement furnishings or materials.** Depending on what already exists in the room, furniture, upholstery, carpets, wall-papers, painted decoration and pictures may be needed. All will need to be sourced with an understanding of authentic manufacture and also of what is technically feasible. These constraints are becoming more rigorous: many specialised, traditional or craft-based businesses are struggling to stay economically viable; traditional raw materials are becoming more expensive and harder to source; and UK and European legislation will only allow lead-based traditional paints to be used under licence, and a tightening up of the use of solvent-based paints and varnishes will soon follow.[4]
- **Conservation of existing furnishings, fixtures and applied decoration.** Leaving aside the technical complexities of the different conservation disciplines, and the various acceptable ways of cleaning and making good, conserved objects ultimately have to be accommodated within a decorative scheme. How will original items integrate visually with new finishes? Furthermore, responsible conservation criteria set certain environmental controls on historic rooms that can be very intrusive. Room barriers and sacrificial floor covering are part of the accepted paraphernalia, but the desirable limiting of natural light may prevent a recreated scheme from being enjoyed as intended. The latter was overcome at Attingham Park, Shropshire, when the dining room was redisplayed as if after dark, with curtains drawn, the table laid for dinner, and the fire and Argand lamps lit. Apart from the wonderfully intense atmosphere this has created in the room, it has also eliminated the risk of light damage to the furniture and particularly to the fragile, two-hundred-year-old Axminster carpet (Figure 13.3).
- **Artificial lighting.** The reinstated scheme needs a consistent environment, and artificial lighting may serve to reinforce an authentic feel, or undermine it, both in the fittings supplied and in the type, colour and quality of the light produced. Often pre-electric fittings are needed,

Figure 13.3 The Dining Room at Attingham Park, Shrewsbury, Shropshire. Courtesy of the National Trust.

but even when the hardware is genuine it is rarely possible to include the correct power source, whether oil, candle or gas, that originally allowed the room to function after dark. The issues surrounding artificial lighting in all houses, and in all levels of society, provide fascinating themes that are still largely unexploited in historic room displays. They can explain the effect that natural and artificial light had on the ways rooms were planned, decorated and used, and throw into relief all those conveniences and technologies that we take for granted today.

- **Gaps in evidence.** Well-argued cases need to be made to fill gaps or doubts, as the evidence base for a room's reinstatement is rarely complete. The final choices become easier once the project team has an understanding of the situations and taste that shaped the original scheme.
- **Explaining a scheme.** There are many interpretative devices that may explain a room's display. These options may need to evolve, and a display be fine-tuned, in response to changing technologies. The main criterion is that no devices affect the practical conservation of the

architecture or collection and that all imported hardware and display material is fully reversible. (See also **Recreating and interpreting historic schemes**, below.)

Teamwork is vital and a project manager should arrange an initial meeting with all the various researchers, encourage cross-fertilisation of material during the analysis stages so that everyone can benefit from breaking news, and keep researchers involved in the subsequent interpretation process. It is important not to allow different research themes to be pursued in isolation, only to be collated on completion. Assembling a team of researchers and advisers can seem logistically and financially daunting, but a cohesive project team provides good value: it can magnify individual efforts, help focus the research at an early stage, and remove inconsistencies. It also helps to ensure a well-rounded and self-critical response to the research and its assessment. Teamwork can and should extend to external professional feedback.

Recreating and interpreting historic schemes

Every project is different, and there are always varying parameters to research, depending on resources, the surviving evidence and the aims for the recreated scheme. Despite this, there are still matters concerning the buildings, owners, collections and furnishings that will be shared by all projects. Also, there is a common dilemma in the recreation of all historic schemes: is it actually possible to recreate faithfully a previous scheme of decoration? There is a need to recognise that all such work is likely to be limited by current knowledge, by the influences of contemporary taste, and by the intrusions that accompany the formal rescue, conservation and display to visitors of a historic interior.

In addition to the physical presentation of an interior itself, there are further levels of interpretation to help the visitor feel involved in the story of how the room was first created, and how it came to be recreated. There is frequently a guidebook or room notes that articulate the main history and describe the principal facts. The level of detail that is provided depends on the energies, enthusiasms and resources of the curatorial team that cares for the house. To reach as wide an audience as possible, information has to be delivered in a series of tiers, perhaps starting with the guidebook as an overview, and using additional leaflets to cover conservation concerns, family-orientated material, new acquisitions or particular themes in a house's collection. A room steward or guide may provide a more personal account, and be able to respond to questions. Exhibitions, either in the form of small, discreet displays within the recreated room or larger, separate exhibitions covering broader aspects, can add to the understanding of a recreated scheme within a house. New technology has the potential to change the way research is made available in a cost-effective way. Digital audio-aids and podcasts are increasingly popular as providers of individually managed information in museums and galleries, although headphones have been criticised for their tendency to turn visitors into passive spectators, disengaged from the primary material. However, advances in technology will no doubt provide more sophisticated and finely tuned hardware and software which will enhance interaction and improve the delivery of information.

An allowance needs to be built into a project to record the research and interpretation so that the process can be archived and understood by those who follow on at a property. This ideally requires a concluding essay, accompanied by an indexed set of the research papers and primary documents that guided the project.

There are many flaws in the stated aim of recreating a historic scheme of decoration. These flaws can trickle through all the various attempts to remake superficial appearances, and often from our earnestness to explain them. The very process of 'presenting' a room usually sets it apart from the way in which it was originally used and enjoyed. Exceptions might be the most formal historic interiors, such as the State Rooms at Kedleston Hall, Derbyshire, in a political powerhouse designed almost exclusively for show and status, and open from an early stage for general visitors, not just guests of the owner. But most homes were more private and modest, and centred on the interests, wealth and social status of the occupants. Everyday living generated light, warmth, smells, movement, bustle and social activity just as homes do today, and the game of re-presentation must allow for some of these tactile responses in order to engage the visitor fully and make the experience credible.

Both recreated and preserved historic schemes are not just the sum total of collated and analysed facts. They need social and emotional 'glue' to make the whole artifice cohere, and visitors need to be informed about their purpose. The historic function of rooms is fundamental to the working and appearance of houses. Many had a hierarchy of room usage which was reflected in their decorative schemes. House technology is also popular with today's visitors: bell systems, early central heating, telephones, lifts, gas and electrical installations, kitchen heating equipment. Film and television productions are also realising the appeal of authentic detail and atmospheric lighting in historic interiors.

House versus home

There may always be an imbalance or tension between the aims of historic house guardians and the pressures of 'reasonable access' for visitors – a paradox unintentionally summed up in the National Trust's slogan, 'For Ever, For Everyone'. Conservation demands do not square easily with an authentic room display: risk assessments will prohibit a real fire burning in a grate on an autumn day. Another tension lies in comparing houses that are not lived in with those that are. Houses that are conserved and 'preserved' as historic shrines lose an indefinable character of ownership and use, while historic houses that are still inhabited retain a valuable 'household genius'. An attempt to replicate the lost sense of family occupation, with a table laid for tea, or a crumpled newspaper, never fools; but genuinely muddy boots in the hall, or a half-drunk mug of coffee on a windowsill, lend legitimacy to a house, provide glimpses into a family's life and have become strong currency for marketing a house to the visiting public. How many times have you heard a house highly rated simply because it feels 'lived in'? A house that is unoccupied as a home can quickly become institutionalised, dulled by such ephemera as merchandise, official notices, pamphlets and signboards. The sense of occupation is so desirable that the temptation is to fake it up even when the thread of family occupation has broken, though ultimately this fails to convince. The 'Country House Look' has encouraged veneration of 'shabby chic' interiors, but the genuine assemblage of high-value artefacts, family photos, Aubusson carpets and dog baskets can rarely be mimicked or even preserved once the occupying family has left.

Over the past thirty years, successive attempts to perfect the 'conserve as found' aesthetic have been made at many unoccupied houses, including Canons Ashby, Northamptonshire; Erddig, Clwyd; Calke Abbey, Derbyshire; Brodsworth Hall, Yorkshire; and probably at Tyntesfield, Somerset. This is a fail-safe, easily specified strategy for the display of historic houses and gets round the problem of the lack of life by fixing the patina of the last phase of ownership. The fabric may require sensitive, invisible repair, but with a ruthless end result of 'no change'. This enshrining of decay and decline can be confusing to the understanding of authentic historic schemes. The approach satisfies many conservation aims, but more significantly reflects contemporary taste. At best, the 'conserve as found' approach preserves a rich undercurrent of clues for us and future generations to analyse and interpret, and adds to the variety of presentation options. It also honestly records the perilous state that many houses have reached before being rescued, and could in some cases be the only option for display, owing to decay and dispersals. At worst, it can warp our appreciation of a house and its collection, and the care that was taken over its creation and assembly.

Conclusion

Research satisfies the duty to record, understand and care for historic houses, collections, schemes and tastes, and helps to unlock depths of meaning and value behind the display of interiors. It not only illuminates artefacts and craftsmanship, but also opens windows on history, customs, people and social interaction. Dissemination of research can supplement the presentation of interiors and engage the visitor's interest in some of the decision-making processes.[5] This forensic approach, coupled with sensitive interpretation, honestly acknowledges the artificiality of displaying historic interiors while providing opportunities for catching the visitor's attention. The fruits of research, requiring time and an ingenious eye, successfully blend re-creation with interpretation, to the gain of the visiting public.

Endnotes

1. These policies are usually described as Conservation Management Plans, Conservation Plans and sometimes 'Spirit of the Place'.

2. See 'The Philosophy of Repair', in *Materials and skills for historic buildings conservation*, for the main types of approach to treating historic building fabric.

3. Useful sources are the glossaries in the volumes of Pevsner's Buildings of England series; *The Penguin Dictionary of Architecture and Landscape Architecture* (various editions, 1966–); A.L. Osborne, *A Dictionary of English Domestic Architecture* (Country Life, 1954), W.H. Leeds, *Architecture for the Use of Beginners and Students* (Doubleday, 1954); and J. Lever and J. Harris, *Illustrated Dictionary of Architecture 800–1914* (Faber & Faber, 1993).

4. EU Directive 2004/42/CE (phase 2) came into force on 1/1/2010, with the aim of further reducing the amount of volatile organic compounds (VOCs) emitted through decorative products such as paint and varnish.

5. Varied interpretation techniques and displays are currently being trialled at Attingham Park, Shropshire, and at Lyme Park, Cheshire, to celebrate the return of Caxton's fifteenth-century Missal to the Library. Both houses are properties of the National Trust.

14 Environment in the historic interior

David Drewe

Introduction

Historic buildings have a life expectancy several orders of magnitude greater than human beings; sometimes buildings retain their original use and sometimes they are adapted to new uses through modification and alteration, which enables them to remain with us. Installed mechanical facilities, including space heating systems, are intended to improve the usage of old buildings by providing an acceptable level of comfort for the occupants, the predominant measure being air temperature. But the need to provide comfort temperatures, and the effect of this on relative humidity, tends to conflict with the conservation of historic building fabric and building contents in both the short and the long term; this chapter will consider that conflict from a building services engineer's perspective.

Heating may be installed into buildings generally to control the internal environment for a number of reasons.

- human comfort
- protection of objects, including internal finishes and furnishings
- protection of the building fabric.

It is often the case that the differing needs of these three require a level of compromise.

Considerations with respect to people, collections and the building fabric

Human comfort is governed by a number of factors, namely air and mean radiant temperatures, air movement and relative humidity (RH). Air temperature is the most well known of the comfort indicators and is easily measured. We can deal with a reasonably wide band of air temperatures,

Interior finishes & fittings for historic building conservation, First Edition. Edited by Michael Forsyth & Lisa White. © 2012 Blackwell Publishing Ltd. Published 2012 by Blackwell Publishing Ltd.

but this is dependent on levels of activity and clothing. What is not always considered is the mean radiant temperature of the cold or warm surfaces that surround us and the effect we feel from this radiant heating or cooling effect. Where the difference in temperature experienced between different sides of the body is extreme it will be perceived as discomfort. This concept of the radiant effect of surfaces is of particular importance with older buildings that tend to have higher thermal mass and so experience lower surface temperatures.

Air movement is closely linked to evaporation of perspiration from the body, so this also interacts with temperature and RH. However, what might be a cooling and welcome summer breeze when experienced face on would, with the same conditions of temperature and air speed, be perceived as a cold draught if on the back of the neck or around the feet or ankles.

We have all experienced the problem of discomfort during hot summers as a result of high RH. For us, the main issue with RH is that it interferes with our body's ability to sweat, which is one of the main mechanisms we have for controlling our body temperature. While the moisture content of air remains constant with changes in temperature, RH varies directly with such changes, decreasing with a rise in temperature and increasing with a reduction in temperature. If moisture is added but with no increase in air temperature then eventually the air will become saturated (100% RH). The same effect is also reached by reducing the air temperature. The point at which the air becomes saturated is known as the dew point temperature; at this condition, the air can hold no more moisture.

In general, RH is a much more important factor than temperature when considering the needs of collections. Many materials are more structurally sound over a range of temperatures, the exceptions being when subject to high or low extremes that fluctuate rapidly, such as where the rapid rise in temperature gives rise to a lowering of RH and drying of sensitive materials; or the reverse, when low temperatures and high RH can result in moisture problems and the possible results of mould growth and other problems. It is the problems associated with these rapid changes that give rise to the need to maintain a relatively stable environment, where any changes that take place do so in as gradual or controlled a way as possible.

The last consideration is that of the building fabric. Moisture can enter a building in a number of ways – from the external air, introduced via natural or forced ventilation; from the occupants or processes contained within; and via the moisture exchange between the fabric and the space – all of which add up to give the resultant relative humidity. Heat, air and moisture are constantly being exchanged between indoors and outdoors in an attempt to reach a balance. At the dew point, condensation can appear as water on cold surfaces, including windows, walls and metalwork, or be absorbed into parts of the structure; it can also form within the structure, when it is termed interstitial condensation.

Buildings materials and their contents have an ability to buffer the effects of RH/moisture movement through the capture (absorption) or release (desorption) of local water molecules. Usually a material will retain more moisture during desorption than it absorbs at the same temperature and RH. This effect will tend to stabilise the internal moisture levels during times of high moisture gains. A building could therefore store moisture over a longer period before problems become evident, by which time the situation might be more difficult to reverse. Buffering is dependent on the air change rate in the space as high air change rates transport far greater quantities of moisture in relation to that absorbed/desorbed by buffering; therefore in this case buffering has little effect on daily variations. As a rule of thumb, for buffering to be of any significance in stabilising room conditions the air change rate needs to be no more than 0.5 air changes per hour, a figure likely to be exceeded in many buildings.[1]

Heating buildings can encourage the movement of moisture between the outside air and the building fabric and crystals from the salts in the original water used for construction can be re-formed through the effects of dissolved gas in rain water reacting with the masonry, or in ground water adjacent to the building. This process can split layers off a masonry surface and is typified by visible fluffy white efflorescence growths.

Heating buildings can also cause the moisture stored within the fabric to be released into the heated space, thereby increasing the amount of moisture in the air; this results in an increase in RH and raising of the dew point temperature. The moisture being carried in the air, particularly once it is warmed, will not always exit the building in the same way that it arrived or in a controlled manner, finding its way out instead through unheated spaces such as roof voids and again increasing the risk of condensation in these areas. Moisture can thus move around a building. For example, moisture removed from masonry may be absorbed by wood/timber, while the opposite is also possible where drying out may cause damage to sensitive interiors.

The interaction of heat, moisture and air movement within a building is complex, being controlled by a number of constantly changing and variable factors:

- moisture generation
- moisture movement
- the sponge/buffering effect
- level of heating
- ventilation rates and air paths
- external conditions.

Conventional heating design is based on an assumption of standard steady-state conditions, with the purpose of determining the needs of occupant comfort where air temperature dominates, but it does not consider the overall impact on the building in both the short and the long term. These effects can combine and result in permanent damage to historic building fabric.

While our raised expectations, and our increasing understanding of how buildings and their contents behave, have impelled the provision of suitable mechanical systems, the biggest influence on building services has been legislation. However, many new regulations are not retrospective, so in most cases you will not be expected to upgrade existing installations unless you are undertaking modifications to or installing new systems during programmes of redevelopment, refurbishment or replacement.

When considering the heating of a building, it is important as far as possible to determine how the building performs, its orientation and which rooms get the most sun. This is especially vital in the case of museum environments and houses open to the public with room settings. By considering a building's natural performance at an early stage it may be possible to influence room layouts to prevent, for example, certain objects being placed in rooms where they will be most adversely affected when an alternative room or space may be available in which they will be subject to less extremes. The result can be a reduction in the need to provide intrusive and possibly damaging services, and the opportunity to identify alternatives to controlling the overall room environment.

So we need to initially consider:

- **an understanding of**
  - the potential use of the building
  - human expectation
  - the building.
- **issues**
  - statutory requirements
  - meeting human expectations
  - aesthetics v. irreversible damage
  - historical integrity.

It is also very important to remember that building services are transitory, having a limited life compared to that of the building and possibly being replaced several times in the building's lifetime. Typically, a historic building may have a services life of fifteen to twenty years and a building life of three hundred to five hundred years, or more.

Heating

In historic buildings heating systems are commonly found that have been installed by former owners, and not always for the purpose for which the building now finds itself being used. When reviewing the operation of existing systems or considering the introduction of any new form of heating into a historic building, the following issues, in addition to the comfort of the occupants, must be taken into account:

- limiting the release of stored moisture from the fabric
- limiting the amount of moisture added directly to the internal space
- limiting the physical impact on the building and interiors.

As noted above, heating the air within a space can release moisture stored within the building fabric, and this is one of the reasons why heating an interior – perhaps contrary to intuition – can increase moisture-related decay problems. Moisture can be added directly from the following sources:

- natural ventilation
- the occupants
- direct water ingress
- forced fresh air from a mechanical ventilation heating system
- the use of flueless heaters.

It is unlikely that much can be done to control the moisture introduced by natural ventilation and occupants, while direct water ingress will require the source to be found and the appropriate remedial works carried out to rectify the problem. The use of any warm air ventilation system that introduces outside air into the space will be adding the moisture contained in this air into the space. This will only be problematic when the external moisture content is greater than that inside the building.

The selection of the type of heating system will involve a number of factors, including:

- size and construction of the building
- intended use
- operating times
- location
- fuels/energy available
- capital and running costs.

There are many variations of heating systems types, but they can be divided into the following basic groups.

Radiant systems consist of a number of heater units, mounted at high level that radiate heat at short wavelength, with anyone in the direct path of the radiant heat absorbing this heat and therefore feeling warm. This system can be controlled to switch on when needed and does not require any preheat time. If left running, the radiant heat would in time warm the structure, which would result in heat being released into the space, with a corresponding small rise in air temperature. This would give very high running costs and defeat the object of radiant heating, its purpose being to provide heating as and when required for the occupants without the need for high air temperatures. Examples of this type of system include infrared electric panel and plaque heaters, electric- and gas-fired radiant tube heaters and wet radiant panels.

Warm air systems require that a certain volume of heated air be supplied to offset the heat losses from the space; the air is heated first, and in turn warms the structure. The air volume supplied is a function of the temperature difference between the space and supply air temperatures: the higher the supply air temperature, the lower the required air volume for the same space condition.

Some forms of warm air systems can make use of a measure of recirculated air to reduce energy and fuel used. Direct gas-fired heating, which burns gas in the air to be supplied to the space, uses full fresh air, adding both the moisture contained in the outside air and that released during the combustion process, as well as any other products released or present in the external air, directly into the heated space. There is therefore a possible increased risk of condensation, and the consequential effects this may have on the building fabric, both in the short term and the long term, make gas-fired systems the less favoured option in buildings with sensitive interiors and finishes. Examples of such systems include direct and indirect warm air ventilation systems, and electric and low-temperature hot-water fan coil and fan convector systems.

Convection systems use the convective air currents set up from the heat emitter to circulate heat throughout the space using electric panel or storage heaters, wet radiator and convective tube or skirting heating systems, or underfloor electric or wet pipework systems. Where hot water is needed this is normally generated by an oil- or gas-fired boiler. This system generally warms the air, which in turn heats the structure, except where underfloor heating is used, when the structural floor warms up first then heats the air by convection, although a small percentage of radiant heating effect is available.

The options

When looking at services installations, there are two possible options. In some cases the building may already have services installed, so the first option is to consider the use of existing services. Otherwise, a new system must be installed.

Let us look at the option for using existing systems where they are available. Each year we lose much of our engineering past, normally owing to a lack of understanding of the importance that a particular system or piece of equipment may have. When a building is listed, all existing fixtures and fittings including services installations are then protected and wherever possible we encourage the continued use of historically important engineering installations or systems, subject to health and safety concerns, improvement where possible, or at least retention in situ with new systems installed alongside the original. This course of action is not always possible, so here recording is important before the installation or system is lost.

However, most existing installations will not in fact be significant, being already a second- or third-generation installation. While reuse or modification of existing services may be seen as a cheaper option, their condition may not make them suitable for reuse, and compliance with current legal requirements may make reuse more expensive than installing completely new systems. There could also be hidden dangers of toxic or hazardous materials that were used in the past and are now banned, including asbestos insulation and lead-based pipework. Access for upgrading or improvement may also be difficult, as services installations were sometimes fixed and the building constructed around them, and undertaking works would require major opening up of the historic building fabric, with consequent unjustifiable damage. But there is always the chance that early installations can be upgraded, such as a Victorian coal-fired furnace located below the floor grate being converted to oil-firing, cast iron free-standing coal stoves converted to use with natural gas, and gas lighting converted to electric.

However, making use of parts of an existing system, and adding on or updating certain key parts, is not always as easy as it at first seems. Determining the performance of the older or existing parts of a system may be difficult or may require an extensive amount of research to determine performance and suitability for further use.

Having considered existing situations, we can now turn to the more usual situation of installing new services in older buildings. Installing new building services in historic buildings involves an approach similar to that for a new building. There are six key areas.

- planning
- survey
- services routes
- builders' work
- aesthetics
- reversibility.

As with any new-build or historic project, planning ahead is essential, but the main difference with a historic building is the reward of working with the full-scale model, together, where possible, with historic records.

It is in this early stage of design that the designer needs to take more time than with new-build. The survey is important to identify proposed services routes so that contractors can adequately cost the installations, which may need to be longer than simply the shortest distance between two points to prevent avoidable damage to historic fabric. It is essential that provision is made within the programme for an extensive survey of the existing building. Time is well spent on this to identify potential services routes but also to uncover the history of how the building may have been serviced in the past. The survey may identify areas and spaces where services, plant and equipment could be installed, and identify parts of the historic fabric not normally visible but no less significant, such as timber structural supports within floor voids that would prevent the running of services.

It is the services installation that tends to cause the most serious scars in historic building conservation and it is essential that detailed design information is made available before the appointment of the undertaking contractor; this is a standard condition of building services consultants employed on English Heritage works.

In terms of appearance, it is often totally inappropriate to try to provide a period look. Services are relatively new, only being with us in the last 150 years and it would be false to introduce Victorian-style radiators in a Norman church or Tudor house. It is far better to be honest and show that this is a modern addition to the building. It is also now becoming much easier to successfully integrate services into building in such a way that they are almost unnoticeable. Possibly the most important consideration, and one of the most difficult, is that of reversibility, whereby the installations could be removed and leave little or no evidence that they had been there.

At the design stage it is also important to remember that, in addition to the appropriate listed building or scheduled monument consent, it is necessary to meet the needs of building control, many systems now being classed as controlled services under Building Regulations, fire, health and safety, and environmental regulations, and possibly nature conservation.

Maintenance and statutory requirements

Building services range from a simple domestic electrical system to complex electrical installations that may supply power to a passenger lift, central heating system, and air conditioning and ventilation plant. Natural gas is used for heating in certain buildings, and these systems may make use of pressurisation equipment. Artefact stores could be equipped with mechanical lifting equipment. Fire detection and emergency lighting are also installed in many properties.

All systems need to undergo regular maintenance and inspections, not only to ensure that they operate as efficiently as intended but also to ensure that they remain safe. All equipment provided in the workplace should be regularly checked and maintained and this could include:

- daily or weekly visual, operational or functional checks
- routine maintenance carried out, by trained and competent persons
- formal planned inspections and testing, by competent and approved persons.

The wide variety of services that may be installed in a building are governed by legislation, and many of the Acts of Parliament are supplemented by Regulations (Statutory Instruments) that give guidance as to how the law may be complied with. There are various authorities that are empowered to enforce the Regulations. The majority of Regulations that govern building services come under the Health and Safety at Work Act, and this is enforced by the Health and Safety Executive, which publishes a number of guides and Approved Codes of Practice that, if followed, should ensure that we are able to maintain services in a safe condition.

Conclusion

The normal main concern when considering the effects of heating on historic building fabric is to restrict large temperature swings that arise when satisfying the needs of people in the space, especially when the building is used intermittently. These changes in temperature encourage the movement of moisture and possible salts into and out of the structure, with the consequential risks of condensation, fungal growth and other damage.

The provision of a heating system that provides a constant low level of background heating in the order of 10°C to 12°C, known as conservation heating, will over a period of time elevate the temperature of the fabric and thereby reduce the effects of temperature swings. While this will encourage the movement of moisture out of the fabric, it reduces the risk of surface and interstitial condensation. Conservation heating is sometimes provided to reduce the relative humidity within a space, and a timed over-ride can be provided to give acceptable human comfort levels, say 15°C to 18°C, during occupied periods. Both warm air and convection heating systems can be designed and controlled to provide conservation heating with the necessary top-up for occupant comfort.

It can be seen that the installation within a historic building of a heating system, as well as other systems to control the internal environment, is normally a compromise between the need to preserve the building fabric and interiors and providing the comfort required by the users and occupants to ensure that the building continues to fulfil a function and purpose that guarantees its continued use.

Endnote

1. W Bordass and T Oreszczyn, *Internal Environments in Historic Buildings: Monitoring, diagnosis and modelling* (English Heritage, 1998).

15 Fire safety in Georgian houses

Peter Norris

Introduction: legislation and guidance

The control of fire safety measures in buildings comes, in the main, from Part B, *Fire Safety*, of the Building Regulations.[1] The main purpose of these regulations is to ensure the health and safety of people in or about a building; therefore the main focus relates to life safety. The Approved Documents that accompany the regulations give practical guidance about some of the ways of meeting the functional requirements of the regulations. Conflicts often arise between these requirements and those of conservation. Approved Document B does recognise the difficulties when the requirements are applied to historic buildings and suggests a flexible approach may be adopted. Part B, *Fire Safety*, is arguably the most important section of the Building Regulations as many lives are lost in fires and one therefore cannot over stress the importance of fire protection measures and means of escape. For historic buildings there is a need to seek solutions to Building Regulation requirements that ensure that health and safety are achieved without adversely affecting the building's historic character and setting. The fire safety measures taken to protect the occupants of the building often protect fabric and contents, which for historic buildings is of significant importance in preserving our heritage for future generations.

Now replaced by Planning Policy Statement 5, the former Planning Policy Guidance: Planning and the Historic Environment – PPG 15, under Part 1, usefully related to Building and fire legislation; access for disabled people; and house renovation grants. With regard to listed building control it stated:

> In exercising their responsibilities for the safety of buildings under the building and fire legislation, local planning authorities should deal sympathetically with proposals for the repair or conversion of historic buildings. The Building Regulations should be operated in a way which avoids removal of features which contribute to the character of a listed building and are part of the reason for its

Interior finishes & fittings for historic building conservation, First Edition. Edited by Michael Forsyth & Lisa White. © 2012 Blackwell Publishing Ltd. Published 2012 by Blackwell Publishing Ltd.

being listed. Sufficient flexibility exists within the Building Regulations and Fire Precautions Act systems for authorities to have regard to the possible impact of proposals on the historical or architectural value of a building, and authorities should consult their own conservation officers, or seek expert advice from other sources, when handling difficult situations. It is particularly important that there should be a flexible approach to structural matters, to ensure that any changes are in character with the rest of the building and that there is no unacceptable damage to the fabric. In order to ensure that requirements which are unacceptable in terms of a historic building can be considered as part of a listed building consent application, the precise Building and Fire Regulations requirements should be made explicit *before* an application has been determined. A successful outcome is more likely to be negotiated if the authorities have been consulted from the outset.[2]

The document encourages early consultation between the local authority planning or conservation officer and the building control body (local authority or approved inspector) to ensure that fire safety matters, in particular, are resolved before an application has been determined.

The importance of fire safety is also recognised in British Standard 7913: 1998, *The Principles of the conservation of historic buildings*, which states: 'Fire is the greatest single threat to the fabric and contents of any building and, in the case of an historic building, the loss of authentic fabric in a fire is irretrievable.'[3]

Fire protection

There are two areas of fire protection, passive and active, and both have an effect on means of escape.

- **Passive fire protection** is supplied by the material construction of the building, which needs to be able to check the spread of heat, smoke and fire for specific periods of time and protect safe exit routes for a sufficient period to allow all building occupants to escape to a place of safety.
- **Active fire protection** takes the form of mechanical suppressants such as sprinkler systems which are automatically activated when a fire is detected, and automatic fire detection systems such as smoke and heat detectors that give early warning of a fire.

Where alteration of the historic building necessitates upgrading existing elements, such as in flat conversions, some intervention into the fabric will invariably be necessary. The upgrading for passive fire protection can cause conflict between the Building Regulations and conservation, with the upgrading of elements of structure such as floors and doors and the need to provide lobby protection to staircase enclosures. Clearly, it is how these operations affect the historic fabric and overall effect that is the chief concern from a conservation point of view.

For upgrading purposes, passive measures are a particular problem in historic buildings where fine architectural features and design are involved.

This is particularly so in Georgian terraced properties. The height of these buildings is such that the minimum period of fire resistance would be 60 minutes (where the top floor is more than 5 metres above the ground for flat conversions and offices). The upgrading of existing floors can be problematical where there is decorative ceiling plasterwork to the underside. This particular problem became rather acute when the requirement for the 60 minutes' fire resistance for existing floors undergoing a change of use to flats was first introduced in the Building Regulations 1965 (Table A to Regulation E5). In Bath, the then Bath City Council were proactive in resolving the issue by undertaking an in situ fire test on 12 Chatham Row (built c. 1760) to establish the fire resistance afforded by a typical Georgian floor. Various bodies were involved in supervising the test including, among others, the Fire Research Station, or the Joint Fire Research Organisation as it was then known.

In order to simulate as closely as possible the conditions and development of a normal fire in a dwelling, it was decided to allow the fire to burn unhindered for a prearranged period of 45 minutes from the time of ignition. The ceiling was prepared for decoration, as would happen in a conversion.

The timber upper floor construction consisted of:

- 175 × 25 mm square edge boarding
- 200 × 50 mm floor joists at approximately 400 mm centres
- 25 mm lath and plaster ceiling with an ornate cornice.

The pyres were set up in the ground floor reception room to test the floor over. Thermocouples (a widely used type of thermal sensor) were installed in the floor, and the measuring and monitoring equipment was set up in a remote first-floor room. About 25 minutes into the test the fire began to die away, probably owing to the lack of oxygen, so a window was opened from the outside. With the availability of oxygen the fire further developed, and at its peak the temperature reached 1000°C – probably hotter than a normal domestic living room fire. At the time of extinguishing the fire, some smoke had percolated to the floor above but no flame penetration had occurred. The ceiling was still apparently sound, but immediately water was applied to extinguish the fire the rapid cooling of the surface resulted in extensive cracks appearing and part of the ceiling collapsed. With the knowledge gained from the test, Bath City Council adopted a policy that where 60 minutes' fire resistance was required the existing square-edge boarding would be upgraded by the overlaying of hardboard to achieve a 'modified' hour (in more recent times the hardboard has been replaced by an acoustic board system to comply with the requirements of Part E in respect of impact and airborne sound insulation[4]). Clearly, major intervention is not necessarily required to achieve a reasonable standard of fire protection from floors with this type of construction. When the in situ fire test was carried out, 12 Chatham Row was due for demolition as part of a new traffic relief scheme for the city. Fortunately, the scheme did not take place: Chatham Row was saved from the bulldozers and number 12 was subsequently renovated to its former glory after the test.

We perhaps think of in situ fire tests as a comparatively modern method of assessing the fire resistance of elements within a building. The designers of buildings constructed during the Georgian period, however, were conscious of the destructiveness and dangers of fire. In July 1793, the Association of Architects produced a report, *To consider the causes of the frequent fires and the best means of preventing the like in future.*[5] The report outlines various tests carried out on floors, walls and fireplaces and the construction methods adopted as a result. The Association of Architects at that time had a very eminent membership including Sir William Chambers, Sir John Soane, James Wyatt and Earl Stanhope.

Fire-resisting doors

Fire doors are one of the most important links in the chain of fire precautions and have at least one of two functions:

- to protect escape routes from the effects of fire so that the occupants can safely reach a final exit
- to protect the contents and/or the structure of a building by limiting the spread of fire.

An existing door needs to be assessed to determine its suitability for upgrading to fire-resisting standard, which is dependent not only on design and materials used but also, very importantly, on its current condition.

The practical considerations for assessment are:

1. Will the building control body and the fire authority accept an upgrading solution?
2. What appearance is required by the conservation officer?
3. What are the requirements with regard to fire and smoke resistance?

Upgrading door check list:

- condition of the door and frame/lining assessed for suitability, i.e. thickness, construction, gaps between frame and wall, etc.
- no gaps or loose joints
- damaged or out-of-square edges – repair or re-lip
- glue used in door construction (if animal glue, ensure that the jointing is adequate – mortice and tenon with wedges)
- check timber species and density (not less than $400 \, \text{kg/m}^3$)
- check detail of panel and beading
- check suitability of ironmongery.

The main problem associated with upgrading panelled doors is the comparative weakness of the panels with regard to fire resistance. It is possible that a fire will consume the timber panel more rapidly than the rest of the door components and thus the 'burn-through' is likely to take place within the required fire-resisting period. In many cases the timber panel would either have to be replaced or be backed up with a fire insulation board or other proprietary method, the position of which would depend on the appearance required for the door.

The application of an intumescent paint or varnish can upgrade certain doors for fire protection. Modern-day products are now much more robust and, from a conservation point of view, do not require any intervention into the fabric. The existing substrate can remain (except for polished finishes) and the protective paint or varnish applied can be decorated with 'normal' paint.

In recent years various guidance notes have been produced on the upgrading of panelled doors that are typically found in the Georgian period. In particular, methods have been developed so as not to significantly change the appearance of the doors. English Heritage has produced a technical guidance note entitled *Timber panelled doors and fire*[6] and others are in existence (Peter Norris, *Upgrading Existing Panelled Doors for Fire Protection* – personal publication). At present, further research is being carried out by Historic Scotland into the upgrading of historic doors that is likely to be introduced by the Institution of Fire Engineers Heritage Special Interest Group.[7] There is also a school of thought that historic doors, while not achieving the designated fire resistance without upgrading, would function adequately in affording sufficient protection for means of escape purposes without intervention or upgrading. The reduction in fire resistance can be off set by the use of automatic fire detection giving early warning of a fire or by sprinkler systems that suppress fire growth. This approach does, however, need an enlightened approach from the controlling bodies (building control body and the fire authority).

The upgrading of elements such as doors within a historic building requires a high standard of workmanship and attention to detail. This will ensure that the effectiveness of the upgrade is maximised and that the quality and respect required for the historic building is maintained.

Code-compliant solutions to fire safety and means of escape

Georgian four- and five-storey terraced properties that contain living accommodation and have single staircases are, with their sleeping risk, among the most onerous situations with regard to fire safety. Flat conversions of these types of buildings and those associated with mixed uses involving living accommodation present particular difficulties when endeavouring to comply with the prescriptive guidance of Approved Document B.

Flat conversions

It is perhaps the provision of lobby protection to staircase enclosures and exit routes that presents the greatest problem – most notably in flat conversions and buildings of mixed uses involving a single staircase and common escape route. The first modern guidance on means of escape came in the form of CP3. Chapter IV: Part 1: 1971 related to flats. The code required a lobby between the flat entrance and the common staircase, which is a particular problem in Georgian buildings as the landings, even on grand staircases, did not have sufficient space for the construction of a fire-resisting screen and door.[8] This requirement was often relaxed by the building control body on condition that a protected entrance hall was provided within the flats. This design philosophy was adopted by BS5588: Part 1: 1990 and later was also included in Part B, Building Regulations 1991 and later editions,[9] with the proviso that the top-floor flats were no more than 11 metres above the ground and had no more than three storeys above the ground-level storey (i.e. four storeys). Also, Part B introduced smoke detection as a requirement for flats but it is limited to self-contained smoke alarms to BS5446: Part 1 within the flat and does not extend to the common areas.

Internal arrangements within flats also cause problems from a listed building point of view, in particular where lobbies are required as these are seen as undesirable in principal rooms from a conservation point of view. Their absence, however, can create significant problems from the viewpoint of Building Regulations generally in the creation of an inner room situation or the lack of protection to the staircase – the tenability of which is of paramount importance.

Figures 15.1 to 15.4 show a typical property dating from the Georgian period selected for the research on conversion to flats and the possible scenarios relating to staircase protection.

Figure 15.1 indicates a floor on one of the principal storeys (generally ground and first floors) prior to conversion. The two reception rooms are linked by double doors and generally have generous ceiling heights.

Figure 15.2 indicates a minimal intervention flat conversion providing living room, bedroom, kitchen, bathroom and entrance lobby. This layout would normally be favoured by conservation but is non-compliant owing to the lack of lobby protection to the staircase with a single door to the bedroom.[10] If the door were sealed up the bedroom would become an inner room (a room from which escape is possible only by passing through another room – the access room – which in this case in the living room), and not acceptable under the regulations owing to the risk of having to exit via the living room.[11]

Figure 15.3 indicates a code-compliant solution. The door between staircase and bedroom is sealed up and upgraded to 60 minutes' fire-resisting standard. The fire-resisting entrance lobby is extended to include a door giving access to the bedroom. This layout is unlikely to be acceptable to conservation owing to the loss of the double doors between the original reception rooms as these are often an important architectural feature of the building.

Figure 15.4 retains the double doors and addresses the issue of a single door from the bedroom to the staircase by the provision of an 'inner room lobby'. The provision of this alternative exit from the bedroom addresses the inner room situation. Doors are upgraded (including those between the living room and bedroom) to the standard indicated and a protected

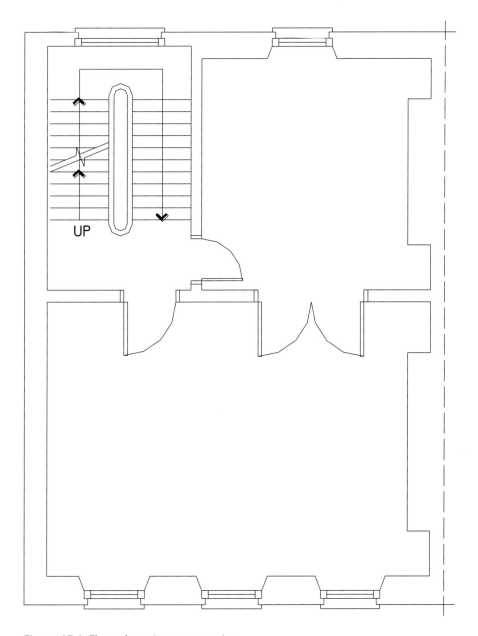

Figure 15.1 Floor plan prior to conversion.

entrance hall is formed. The outer door of the 'inner room lobby' is rehung to open outwards and secured with egress ironmongery. Both doors to the lobby are fitted with self-closing devices. The lobby would not need to be full height, and as such would need to be fitted with a fire resisting ceiling and deck. This solution has been adopted in Bath, in particular, many times and on occasions conservation have requested that a similar arrangement be constructed as a wardrobe at the opposite end of the same wall to balance the room interior. To ensure that anyone in the bedroom is alerted to a fire in the high-risk rooms (living room and kitchen), a smoke detector

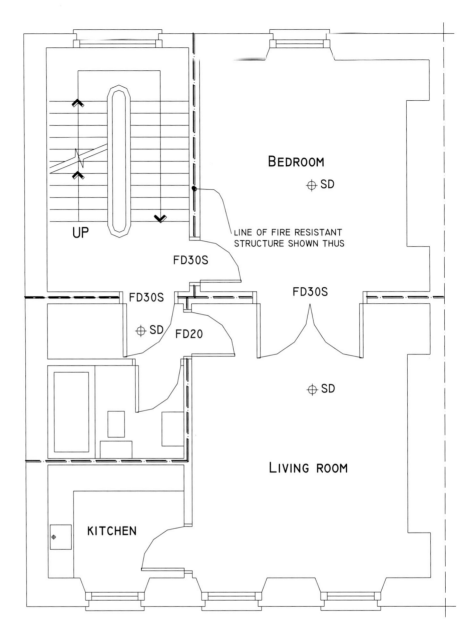

Figure 15.2 Non-code-compliant layout.

should be installed in the living room in addition to the smoke alarm in the flat entrance hall. This 'inner room lobby' code-compliant option is more respectful and sympathetic to the existing interior. One real concern, however, is the need for the lobby to be kept free of obstacles for unimpeded exit, and when one considers the limited storage in flats of this nature there would be a temptation to utilise all available space.

The inner room lobby approach, while successfully adopted many times, still presents intervention insofar as additional elements are being added

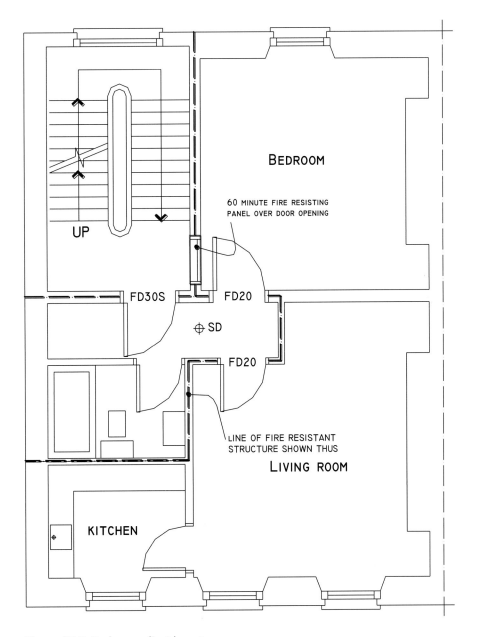

Figure 15.3 Code-compliant layout.

to the interior. As such, there was reluctance on the part of conservation to accept the solution. The author considered that a fire engineering approach might be a way forward.

Fire engineering

One has to be aware that the present-day codes are still based on the *Post-war Building Studies* publications for the 2½-minute evacuation period

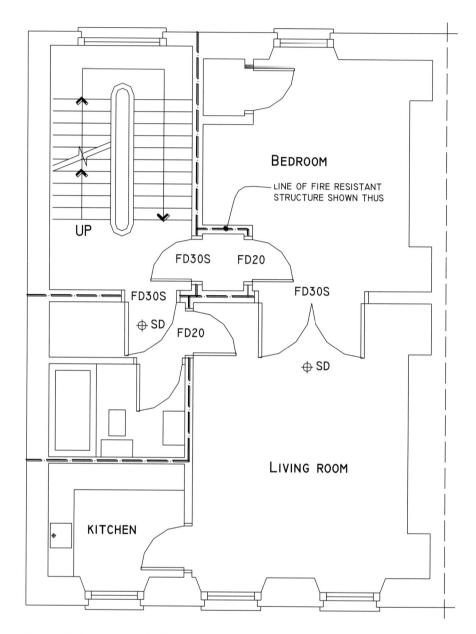

Figure 15.4 Inner room lobby – code-compliant layout.

derived from the fire at the Empire Palace Theatre in Edinburgh in 1911. Here a fire broke out on the stage and the time taken to clear the building was 2½ minutes – the approximate duration of the National Anthem. Also, Approved Document B does not take into account such things as ceiling heights and room volume. The principal storeys of Georgian buildings have high ceilings which, in a fire situation, would act as a reservoir and would allow more time before the smoke layer became a hazard, thus providing more escape time.

Approved Document B – *Fire Safety*, Building Regulations 1991 – introduced a fire engineering approach to fire safety and makes particular reference to its application in buildings of special architectural or historic interest where compliance with the approved document might prove unduly restrictive; it is contained in the current edition.[12] Also, British Standard 7974: 2001 'provides a framework for developing a rational methodology for design of buildings using a fire safety engineering approach based on the application of scientific and engineering principles to the protection of people, property and the environment from fire'.[13]

There is, therefore, an alternative approach to fire safety in addition to the more traditional code-compliant method.

The factors that should be taken into account include:

- the anticipated probability of a fire occurring
- the anticipated fire severity
- the ability of a structure to resist the spread of fire and smoke
- the consequential danger to people in and around the building.

A risk assessment approach should take into account:

- the nature of the building structure
- the use of the building
- the processes undertaken and/or materials stored in the building
- the potential sources of fire
- the potential of a fire to spread through the building
- the standard of fire safety management proposed.

In Georgian terraced properties being converted to flats, being mindful of the obtrusive nature of lobbies within existing rooms in the 'inner room lobby' solution and the unwillingness on the part of conservation officers to accept their inclusion in historic buildings, the author sought to find alternative solutions and became involved in research on this particular subject. Jeremy Gardner Associates, Fire Engineering Consultants, were commissioned by the then Bath City Council to look into alternatives to the code-compliant solutions for fire safety along with the author.[14]

A fire engineering approach can provide alternative measures at least as effective as the 'lobby' code-compliant solution. With the aid of a computer modelling system the fire engineering approach involved the following analysis:

1. modelling the existing situation
2. modelling the code-compliant solution
3. modelling alternative fire engineering solutions
4. sensitivity analysis of the key assumptions made.

Fire safety measures should be seen as methods of either increasing the time available before escape routes become hazardous – the available safe egress time (ASET) – or reducing the time needed from ignition of the fire to escape to a place of safety – the required safe egress time (RSET).

Measures to increase the available safe egress time typically include:

- fire suppression – sprinklers, water misting, etc.
- pressurisation
- smoke venting
- smoke dilution
- ceiling heights and room volume
- containment/compartmentation.

Measures to reduce the required safe egress time typically include:

- automatic fire detection
- voice alarm systems
- escape lighting/signage, e.g. directional low-level escape lighting
- reduced travel distances
- increased exit widths
- management procedures.

From the research by Jeremy Gardner Associates, the alternative measures generally considered to be equal to or better than the code-compliant approach were:

1. domestic sprinkler system in the bedroom
2. smoke ventilation to the staircase enclosure
3. smoke dilution in the staircase enclosure.

Solutions 2 and 3 would require a mechanical ventilation system in the staircase enclosure, which would be difficult to accommodate sensitively. The inclusion of a residential sprinkler head in the inner-room bedroom, which could be connected to the domestic water supply system, could be accommodated without significant alterations to the appearance of the room or its architecture. The sprinkler system could involve a side-wall sprinkler head, which would have minimum intrusion and appearance. In addition to the solutions indicated above, an automatic fire detection and alarm system was also considered necessary in the fire strategy for early warning (Figure 15.5).

The side-wall sprinkler-head installation produced a level of protection between the bedroom and staircase at least equal to that in the lobby. This was essential to ensure that the protected staircase remained tenable as a means of escape for the occupants of the building and for the protection of fire-fighting personnel.

One downside of this solution is that it provides only a single door between a common area (staircase enclosure) and a bedroom. With this approach there is an obvious weakness with regard to sound insulation. The smoke seals on the doorset will assist with the acoustics, but consideration should be given to ensuring a closely fitting seal at the bottom of the door to reduce sound paths.

The inner-room bedroom situation has recently been addressed in a publication by the NHBC Foundation and the BRE.[15] This research is the result of a study examining the options for satisfying the requirements of the Building Regulations. It addresses layout, size, travel distances,

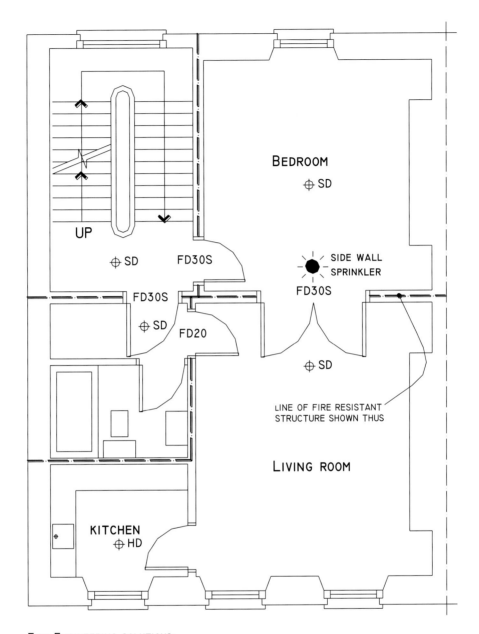

BEDROOM

⊕ SD

UP

⊕ SD   FD30S

FD30S

⊕ SD   FD20

KITCHEN
⊕ HD

☀ ●   SIDE WALL
        SPRINKLER

FD30S

⊕ SD

LINE OF FIRE RESISTANT
STRUCTURE SHOWN THUS

LIVING ROOM

FIRE ENGINEERING SOLUTIONS:
1. DOMESTIC SPRINKLER SYSTEM
   IN BEDROOM;
OR

2. SMOKE DILUTION SYSTEM IN
   STAIRCASE ENCLOSURE.

AUTOMATIC FIRE DETECTION
AND FIRE ALARM SYSTEM
TO BS 5839; PART 6 REQUIRED

Figure 15.5 Fire engineering solution.

enhanced detection options and sprinkler use. In addition, it addresses the human implications, including the various reactions, wake-up and response times from people occupying the building. This document gives alternatives to the code-compliant solutions that have been modelled to demonstrate that they are equal to the code. The publication gives greater freedom to designs in providing flexible interiors for loft-style living with the introduction of automatic fire detection (to BS5839-6[16]) and residential sprinkler systems (to BS9251: 2005[17]).

Mixed-use buildings containing living accommodation

Within historic town and city centres there are many properties that have shops on the ground floor which share a common entrance with the storeys above. Many of these upper storeys are unused owing to the problems associated with means of escape but present opportunities for flat conversions. Planning Policy Guidance (PPG 15) encourages the use of this valuable accommodation so that the building is not left vacant and possibly decaying as a result. Also, such endeavours would bring life back to the town or city centre in the evenings in addition to increasing the potential housing stock. For mixed uses, Regulation B1 (2.47)[18] requires lobby protection to staircases and escape routes. This presents a problem where the provision of a lobby within the ground floor shop would reduce the commercial floor area and would also be obtrusive where the shop has a narrow frontage. Where the shop front is listed, it is unlikely that an independent entrance to the upper storeys is possible. Initiatives for converting the upper storeys to flats have proved problematical regarding means of escape for code-compliance situations. However, there are further opportunities to consider alternative fire engineering solutions in place of conventional protection to the escape route in lobbies, where the latter may involve undesirable physical intervention within the historic interior. The terraced building with a shop on the ground floor and the potential for the upper floors to be converted to flats can benefit from a fire engineering approach with potential solutions such as automatic sprinkler systems or fire ventilation systems in the ground-floor shop. The doors between the shop and the escape corridor would need to be upgraded for fire, smoke and radiant heat. The combination of passive protection to the shared escape corridor and active measures within the commercial ground floor use can provide a solution equal to the code-compliant lobby with minimal intervention.

BS9999: 2008 Code of practice for fire safety in the design, construction and use of buildings

This new British Standard recognises the issues faced when dealing with historic buildings, and while not applying to dwellings can be used for the commercial areas of a mixed-use building or complex. The document states:

> Historic buildings present particular challenges, as many are listed, and permitted alterations are limited without the agreement of the appropriate authorities. The advice of consultative bodies, such as English Heritage, should be sought in the early stages of design. The appropriate authorities sometimes agree to limited modifications to improve life safety where, in turn, there will be added long-term protection and preservation of the original building fabric. Specific issues relating to historic buildings can be divided into four areas:
>
> 1) the preservation of the ambience and important features of the building such as timber linings to accommodation stairs and slender cast iron structure, both of which can sometimes conflict with the desired fire safety construction but can be accommodated with suitable compensating features;
>
> 2) the existing construction of the building, including hidden features such as the extent of cavities through which fire could spread and the quality of walls, partitions and floors the fire resistance of which might be unknown or questionable. Life safety can often be addressed by the use of suitable compensating features, but these do not always cover property protection and business interests;
>
> 3) the fire performance of the building structure. Although modern construction standards seldom apply to historic buildings, action to improve the level of fire and life safety might be necessary based on change of use or due to the need to reduce the fire risk and potential for loss of the structure and/ or interior in any other context;
>
> 4) the sensitivity of historic structures and interiors (finishes and contents) to fire and smoke damage.
>
> In both new construction and upgrading existing buildings, the various aspects of fire precautions are interrelated and weaknesses in some areas can be compensated for by strengths in others. A higher standard under one of the areas might be of benefit in respect of one or more of the other areas. BS 9999 provides a level of flexibility that allows the fire protection measures and the risks to be assessed to enable reasonable practical solutions to be designed.[19]

BS9999 outlines many of the fire safety concerns for historic buildings and fabric and seeks to offer solutions. It also recognises the benefits of high ceilings and automatic fire detection as compensatory features for justifying extended travel distances and reduced exit and stair widths.

Conclusion

The requirements of the Building Regulations and associated legislation and guidance need to be balanced against the guidance contained in BS7913: 1998 *The principles of the conservation of historic buildings* and PPG15. Clearly, professional experience and judgement will be required from all parties involved. This will include the architect/designer in their approach to and justification of the building proposals; the building control body in applying the requirements of the Building Regulations (and the involvement of the fire authority in consultation); the local planning authority conservation officer (and English Heritage in consultation) in seeking to preserve the nation's heritage in relation to historic buildings and architecture; and other related construction professionals. Such proposals and solutions should adopt wherever possible the principles of minimum intervention and reversibility.

Endnotes

1. *The Building Regulations* 2010 – Approved Document B, *Fire Safety*, Vols 1 and 2 (2006 editions).
2. *Planning Policy Guidance: Planning and the historic environment 15* (September 1994), paragraph 3.26, pp. 11–12.
3. British Standard 7913: 1998, *The Principles of the conservation of historic buildings, 7.2.2 – Protection against fire*; Paragraph 7.2.2 *Protection against fire*, p. 9.
4. *The Building Regulations 2010*, Approved Document E, *Resistance to the Passage of Sound* – (2003 edition).
5. *Resolution of the Associated Architects with the Report of a Committee by them appointed to consider the causes of the frequent fires and the best means of preventing the like in future* (1793).
6. *Timber Panelled Doors and Fire* (English Heritage, May 1997).
7. Institution of Fire Engineers Heritage Special Interest Group is involved in the research and development of fire safety in historic building.
8. CP3, Chapter IV: Part 1: 1971, Fig. 19.
9. Approved Document B *Fire Safety*, Vol. 2 – *Buildings other than dwellinghouses*, paragraph 2.21, Diagram 9.
10. *Ibid.*, paragraph 2.17, p. 25.
11. *Ibid.*, paragraph 2.5, p. 22.
12. *Ibid.*, paragraph 0.35, p. 14.
13. British Standard 7974: 2001, *Application of fire safety engineering principles to the design of buildings*, p. 1.
14. Norris, P., Gardiner, J. P., Davidson, M., *Fire Safety in Historic Dwellings in Bath – A Fire Engineering Approach* (Bath City Council Seminar Paper, March 1996).
15. NHBC Foundation, *Open plan flat layouts – Assessing life safety in the event of fire* (September 2009).
16. BS5839-6: 2004 *Fire detection and fire alarm systems for buildings – Part 6: Code of practice for the design, installation and maintenance of fire detection and fire alarm systems in dwellings.*
17. BS9251: 2005 *Sprinkler systems for residential and domestic occupancies – Code of practice.*
18. Approved Document B *Fire Safety*, Vol. 2 – *Buildings other than dwellinghouses* (2006), paragraphs 2.50–2.51, p. 32.
19. BS9999: 2008 *Code of practice for fire safety in the design, construction and use of buildings*, paragraph 0.1, pp. 1–2.

Index

Interior finishes & fittings for historic building conservation, First Edition. Edited by Michael Forsyth & Lisa White. © 2012 Blackwell Publishing Ltd. Published 2012 by Blackwell Publishing Ltd.